An OPUS book

METROPOLIS

Metropolis

EMRYS JONES

Oxford   New York
OXFORD UNIVERSITY PRESS

Oxford University Press, Walton Street, Oxford OX2 6DP

Oxford New York Toronto
Delhi Bombay Calcutta Madras Karachi
Petaling Jaya Singapore Hong Kong Tokyo
Nairobi Dar es Salaam Cape Town
Melbourne Auckland

and associated companies in
Berlin Ibadan

Oxford is a trade mark of Oxford University Press

First published 1990 as an Oxford University Press paperback and
simultaneously in a hardback edition
Paperback reprinted 1992

British Library Cataloguing in Publication Data

Jones, Emrys, 1920–
Metropolis. — (Opus)
1. Cities
I. Title II. Series
307.7'64

ISBN 0-19-282578-X Pbk

Library of Congress Cataloging in Publication Data

Jones, Emrys.
Metropolis/Emrys Jones.
p. cm.
Includes bibliographical references.
1. Metropolitan areas. 2. Cities and towns—History. I. Title.
307.76'4—dc20 HT330.J66 1989 89-22863

ISBN 0-19-282578-X (pbk.)

Printed in Great Britain by
Biddles Ltd.
Guildford and King's Lynn

To Catrin
and in memory of
Rhianon

Preface

There has never been a dearth of books on cities, but in the last few decades they have proliferated as never before. In particular cities have become an academic field of study, their origin, history, economics, and social life endlessly examined and re-examined. Since our growing awareness of the urban explosion in the Third World and the degradation of the inner city in our own, the problems of cities have stimulated popular, academic, and governmental responses in bewildering variety. Another book has to be justified. I have confined myself to discussing great cities, the giants among cities, for several reasons. There would be a ready consensus that historically a handful of cities stand out above all others, not merely by size, though most of them were immense by the standards of their day, but because they represented peaks of cultural achievement and were centres of creativity which transmitted many of the values of civilization to succeeding generations. Many scholars think that it is still so in our own time, that there is a discrete group of super-cities which are in a class of their own. Today we are rather overwhelmed by cities with immense populations. The 'million city' which was once so rare has become a commonplace, and we have become used to thinking in terms of multi-million cities. But the really great cities, those which are qualitatively outstanding, are still relatively few. In any historical period the tip of the pyramid is small; élitism is exclusive by definition.

The word 'metropolis' seems a convenient one to identify these great cities in any period; and the thread that runs through this book is that their greatness stems from the way in which they express the greatest achievements of the particular societies and cultures of which they are the culmination. The first chapter considers a number of studies which have dealt with great cities from several aspects, in order to identify their characteristics. I have deliberately avoided creating an exclusive class of cities but rather looked for a range of qualities which may be present in varying degrees. There is a brief account of the metropolis in proto-history and in European history, leading to the metropolis in modern times and then the contemporary metropolis, including examples in the developing world. A further chapter speculates on changes and trends which will affect the shape and function of the metropolis of the future. Lastly I deal with the problems of the great city, most of them shared both by the city in history, and by the modern Western and Third worlds. In spite of the search for common characteristics, a feature which I hope will be self-evident is the fact that the metropolis is always the expression of a particular society and culture—that each one is in fact unique. There is no attempt to be comprehensive. I stress what I think are the important criteria and I illustrate these by case-studies.

The emphasis on individual cities by no means implies that they can be divorced from the entire systems of cities of which they are the centre. For the purpose of this book there was enough of common interest in those cities which had reached pre-eminence to warrant dealing with them as a distinct phenomenon, however much they were also part of wider national systems which often helped sustain them. Indeed, today we must also see them as part of a world-wide urban system with a degree of interaction, and even of interdependence, which often challenges their uniqueness. The references, though very selective, are some indication of the wider interests against which my theme has been developed; there is ample material to pursue interests in many directions, and if the book awakens such interests it will have served its purpose.

The maps were prepared in the Department of Geography at the London School of Economics, and I am very grateful to Mr Gary Llewelyn for the care with which they were drawn.

Contents

Illustrations

1

The Measure of Metropolis

The measure of a city . . .

ARISTOTLE

i

What is a 'great city'? How do you describe those cities which seem to tower above their fellows, cities that are in a different class, that evoke superlatives? Do we call them great cities, super-cities, giant cities, megacities, cities of destiny? I use the plural, for though at any one time one city may seem to dominate all others—Athens, Rome, or London—from a more general perspective they form a group of cities, all of which have been pre-eminent at some time. Unwittingly I have created a class of cities. This in spite of the fact that the most obvious thing about any city is its uniqueness. Each city has its own particular location, each occupies a particular niche in time. Each city has a name which conjures up qualities often impossible to define. An American author recently wrote a book on New Orleans in which he referred to that city as 'she' and 'her', a compelling device to signify its differences from other cities, but also demonstrating that our view of cities can be empathetic and emotional and often denies rational academic analysis.

Very few people are interested in consciously classifying cities; a handful of social scientists perhaps, trying to measure certain attributes to understand better what makes them function. Yet most of us unconsciously classify cities in a common-sense way as an essential part of describing them. If I say that Manchester is a big industrial city then I have conveyed quite a lot of information about Manchester even if it is rather generalized. I have 'classi-fied' it by size, by function, and by corporate status. Each of these terms can convey a wealth of meaning to other people living in Britain, and a lack of precision in the definitions bothers no one but the academic specialist. More evocative descriptions would defy classification; the liveliness and excitement of some cities and the dullness of others have to be experienced rather than measured, but they are an essential part of the personality of a city and often mean more than prosaic measurements.

It is in this way that everyone responds to 'greatness' in a few cities, past and present, and would not hesitate to express an opinion on it. The word 'great', however, has two meanings; the first is size, something which is vast or colossal; the second is quality, something that is eminent, exalted, principal, primary, or marvellous. That all these are relative terms need not concern us for the moment, though later it may be necessary to find more objective criteria. But we can start by recognizing that there are 'greater' and 'lesser' and that greatness has something to do with both size and quality.

Size is a very elastic concept. It is probably the first thing to strike a layman but the last thing he is capable of assessing accurately. To a traveller entering a city the view is very limited; the horizons are too close, observations are too circumscribed for him to imagine the city in its entirety. Air travel has improved our perspective. Magically we can now see an entire city, as if on a map. Nothing is more spectacular or awe-inspiring than to approach Tokyo by air and see the entire city spread around Tokyo Bay; or to leave Montreal airport by night and see a chequer-board of coloured lights, breath-takingly beautiful, etching out every street and avenue. But when it comes to assessing their size the whole is as baffling as the part. Size has an immediate and powerful impact, but we are usually at a loss to measure it. We have to fall back on numbers in census tables, which are themselves often meaningless because they outstrip our comprehension.

When Marco Polo described his journeys in China, either words failed him because of the sheer magnitude of some of the cities he saw or he resorted to guesses so wild that they too merely indicate the wonderful and the unimaginable. In Taidu there was 'such a multitude of houses and people . . . that no-one could count their number' (Lathum, p. 106). In Kinsai there were 'such crowds of people . . . that anyone seeing such a multitude would believe it a stark impossibility that food could be found for so many mouths' (Lathum, p. 179). There were so many prostitutes in Taidu that 'no-one could believe it'—but he makes a gues~ at 'twenty thousand'! Doesn't this really mean 'a very la₁ₑe number', as does his count of 12,000 bridges or his statement that in every one of the twelve guilds there were 12,000 establishments of between ten and forty people? There is an arbitrariness about such numbers which suggests that all Marco Polo was doing was justifying his feeling that Kinsai, another major metropolis, was 'without doubt the finest and most splendid city in the world'. It was, in every way, so far beyond his experience of fourteenth-century Venice that he had to search for the language to convey his impressions to his fellow merchants at home.

Even when exact census figures give us a reasonably accurate count of the population of cities there is an arbitrary element in where we draw the lines between classes of city size. What is 'big'? Where did the United Nations conjure up the figure 200,000 which it uses officially to distinguish 'large' cities? Why are we so impressed with the figure '1 million'? This last has a magical quality. The numerical system of the West enables us to count—theoretically at least—almost indefinitely, and certainly well beyond the point where we can match numbers to comprehensible images. We have advanced far beyond the Australian aboriginal's 'one, two, three, four, five, a lot'. But I think everyone would agree that when we say 'a million' we mean 'a lot'; it is virtually impossible to imagine a million people. In population counts there is a sort of barrier beyond which there is a change in significance. The 'million city' is such a barrier. Until recently the cities which came into this category were few indeed, and the word conjured up wonderment and awe.

Very few cities in earlier history even approached this number, some would say none (Chandler and Fox). The more conservative estimates make classical Rome no more than 650,000 at its peak (about AD 100). Alexandria's population may not have been greater than 400,000. Between AD 900 and 1500 Baghdad may have been as much as 900,000; Ch'ang-an at the same period was about 750,000, and Constantinople at the height of its powers about 300,000. Not until 1750 did the first million city appear, and that was Peking. Some estimates do exceed those I have given, and Hankow and Tokyo were certainly of the same order of magnitude as Peking by the mid-eighteenth century. All these cities were the products of the 'first urban revolution'—that is, their economy was pre-industrial and based on agricultural communities. The giant cities of the 'second urban revolution', based on industrialization, began when London reached the million mark soon after the beginning of the nineteenth century. It was followed by Paris in 1853, New York in 1857, and Vienna in 1870. The era of the million city had arrived.

This century opened with perhaps a dozen cities claiming a million people. In fact it is not easy to decide on the exact number, so much depending on whether the definition of the city is by administrative boundary or whether suburban extensions are to be included. On the conservative estimate eleven cities entered the twentieth century as million cities: London, Paris, Berlin, Vienna, Moscow, St Petersburg, New York, Chicago, Philadelphia, Tokyo, and Calcutta. Twenty years later the number was 20; in 1940 there were 51, and in 1961, 80. This trend has itself increased dramatically and in the mid-1980s the count was 226. One can hardly call it an exclusive class any more. Again, different definitions of what constitutes a city give slightly different numbers. Some of the population figures in the United Nations data are for the 'city proper', some for administrative areas extending beyond this to include urban areas which are nominally independent yet part of a single urban system. For example, whereas Boston 'proper' has 508,000 inhabitants its urban system has over 4 million. The interrelationships giving reality to the second figure will become apparent later, but the larger figure is the more acceptable as a true representation of a single urban agglomeration. I have adopted these larger figures given by the United Nations to arrive at the total of 226.

Their world distribution tells us many interesting things about urbanization in general (Fig. 1). The shift of emphasis from Europe is the most obvious, for, excluding the USSR, this continent which once dominated the big-city league now has only twenty-nine (13 per cent) of the million cities, and some cities (for example, Glasgow and Birmingham) have both achieved and then lost this status within this century. The United States has 37,

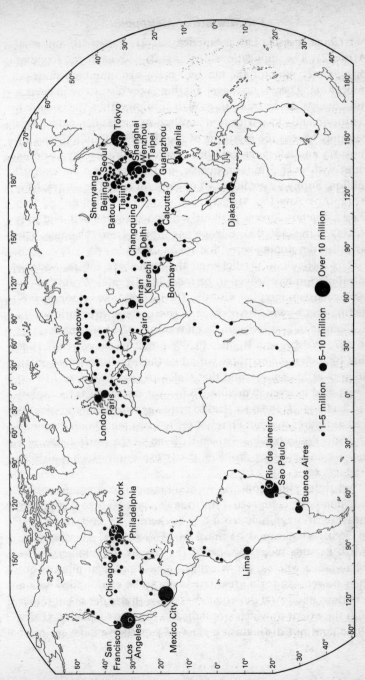

Fig.1. The world's largest cities.

but China has 45. Latin America has 21, Japan 10, and even Africa 21. The implications of this shift lie outside the scope of this chapter, but for the moment mere size, numbers alone, is interesting. There is no longer anything very distinctive in being a million city. If the trend in growth continues then the twentieth century could close with five hundred or more such cities. This certainly lessens the mystique of the figure of a million, and we must try another magic number. There are already twenty-seven cities with over 5 million people, and six of these are over 10 million. Surely we are in a class of giants at last? The six are: New York, Los Angeles, Mexico City, Tokyo, Shanghai, and São Paulo. Buenos Aires is perilously close with 9,968,000, and so is Peking with 9,180,000. Europe has slipped from the scene. The so-called developing world has taken over.

It is difficult to predict even the immediate future, because intrapolation has proved to be a doubtful guide. Writing in the 1950s, the demographer Kingsley Davies (1955) was gloomily predicting that by 1985 one person in five in the entire world would be living in million cities; in fact it was far less, about one in eight. In 1975 Wilsher and Righter (p. 30) predicted on current trends that by the same year there would be three or four metropolitan areas over 25 million, and that Calcutta, São Paulo, or Mexico City could be over 50 million. In fact the last city was the largest at 18 million. Trend lines tend to run away with demographers, as well as figures. Calcutta has not yet reached the 10-million mark, and São Paulo has just passed it. Even so the world is facing a massive and growing problem of city explosion which is already frightening.

Aristotle, philosophizing within a scale of community which was miniscule compared with today's, said: 'There is a proper measure of magnitude for a city as there is for everything else' (p. 266). What would he make of Mexico City? He also said: 'Most persons judge the size of the city by the numbers of its inhabitants; whereas they ought to regard not their number but their power . . . for a great city is not to be confounded with a populous one.' And our concern is not with size *per se* but rather with the extent to which size indicates distinctive quality. If size alone does not distinguish a class of superlative cities we must look for attendant qualities. We must go much further than arranging the world's cities in classes of size, like some immense pyramid, and then cutting off the peak as if those cities alone merited further examination. Size *is* relevant, if only because of the common problems which are a direct result of such concentrations of people, but it is not an acceptable index of greatness, as it could exclude more interesting cities which are lower in the pyramid. On the other hand, if all big cities are not necessarily great, most great cities have been relatively big. The key word is 'relatively', for primacy, dominance, and importance are usually correlated with size.

ii

In trying to define the great city we have already moved from the simple category of over 1 million to three categories: 1–5 million, 5–10 million, and over 10 million, the number of qualifying cities diminishing sharply with each successive class. Lower down the pyramid we can make other categories, using more or less arbitrary figures. But a common-sense approach demands that we also include function in differentiating settlements. A village is bigger than a hamlet but smaller than a market town, and the last is small compared with a regional centre which itself is dwarfed by a capital city. If we add function, then, it looks as if progression goes in a series of jumps, rather like steps, forming a hierarchy of sizes. The first scholar to realize this was an Arab geographer Al Muqaddasi, who wrote a book in 985 on *The Classification of the Knowledge of Regions*. His classification looks very familiar, for he refers to market towns and cities and capitals, as well as villages. His ranking of cities comprised 17 metropolitan cities, 67 provincial capitals, 50 miscellaneous cities which were mainly in the marginal zones of the Islamic world, and a very large category of traditional small cities. He also suggested that these settlements formed a 'nested hierarchy' in which one market town served several villages, a provincial capital controlled several market towns, and a metropolis dominated several provinces (Wheatley 1976). Almost a millenium later the German geographer Christaller dealt with the same idea with all the scientific nicety of a theory. He set out a hypothetical scheme of settlements arranged hierarchically by size and by function, controlling a hierarchy of regions which nested one in the other. Such a system has been tested empirically, and where there are no great physical and social constraints on communication and exchange there is a reasonable fit between theory and reality. Great cities are the top step in the hierarchy, and there are all kinds of functional reasons why they are sharply differentiated from other cities.

Other scholars have thought that the breaks in sizes are much less important than this, that the sequence of increases is more smooth, and that it might be possible to describe the relationship mathematically as a generalized law. The best known is Zipf's rank–size rule, which states that if the cities and towns of a country are ranked in descending order by size, then the nth town will be nth the size of the largest city; that is, the second city will be half the size of the first, the third one-third the size, the fourth a quarter, and so on. The relationship is such that if the logarithmic scale of population is plotted against the rank on logarithmic scale, the result will be a straight line. Such a graph of the cities of the United States of America does indeed approach a straight line.

This is little more than plotting observations or empirical evidence. But the relationship revealed tempts speculation that in some way there is order inherent in the system which reflects the outcome of a very large number of processes which reach equilibrium at this point. Or is it no more than a reflection of an innate desire in ourselves to perceive order, or even to impose order, and to simplify an otherwise very complex universe?

Having reduced the relationships between cities by size to lines on graph paper we can now compare them. The Zipf line is a simple continuous progression whereas Christaller's hierarchy is broken, or stepped, each step being functionally distinct from the last. When dealing with a very large number of cities and towns the prominence of the steps may seem less, whereas hierarchies may reveal themselves more clearly when the number of settlements is small.

Being at the top of a hierarchy or the first-ranking city in a particular urban system does not necessarily mean 'greatness'. But there are arrays in which there is an enormous quantitative leap between the first city in the system and the next, an immense step in the hierarchy. This indicates a city quite disproportionately greater than any other in the system and this is sometimes called a 'primate city'. The pre-eminence of a single city in a state often accords well with the layman's intuitive approach. 'Paris is France' is a phrase which expresses this very well, recognizing that city's pre-eminence. It was an American geographer, Mark Jefferson, who first dealt with this phenomenon in a more objective way when he proposed the 'Law of the Primate City'. According to this, the 'largest city shall be supereminent'. The disproportionate size of the primate city is an expression of self-sustaining growth based on national pre-eminence. As an example, London is seven times larger than the second city in Britain and encapsulates all that is important in the economic and cultural life of the country: it is a 'primate city'.

Paris is another example from the Western world, but primacy is found more particularly in developing countries in which the capital city has a disproportionate share of the state's economic and political activities. For example, Cairo, with 5.1 million people, has 13.8 per cent of the entire Egyptian population and is three times the size of Alexandria, its nearest rival. Moreover it has 27 per cent of the hospital beds in Egypt, 33 per cent of its doctors, 52 per cent of its telephones, and 62 per cent of its graduates (Khalifa and Mohieddin): this gives some indication of the disproportionate resources of a primate city.

A comparison of hierarchy, rank–size ratios, and primacy is possible in a simple diagram (Fig. 2). Primacy is rather like a single-stepped hierarchy: it is also like an obtuse-angled rank–size array. Following the latter comparison some scholars have suggested a developmental model for city size distribution. The assumption is that primacy is usually a feature of countries low on the developmental scale (e.g. Thailand) and that log-normality—the straight line in the rank–size rule—is mainly the characteristic of developed countries (e.g. the United States). The latter is described as a 'condition of entropy, the result of many forces acting randomly, in contrast to primacy which is the end

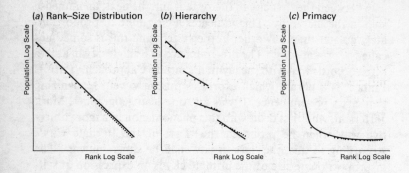

FIG. 2. Comparisons of size and rank of cities.

result of a few simple processes' (Berry, p. 73). Theoretically, then, increasing and more complex processes in society such as industrialization will enhance the status of intermediate cities and will eventually eliminate the great disparity between the primate city and the others. However true this may have been in the urban history of several highly developed countries like the United States, West Germany, Italy, Poland, or Belgium, it is not true of Denmark, Holland, Sweden, or even the United Kingdom. Conversely, while there are many classic examples of primacy in developing countries, such as Uruguay, Peru, Mexico, Thailand, and Sri Lanka, others such as Brazil, India, Korea, and China have log-normal distributions.

Jefferson made no claim that his 'law' was universal, but said that it was generally true enough to warrant looking for explanations for exceptions to the rule. For example, when a state incorporates more than one major cultural group within its boundaries there could be several cities which were primary to each separate group, but none warranting claims to primacy over the whole. In Canada Toronto and Montreal vie for supremacy, but they can also be regarded as the capitals of the two major social groups in Canada. Historically Spain had several primate centres: Madrid for Castile, Barcelona for Catalonia, and Bilbao for the Basque area.

Scale is important too. In China as a whole there is no obvious primacy because there are many giant cities of almost equal significance in a virtual subcontinent. Even at regional level in China primacy is exceptional (Shanghai in the East Region is one), but on the provincial level there are several examples, significantly in the less-developed provinces (e.g. Cheng).

Primacy is a simple concept which applies particularly to an early stage in urbanization in which the resources of a state are concentrated in and expressed by one city. Historically the city-state is the perfect example. In many ways it is difficult to apply the concept to contemporary experience, but there is at the heart of it a corollary which is essential to our understanding of great cities. According to Jefferson the primate city not only represents an intense concentration of people but also a concentration of resources and of 'national influence'; it is 'exceptionally expressive of national capacity and feeling' (p. 226). It is the embodiment and expression of a society and a culture.

iii

From quantity we have moved to quality. If the surface of the earth were divided into culture regions rather than states we could almost certainly expect a primate city in each one, certainly a major city embodying the best in that culture. Historical processes—war, conquest, empire-building, federation—have all played havoc with such a simple notion. In Spain, for example, Madrid was a conscious effort to establish a centre which would dominate several peripheral culture regions. Washington, DC was a bid to balance the fourteen states in the Union of 1786, and in all respects but that of government it does not rank with the foremost cities of the United States. Canberra, though technically exercising federal control in the whole of Australia, is nowhere near the league of large cities. And Brasilia, a very recent effort to counteract the conflicting influence of several massive coastal cities, has yet to achieve greatness. On the other hand the primacy of some cities has come from exercising control far beyond the cultural hearth. Vienna's greatness relates to a former empire, not to Austria; and so in part does that of London.

Even more than size, the qualities of greatness in a city are an outcome of its history; and as civilizations ebb and flow, expand and contract, and even disappear, so their cities come and go. There is no Ch'ang-an, no Angkor Tom, no Carthage. There are only the ruins of classical Athens and of imperial Rome. Within a historical framework we can discuss the flowering of these cities and how they transcended place and even time. At the peak of their achievement they wielded great power; in their decline they bequeathed a cultural heritage. Size was a result of greatness, not a cause—and not always a necessary condition. So the focus of enquiry must move to the city as a centre of political control and as the peak of cultural achievement.

This is why the historian Arnold Toynbee, when surveying the great cities of the past, called his book *Cities of Destiny*. His examples are great 'in the sense that they have made a mark on the subsequent history of civilization' (p. 5). Size is secondary. Achievement and influence are all, and the assessment of these qualities is the prerogative of the historian. They cannot be measured on graph paper, as Toynbee makes very clear when he comments that to become a city of destiny Los Angeles would have to 'evolve at least the rudiments of a soul' (p. 13). (Some observers argue that it has a soul, but one that the European tradition would not easily recognize!)

Primacy is paramount. It was so in the earliest civilizations when the city-state reigned supreme. Expansion of the city-state into an 'empire' increased the power of the central city. In proto-historic Egypt, after the political union of Upper and Lower Egypt, Thebes was an imperial capital. Conquest gave new power and splendour to Babylon, Rome, and Constantinople. In medieval Europe the city-state again became dominant, only to be eclipsed in modern times by the nation-state, leaving a few anachronisms like the Vatican City.

The emphasis which Toynbee places on achievement and on contribution to civilization not only pin-points specific cities but also quite specific periods in the history of those cities. So his cities of destiny include city-states such as fifteenth-century

Venice, fifteenth-century Florence, and eighteenth-century Weimar; nation-state capitals such as Alexandria under the Ptolemies, Rome in the second century AD, tenth-century Ch'ang-an, Constantinople in the fourth century, Cordoba in the fifth, Paris between 1150 and 1300, Mexico on the eve of the Spanish conquest, Isfahan in the early seventeenth century, Delhi in the seventeenth, St Petersburg in the late eighteenth, and Vienna in the 1840s. Nineteenth-century London and New York are included as products of the industrial era. The relative narrowness of the time period emphasizes the thesis. Although Toynbee explicitly discounts the extreme diffusionist views of scholars of culture in the inter-war period, he accepts a strong element of continuity when he states that most of the civilizations are 'related as parents or offspring to one or more of the others' (Somervell). And modern western civilization owes much to elements which it has directly or indirectly inherited from the past. But our interest in Toynbee's examples lies in his critical concern with the way civilizations have expressed themselves in great cities. The outstanding cities of the past are those which embodied the characteristics of societies and cultures at their peak.

Some of these examples from the past will be the subject of the next chapter because they will help us to understand the nature of the metropolis; but considerable work has been done by scholars on the contemporary city, and one outstanding analysis has been that by Peter Hall, called *World Cities*. The title is taken from the work of an earlier urban visionary, Patrick Geddes, but Hall has made the field his own by examining in detail a number of cities which he considers to be in a class of super-cities, outstripping all others in influence and world dominance. The fundamental characteristic of a world city (*Weltstadt*) is that it has outstripped its national urban network and become part of an international global system. This is a natural progression from the very limited territorial dominance of the city in a city-state via the national dominance of a capital city or the imperial dominance of the centre of an empire. World cities still retain the characteristics of primacy associated with these stages; they are massive in size, centres of political power, and host institutions which embrace and enhance that power. But in addition they are centres of world trade, of communications—usually symbolized by international airports—and are the leading cities in banking and finance. Associated with these features are concentrations of the medical and legal professions, and the world of learning; they are information centres *par excellence*.

In the first edition of his book (1966) Hall selected seven cities for this exclusive class, chosen from a 'short list' of twenty-four cities which had a population of over 3 million at that time. Population still seems a prime attribute of greatness; but it is a necessary condition rather than a sufficient one, for there are many cities which fail to become world cities in spite of their size. In fact it becomes clear that increasing population is often the result of a city achieving the status of world city rather than vice versa. The seven cities Hall chose were London, Paris, Randstad-Holland, Rhine-Ruhr, Moscow, New York, and Tokyo. Two of these are not what one would normally classify as cities. Randstad-Holland and Rhine-Ruhr are both complexes of several cities which together make great agglomerations which have those features which Hall seeks in his super-class. In this way he is anticipating changes in city structure which are already familiar but which may be much more important in the developments of the next half-century.

In a subsequent edition of his book (1984) Hall omits Randstad-Holland for reasons of space, using Rhine-Ruhr as an example of a polynucleated world city. But he adds two cities to the list, Hong Kong and Mexico City—both in the developing world. The change is significant. Hall's first list was closely reasoned on economic grounds, and perhaps for that reason those cities reflect a Western system of values, Tokyo having adopted and completely absorbed that system. In general the first group is a product of Western civilization, in this century world-dominant and with a firm economic control over the entire globe. Economically at least Hong Kong has now also become part of this system, and it will be interesting to see whether China will encourage this role when the city reverts to that country in 1997. Mexico City is different. Its inclusion is a recognition of an urban world outside the western realm which may in many ways supersede the old order; an example, not of the power and wealth we normally associate with the Western metropolis, but of the immense difficulties and problems of an exploding urban system trying to get to grips with a world order.

Hall's main interest is in the interplay of function and form and how this is being interpreted in the planning of these world cities. This kind of analysis is considerably enriched in a study called *Metropolis 1890–1940* (Sutcliffe). It was the outcome of a symposium in which Peter Hall played a considerable part. He wrote the book's introductory chapter and postscript, and his influence is seen in the choice of case-studies: London, Berlin, Paris, Moscow, the Ruhr, New York, and Tokyo. The additional depth and richness come from two facts. First, that much of the discussion comes from trying to 'understand' the metropolis through its architecture, its visual arts, music, cinema, literature, and intellectual life generally. Not only is this wider perception of its role and its contribution to cultural life a necessary part of the metropolis, but its influence on a vast hinterland in each case, explored and exploited in planning terms, is a continuing theme. Secondly, the choice of a specific period, 1890 to 1940, to identify a phase in Western metropolitan growth was perceived as a challenge by some of the contributors and a disadvantage by others: but it did confront the dilemma of whether, after all, the metropolis has only a limited life, whether in accord with organic analogies it must eventually succumb to the effects of growth, and die. Hall's final paragraph in the book is headed 'Towards Necropolis', a distinct echo of Mumford's thesis in which metropolis was part of a cycle of growth and decay, from polis to metropolis to megalopolis and finally to necropolis. It was in Berlin between the wars that Max Ernst produced his awesome picture *The Petrified City*—the city of the dead. And a future of decline is easy enough to envisage. The Greek planner Doxiadis, theorizing on city development, envisaged change as the main ingredient. To be static is to be dead. To him the great metropolitan cities of the past went through a phase of dynamism before becoming static, when their subsequent decline and death was inevitable: 'humanity was not prepared to deal with such complicated mechanisms' (p. 213).

Metropolis 1890–1940 implies that the metropolis in its traditional form, the great city, immense and immensely rich, has reached its peak and indeed has possibly passed it, already beyond our ability to cope with it, already bearing the seeds of its own decay. Today we are more aware of the problems of metropolis than its achievements, and we may well have to invent new administrative structures for it or devise new forms of the built environment to allow it to flourish. World cities already may have become no more than products of the past, unable to adapt to the demands of modern technology or to meet the needs of the next generation.

iv

No one would dispute the strong case which Hall makes for his class of world cities, and certainly the cities he chooses would be accepted by most as major metropolitan centres. But a Western outlook reinforces the idea of the dominance of Western cities. The expansion of Hall's work to include Hong Kong and Mexico City not only recognizes the extension of the global network to include non-Western cities, but it also acknowledges a wave of urbanization in the developing world which will make the urbanization of the Western world seem small. It is clear that some of these immense new cities will not fit easily into concepts derived from Western studies, although it may be premature to try and devise new ones. These cities will no doubt be part of a global system, but they will also be expressions of their own distinctive cultures. To a geographer one of the most interesting aspects of this new wave of urbanization is the shift from the temperate to the tropical zone which I have already referred to. This is the latest in several shifts in areas of urban development which Western civilization at least has undergone; from Middle East to the Mediterranean, to Western Europe and its extension beyond the Atlantic, and to some outposts in temperate Australia and South Africa. Europeans were also responsible for the secondary seeding of cities in the tropical zone, where they sought to exploit resources with the minimum transference of white people. It is here that urbanization has now taken off at a speed and magnitude which makes the industrial era in Europe look sluggish. Size and continuing speed of growth are the most obvious attributes of these cities, but nevertheless they represent comparative wealth, power, and influence, and they express the heart of the cultures they serve. Nor do they lack an element of awe and wonder, hidden though these often are by sheer numbers and the problems they bring. If our exploration of metropolis means anything it must include some of these giants of the non-Western world.

Such cities were the subject of a recent book called, significantly, *The Exploding City* (Wilsher and Righter), and it centred in particular on Calcutta (pop. 9 million), Bombay (8.2 million), Djakarta (6.5 million), Manila (5.7 million), Mexico City (14.7 million), Lima (5 million), Caracas (1.6 million), São Paulo (10 million), Rio de Janeiro (5.6 million), Bogotá (4 million), Seoul (8.3 million), Singapore (2.5 million), and Shanghai (8.2 million). The most alarming aspect of this phase of urbanization is its speed: there is no more apt word to express this than 'explosion'. Not only are the population figures far beyond most Western cities, but projections of growth suggest that there will be no slowing down in the immediate future. Historically many of the cities have much in common. With few exceptions they are ports. An older generation of geographers made much of the significance of site and particularly of the fact that cities grew where there was a break in the mode of transport—in this case from sea to land. This thesis is restated in a chapter called 'Giant Cities as Maritime Gateways' (Dogan) in the most recent work on metropolitan cities, *The Metropolitan Era* (Dogan and Kasarda). Change in mode is an indicator of the coming of Western civilization in the form of colonial powers intent on exploiting tropical resources. This was sometimes done by exercising power in an existing city, as in Shanghai, or, more often, by establishing new settlements, as with Calcutta. They all became points of contact between indigenous and intrusive cultures. Today these cities have considerable elements of Western culture which bring them into the world orbit, but even more importantly they are part of an overwhelmingly indigenous society and culture. Not all these cities share in the transactional network which is the essence of a world city, but they are metropolises in their own right because they embody the achievements of distinctive local cultures, exercise political and social control over large areas, and are magnets which attract millions of migrants.

It may be a characteristic of Western thinking that these cities are seen almost exclusively in terms of 'problems': economic problems because they lack the industrial base on which our own urban expansion depended; political problems in building up the requisite organizational framework to deal with city management; social problems because of their inability to cope with the housing and welfare demands of a frightening agglomeration of people. On the other hand the Western world is well aware of its own shortcomings and the problems inherent in ageing processes. It is significant that in the last two decades academics have shifted their attention more to problems in society as opposed to abstract academic problems within their own disciplines. It is not surprising that an international symposium arranged by UNESCO in 1986 was entitled 'The Pathology of Cities'; and in this context it is interesting to see what they considered to be the world's giant cities (or 'Mega-cities', to quote the title of the published volume [Dogan and Kasarda, ii] of case-studies based on the symposium). The case-studies are: New York, Los Angeles, London, Tokyo, Shanghai, Delhi, Lagos, Cairo, Mexico City, and São Paulo. Five of these (Mexico City, Tokyo, São Paulo, New York, and Shanghai) are the largest agglomerations in the world; London is included largely for historical reasons; Los Angeles represents the automobile-oriented city; Cairo, Delhi, and Lagos exemplify very rapid growth in developing countries. In a companion volume called *A World of Giant Cities* other large cities are referred to, but particular attention is paid to Moscow, Calcutta, Seoul, Djakarta, and Peking.

iv

The lists of great cities I have extracted from recent literature have inevitably differed considerably from one another because they have reflected the thesis or the interest of the writers. But the criteria they chose obviously overlap very considerably. Size is an assumption and a recurrent theme. The fact that we are dealing with such immense cities does not invalidate historical examples because size is relative to particular periods and cultures in the past. Today an absolute cut-off point might be 5 million.

Secondly, metropolises have been singled out for their qualities, particularly the accumulation of achievements which express technological or cultural excellence. And thirdly, they have been singled out for their supranational role. Lastly, they have been grouped together for posing problems which have given rise to common pathologies.

Before discussing these points in subsequent chapters I want to deal with one other general matter, and that is the enlarging of the concept of metropolis to include those areas where the immediate influence of the city is dominant. The very word 'metropolis' originally implied 'daughter cities' under the control of a 'mother city'. In this century in particular, and in the United States more than elsewhere, much attention has been given to the city as a functioning system rather than as a collection of buildings ('bounded by a wall' as the Old Testament describes Jerusalem).

The difficulties of defining a city areally have been referred to already. The days of being able to distinguish easily between what is in a city and what lies beyond it disappeared with the city wall. Rather than pretending that a clear distinction exists where it does not, most scholars now think of the city as the total activities of the people who live and work there, and this includes a very wide area often well beyond the continuously built-up area. The idea of a metropolitan region may be much more realistic than that of metropolis. Indeed, the burden of the story so far has been that the metropolis controls the activities within the region that supports it. The old city-state expressed this most succinctly. Today the problem of defining areal limits is compounded by the ease and rapidity of travel and the extension of the city's domination over so many aspects of our lives. It is extremely difficult to capture the nature of the contemporary metropolis. London is as good an example as any to illustrate the difficulties. There is a historic City of London, which still has its own system of government although it is only a tiny fragment of the metropolis and has an even smaller proportion of its population. Much more realistic is the area covered by the thirty-two boroughs which until 1987 constituted Greater London and is almost coterminous with the continuously built-up area within the green belt. The latter is a deliberate attempt to limit growth, a sort of twentieth-century wall. But although this was containment of a kind it did not prevent further expansion, merely ensuring that this could be more controlled and planned. Beyond the green belt overspill from London was itself contained in orderly communities. These new towns, 40 kilometres from the centre, were meant to have an economic and social existence separate from the capital. They were partially successful in this aim, but there is also no doubt that they remain within London's orbit and influence and there is considerable commuting. A second generation of new and expanded towns was planned 80 kilometres from the city centre. Planners now recognized a metropolitan region, 100 kilometres from east to west and from north to south, and for some time there was a South-East Planning Region which covered the whole of south-east Britain. The three definitions—Greater London, the Metropolitan Region, and the South-East Planning Region—hid a multitude of boundaries showing varying degrees of dependence on the capital. The question is this: is there any one boundary more than another which will give us a clear idea of the extent of London? The answer is 'No'. All activities show dominance increasing towards the centre, with a wide peripheral zone in which the physical dominance of the rural landscape belies an economic and social dependence on the city.

This does not satisfy social scientists, demographers, geographers, planners, and sociologists. They will assert that we are living in a world where everything must be measured, counted, or weighed. Even the most subjective concept must be translated into scales and figures which can be manipulated statistically. Terms like 'dominant' and 'attractive' must be quantified to be academically respectable. So what, in their terms, does 'metropolitan' mean? The most comprehensive attempts to answer this question have come from the United States. Here more than anywhere the traditional notion of the city as a discrete entity which can be studied in comparative isolation has given way to the concept of metropolis as a region within which there is interaction between the central city and the remainder of the region. The prime concern of the US Bureau of Census in 1910, when it first introduced the category of 'Metropolitan District', was to acknowledge that much of the population living outside a corporate city was in fact part and parcel of the life of that city.

This was the first attempt to define the 'greater city', a recognition that urban growth was entering a new phase in which the physical fabric of the city and its social reality did not coincide, and that this was not so much an administrative adjustment as an acknowledgement of the day-to-day involvement of people living outside the city who worked in it daily and were dependent on its resources. In trying to measure this dependence the United States Census was by no means interested in just the great cities, but in every city with more than 50,000 inhabitants. In delimiting the new areas they simply added to the central city all those contiguous areas with a high density (150 persons per square mile). This simple definition was made more elaborate in 1950 and again in 1960, this time equating to that of the SMSA (Standard Metropolitan Statistical Area) (Berry *et al*.). This really seemed to sort out the urban from the rural, for among other criteria the central peripheral area had to have 75 per cent non-agricultural workers in the work-force as well as contributing at least 10 per cent of the work-force of the central city. In other words the metropolitan area had to be integrated with the metropolitan city.

These definitions involve all the difficulties of trying to express social phenomena in statistics; all the thresholds—the number in the central city, the proportion of commuters, and so on—are arbitrary. At best the statistics are only crude methods of trying to understand how far the influence of a city is dominant. Their inadequacy is emphasized by their ignoring the common-sense criteria which laymen apply, based on a perception that the built-up area of a city is very different from the environment which it has displaced. But the most serious criticism now is that the very concept of metropolitan region is trying to capture a relationship which is becoming outdated, that it depends too heavily on commuting links between city and hinterland which are centrifugal and centripetal. As a later chapter will show, this only partly expresses the complex interrelationships which are already manifest. In the near future propinquity may lose much of its significance and force us to think very differently about the nature of urban life.

There seems little point in extending the concept of SMSA outside the United States except as a statistical exercise, and in Europe use of the word 'metropolitan' is at variance with the American concept. For example Robson and Regan in *Great Cities* are very critical of the smallness of the population criterion and the narrowness of the functional definitions. In their words, it has allowed 'too much small fry' to come in (p. 29). It was inevitable that by concentrating on the nature of relationships between city and region, size became irrelevant. In 1981 there were 322 SMSAs in the United States; the only constants were those enshrined in the definition. Otherwise the SMSAs varied from the insignificant—there were twenty in Texas alone—to contenders for world status like New York, Chicago, and Los Angeles. By almost any subjective criterion of greatness or metropolitanism few of the examples qualified. Relying on similar concepts and using data on commuting and the labour market the American geographer Brian Berry has put forward what he terms 'consolidated urban regions' (Berry *et al.*). They are much bigger, numbering thirty-four, and are more likely to include the qualities of life we associate with a metropolis. Their interest to us is in their recognition that urbanism spills over the conventional limits of the city, and metropolitanism affects many more people than are suggested in city statistics.

Robson and Regan begin with the unquantifiable, for they consider that the exercise of political power is the essence of metropolitanism. The bases of such power are most clearly seen in metropolises which are also capital cities, for by definition the latter have assumed political control of the state. In fact only fourteen of the twenty-four cities that Robson and Regan classify as great cities are capitals. In the United States several qualify for greatness without the trappings of political power: indeed, 'national' power is vested in Washington, a city which rates tenth in population and which is included in none of the listings of great, giant, or metropolitan cities.

V

One thing is clear from what has been said so far: the criteria of the greatness of a city vary according to the perspective of the observer or the aim of the exercise. Size is almost always a factor, though it must be thought of relatively if we are dealing with historical examples because scale has increased so dramatically. In early historic times a city of 100,000, like Thebes, would have been uniquely great; in the Christian era and until the nineteenth century any city approaching a million would have towered over every other; in this century there are several cities over 10 million. Today we are a little less dazzled by size.

But we must be careful to distinguish between greatness based on size and size as an outcome of greatness. It is always easier to recognize greatness in the past; the passage of time affords a more balanced view of the entire range of activities and of their contribution to civilization (*pace* Toynbee). In our own period scholars are at pains to measure attributes and define roles and to see this within the framework of world urbanization. Nevertheless the search is also for those indefinable features which have always been part of greatness, what Raymond Williams called 'feeling the grandeur of a city' (pp. 14–15)—'feeling', you note, not 'measuring'.

To many the word 'metropolis' encompasses just this, indicating qualities different from run-of-the-mill cities. It enables us to forget size *per se* for the moment. Originally the word signified the see of a 'metropolitan' bishop, and the fact that etymologically it combines the words for 'mother' and 'city' indicates an extensive, beyond-the-city influence. This is what the Americans are searching for in redefining their urban regions. The word is now useful to suggest the way in which the exclusiveness of the city as opposed to the country is disappearing. Even in the traditional secular use—as 'chief town or capital' (*OED*, 1590) or the 'chief centre of activity' (*OED*, 1675)—there is implicit the sense of control and dominance at the centre and the idea of the dependence of the periphery.

The word 'metropolis' will be used in this book, but in a general rather than a specifically defined way, to denote those

cities which have been or are great cities. It is not my purpose to
select a list of those which qualify for greatness. What I have said
so far is ample evidence of a degree of arbitrariness in classifying
cities, whether this be done by a numerical cut-off point or by the
considered opinions of scholars exercising more subjective
criteria. There is no agreed opinion on any of this. Even the data
available for discussion are very uneven; for example, only
recently has information on Chinese cities begun to be analysed
and they are conspicuously absent from most studies on the
topic. The importance of culture-specific aspects will become
apparent in subsequent chapters, indicating my own reluctance to
think only in terms of a world system. It is not enough to put all
cities into one heap and then choose the top ten or twenty, whatever the criteria. A case could be made—as Hall does so well—for
accepting the notion of a world system on the dominance of the
Western city; but I think this seriously diminishes cultural aspects
that lie outside technology and economic and financial control.
Indeed, it may relegate non-Western cities to a second class. On
the other hand, accepting cultural variables does not rule out
cross-cultural generalizations and debate: centralization of
power, accumulation of wealth, the focusing of communications, congestion, attraction of an élite, and many more features
are characteristics of all metropolises. Moreover, pursuing the
culture-specific features will lead to a deeper understanding of
individual metropolises as they are perceived by the distinctive
societies which gave rise to them.

My main purpose in the following text is to discuss the many
aspects of metropolitanism as illustrated by certain cities. The
main features will be illustrated by a limited number of examples,
but this by no means precludes other metropolitan cities. The
chapter on the great cities of the past underlines the theme of continuity and the degree to which we must balance the universal
against the specific: unique though these cities are, it is the
common element which will be stressed. The contemporary
process, with strong antecedents in the last century, will be the
main theme. Again, the supranational characteristics shared by
all metropolitan cities will be a priority, but this must be seen in
the perspective of the radical shift in massive urbanization from

the Western to the developing world. The latter may demand a reappraisal of the part played by indigenous cultures in the development of metropolis. Finally, a consideration of contemporary trends and theories about the future of urbanism may give us a hint about what the metropolis of tomorrow will look like.

2

The Metropolis in Early Civilizations

With walls and towers . . . girded round.
                                    COLERIDGE

i

The starting-point of a brief examination of the metropolis in history is the common-sense notion of the city as an imposing mass of buildings and streets which is the home of multitudes of people and the scene of their myriad activities. The agglomeration of people in this way is what we usually mean by urbanization, but this term also means social changes—the differentiation of labour, an increase in social complexity, centralization of control. And there is no agreement among scholars about the mechanism of change, what sparked it off; there is plenty of speculation. In his list of those criteria which he thought of as distinctly urban in prehistoric settlements, Gordon Childe included increase in size, centralized accumulation of capital, monumental public works, the invention of writing, and the emergence of social classes and representational art. These did no more than describe the characteristics of the first cities, but it is equally clear from his books that Childe thought the key to the innovations—the independent variable which explained the change—lay in technology and economics. Behind the 'urban revolution' lay the 'food-producing revolution', the ability to control the growth of food in permanent settlements as opposed to hunting and collecting. It was this that made cities possible.

In the later history of urbanization, as we shall see, technological changes loomed very large. In referring to these great social changes as 'revolutions' Childe was drawing a parallel with what is accepted as one of the most fundamental changes in man's history, the industrial revolution; and indeed many scholars now refer to the subsequent wave of city growth as the 'second urban revolution', and we are already familiar with reference to the immediate future as being 'post-industrial'. There can be no underestimating the role of technology either in the origins of cities or in subsequent changes in their development. On the other hand, this view of origins is greatly influenced by the archaeology of the Middle East and by a Western bias nurtured on what happened in the Western city in the last 150 years. It also assigns a preponderant role to diffusion as a mechanism of change. Postulating a single hearth of urbanization and its subsequent spread throughout the world is much too simple, and does not even accord with the facts. We may have to look for variables more fundamental than technological change and more universal than the inventions and discoveries which underlay the change. Acceptable explanations must include the ancient cities of China and pre-Columbian America as well as those of the Middle East.

An alternative idea is that urbanization derives from the centralization and organization of social power. These elements are incipient in pre-urban society, they are universal, and they constitute an unbroken link between past and present. Cogent arguments have been put forward by Paul Wheatley (1963, pp. 181 ff.) as to why we should consider religion and magic as playing a critical role, both in social control and in what he calls 'cosmo-magical symbolism'—that is, manipulating space to represent the cosmos, and expressing cosmic values and ideals in the layout of buildings and streets. The evidence for the significance of 'religious' ideas in city layout as well as in the ordering of society and the manipulation of power is overwhelming. It also complements the ideas of an American anthropologist that urbanization is an expression of increasing social class differentiation, which began before the building of cities in priesthood, kingship, élitism, and the exercise of power (Adams, pp. 99 ff.).

Theories of what lies behind the building of cities are relevant for two reasons. The first is that because I subscribe to the power theory of urbanization it will underlie many of the themes in the book. The second is that the theories are as appropriate a way of distinguishing great cities as they are of explaining why there are cities at all. What we know about the ancient city of Ur will illustrate these points.

Sir Leonard Woolley's excavations at Ur in the decades between the wars revealed a city which, by any standards, could be considered great. It was probably established before the fourth millennium BC, but during the Early Dynastic period (2900–2400 BC) it became the capital of lower Mesopotamia and the seat of a powerful king. The royal tombs (2500 BC) which Woolley excavated were those of a magnificent metropolis. It covered a compact area of about 80 hectares, and may have had a population of between 30,000 and 50,000. The most striking feature of Ur was the astonishing wealth of the royal tombs. Adams puts these into perspective when he points out that for the Early Dynastic II and III periods 588 burials have been described which are very poor in grave goods, one in eight having no stone or metal object. These graves represent a peasantry which, although living in the city, had acquired very few of the tangible symbols of wealth. Between the two extremes of the royal tombs and these peasant burials were two other 'classes' of graves. About twenty, though not royal, revealed considerable wealth in the form of gold ornaments, copper vessels, beads, bronze tools, and gold- and silver-mounted daggers. More numerous than these were those graves which Woolley himself described as 'typical middle class', with some copper and bronze tools and utensils and some pottery. The distribution of wealth in these several 'classes' of graves shows a very high degree of social differentiation; in other words they reflect a class society. It is also significant that 94 burials recorded at al'Ubaid, a nearby site, had very little metal at all and only one had precious metal: 'Al'Ubaid, it would seem, was a rural dependency of the capital at Ur, with much of its wealth drained off to support urban specialists and administrators' (Adams, p. 101). This is the very essence of metropolitanism.

The outward expression of the greatness of Ur was more apparent in the Third Dynasty (2200–2100 BC) when the great ziggurat was built. This was rather like a stepped pyramid made of sun-baked bricks set in bitumen. Its base, or lower stage, measured approximately 64 by 46 metres and its height was 12 metres. The north side was not sheer like the others but had three great stairways converging on the second stage. From this a single stairway approached the third stage, on top of which was a shrine. The sophistication of the whole is astonishing. The subtle slopes of the wall lead the eye to the summit; and all the vertical lines have a slight convex curve which adds an impression of enormous strength and stability, a principle of 'entasis' which was to appear much later in the Parthenon at Athens.

The significance of the ziggurat is twofold. It clearly indicates the religious importance of the city and that worship was central to the lives of the people; priesthood and kingship were probably impossible to separate at this time. It also demonstrates the way in which surplus resources could be organized to produce monumental structures. Ur was the focal point of a state, and then an empire, on the lower Euphrates, the centre of a land rich from irrigated agriculture and ideally placed for trading and communications. There is evidence that trading extended far beyond Mesopotamia: seals from the Indus valley have been found here as well as copper and ivory from the east. At the heart of this prosperous empire power was concentrated in the hands of an élite which dominated a structured society and exercised control through religio-magic precepts.

These features recur time and time again in the prehistoric Middle East, magnified greatly in those cities which attained ascendency beyond their own small states. The latter became the great metropolitan cities. Babylon, at the height of its power in the sixth century BC, probably had a population of about 350,000. Under Nebuchadrezzar II it was a major imperial power. It fell to the Persians in 539 BC but regained its riches and power under Alexander (d. 323 BC), who wanted to make it his imperial capital. Nebuchadrezzar's Babylon covered 10,000 hectares and was carefully planned. We have Herodotus' description of what the greatest city on earth was like:

The city stands on a broad plain and is an exact square, a hundred and twenty furlongs each way . . . it is surrounded in the first place by a deep moat, full of water, behind which rises a wall fifty royal cubits in width and two hundred feet in height . . . In the circuit of the wall there are a hundred gates, with brazen lintels and side-posts . . . The city is divided into two portions by the river [Euphrates] which runs through the middle of it . . . The houses are mostly three or four stories high, the streets all run in straight lines, not only those parallel to the river, but also the cross-streets which run down to the water-side . . . The centre of each division of the town is occupied by a fortress . . . In the one stood the palace of the kings, surrounded by a wall of great strength and size; in the other was the sacred precinct of Jupiter Belus, a square enclosure, two furlongs each way, with gates of solid brass. [In the middle of this precinct was a ziggurat of eight platforms.] At the topmost tower there was a temple. (i, pp. 90–1)

The ziggurat was, of course, the Tower of Babel, with a base of 100 metres and a height of 91. It stood by the great temple of Marduk, one of several in this part of the city. There were also two great palace complexes. As in Ur the astonishing feature in Babylon is the vast accumulation of resources which all this represents, both in materials and manpower. The wall which Nebuchadrezzar built when he extended the city was over 11 kilometres long. Babylon's hanging gardens were one of the seven wonders of the ancient world. This city was a miracle of power and control, of organization and management, that culminated in the building of temples and palaces. The former, in particular, were a focus of identity. In the words of Nicholas Postgate: 'The artistic and architectural genius of the community was directed to the benefit of the houses of their gods', and they 'functioned as a repository for the surplus wealth of the community and as a source of capital' (p. 17).

ii

The wealth and splendour of the metropolitan cities of the proto-historic Middle East have to be reconstructed from archaeological fragments, but enough remains of the classical cities to allow us to experience at first hand at least some of their glory, whether in remains of architecture and planning or in ideas transmitted through the written word. Athens was comparatively smaller than some great cities of the past, probably housing around 100,000 persons at its greatest in the fifth century BC. It emerged as a city-state, vying for supremacy with Corinth and Sparta. The city had direct control of perhaps 200,000 people in Attica and, at the height of its influence, hegemony over 2 million in and around the eastern Mediterranean. Athens had all the attributes of a great metropolis, based on a sound economy and trade in grain, oil, wine, timber, leather goods, precious stones, ivory, spices, incense—and slaves. It was a wealthy state with a powerful army and navy. Life was focused on two sites in the city, the acropolis and the agora. The first was a fortress with temples, the second the market-place, the social and political hub of the community. In the first, Pericles (461–429 BC) created an architectural gem, the Parthenon, which could well be a symbol of Athens—modest in size but perfect in conception and in execution. This was the age of Aeschylus, Sophocles, Euripides, Socrates, and Aristophanes. Later there were intellectual leaders like Plato, Aristotle, and Zeno. Not only, therefore, was it a centre of power and wealth, but, as Milton said: 'Mother of arts and eloquence'. This was a community which set new frameworks for political, philosophical, and scientific advances which were to be the guidelines of Western civilization.

iii

Whereas Athens remained a city-state, albeit at times the chief city of a hegemony, Alexandria flourished as the capital of an empire. Established by Alexander in 332/1 BC it represented a shift in the centre of gravity of Greek urbanization as its influence encompassed the Levant and parts of North Africa. From this point of view the location was well chosen; moreover, the site was easily defensible, enjoyed a good climate, and commanded the food resources of the Nile valley. It remained a Ptolemaic city until 30 BC, continued to flourish under the Romans, and did not seriously decline until the Arab incursions of the seventh century AD. A contemporary estimate of the free population in the second century BC of 300,000 suggests a total population of around a million, but modern scholars prefer a figure near 700,000. Alexandria exported 300,000 tons of wheat annually as well as papyrus and cloth. It crafted raw materials and distributed its wares throughout the Mediterranean. In the East and in Africa it traded in precious goods like ivory, jewels, gold, glassware, and perfume. The city had a symbol of its control of world trade in the famous Pharos lighthouse, built in 279 BC. This was a technical triumph, said to be 120 metres high. It was constructed in three stages, a square base on which there was an octagonal tower surmounted by a circular one. Above this there towered the statue of a sun-god. No building subsequently reached such a height until the construction of the medieval cathedrals.

In addition to the lighthouse Alexandria had two features which were evidence of its metropolitan status. One was its emergence as a world centre of learning. The word 'museum' is derived from the *museion* of Alexandria, not only a building to house collections but a centre for teaching and research. Its most famous feature was its library, established by Ptolemy II in the mid-third century BC. Here 700,000 papyrus rolls embodied the whole of Greek literature and all ancient science. Euclid and Archimedes were both closely associated with the library.

The second feature was the cosmopolitan nature of the population. The very circumstances of its founding meant that two great peoples and two cultures—Greek and Egyptian—had come together, albeit in an unequal partnership. On the whole Egypt's chief role was the provision of food and raw materials whereas the Greeks controlled trade, took a major role in organization, and dominated learning. The city's extensive trading activities also brought innumerable merchants from much further afield. The most active ethnic minority was the Jews who came in great numbers to enjoy the parity of privileges which the city afforded. There were indeed some aspects of self-government in the Jewish community which made them almost autonomous. This, then, was a city of truly mixed population, a reflection of its worldwide activity and interest, 'a crackling, broiling world city' as one author puts it (Schneider, p. 122).

iv

Alexandria nearly became the imperial capital of the Roman Empire, but its metropolitan glories were to be outshone by

Rome itself, which in the second century AD reached heights of wealth and sophistication unparalleled in the classical world. Rome's population had increased from about 300,000 in 150 BC to over half a million by the early second century AD. Conservative estimates make it 650,000 at its peak, though some would argue for a figure nearer 1 million. At that point in its history it was twice the size of Alexandria and three or four times bigger than Carthage or Antioch. Its population was sustained by the grain of Egypt and north Africa, the vines of the Greek islands, the oil of Spain, peaches of Persia, plums of Damascus, and the spices of the Far East. It was the centre of vast resources of all kinds and its material culture reflected an empire which covered much of the known world.

Rome's achievements in architecture and in engineering are too well known to be recounted here; we also know considerably more about how people lived there than in most ancient cities. For example, during the second and third centuries AD Rome had expanded upward in a way reminiscent of our own cities in the last century or so. A listing of the fourth century cites only 1,797 private houses but 46,602 *insulae* (apartment blocks or tenements). Both Nero and Trajan issued decrees limiting the height of such buildings to 20 metres and then 17, but the overwhelming impression is of tall blocks, well-built in baked brick with ashlar and tufa, and often covered with thin slabs of marble. Apart from a few processional ways the spaces between *insulae* were irregular, forming 'streets' so narrow that carriages were forbidden to use them by day. This is the first real indication of very high density and overcrowding, features which were to become a regular pattern of metropolitan life. Juvenal's comments, so obviously heartfelt, might well be a description of Oxford Street on a Saturday morning:

> No matter how I hurry, I am hampered by the crowds,
> Who almost crush my ribs from front to back;
> This one strikes me with an arm, another with a heavy board;
> My head is brushed by a beam. Large feet step on mine . . .

> (*Satires*, iii. 242–9)

A Greek, Aelius Aristides, was impressed by the number of

people who could be accommodated by the tall apartment blocks. 'If the city were to be laid out flat,' he said, 'so that the Romans who are now aloft could be deposited side by side on ground level, the remnant of Italy not yet covered by Rome would be continuously filled up' (Toynbee 1970, p. 199).

Of course, some degree of density and overcrowding was necessary. The city's daily round depended on face-to-face communication. All citizens must be within easy reach of the forum and the markets; indeed, it was necessary to live in the city to have the full benefits of citizenship. As the population grew its density increased. All was not unrelieved pressure, of course. There were large and well-maintained private and public gardens. And services were good; there was an excellent fresh water-supply, efficiently distributed, and an advanced sewerage system.

Rome was an opulent city full of superb monumental buildings which reflected the wealth of empire. For those who commanded the wealth conspicuous consumption was the order of the day. Enough classical remains have survived to make all this very clear, but one building alone will suffice to illustrate the achievement of this metropolis. The Pantheon remains very much as it was when it was built by Hadrian late in the first century AD, and it is as breath-taking now as it was nearly two millennia ago. It is basically a vast drum, the height of which is half the diameter of 43.2 metres. This is surmounted by a dome which remained the biggest extant until this century, being larger than that of St Peter's or of Hagia Sophia in Istanbul. The glory of the dome is seen from the inside—'architecture turned inside-out', as one architect described it (Vickers, p. 110)—for it is deeply coffered, both to lighten the structure and to decorate it, and has in the centre an *oculus* open to the sky. Variegated marbles add to its richness.

The remains of innumerable other monuments—baths, markets, temples, the Colosseum, circuses—all remind us of the wealth of this city, its control of resources, its technical and organizational skills. Above all, this civilization reached new peaks in learning and particularly in law. But Rome was essentially a consumer city. It did little to create wealth or industry, or even a stable society. It was prey to its own weaknesses in administration and eventually wide open to the threat of invasion. By the time the city was sacked in 455 AD its population had dwindled to a quarter of a million. The loss of Rome's ascendancy was symbolized by the founding of Constantinople, and it was this city that now took pride of place as the world's greatest metropolis.

V

For some time after its founding in 330 AD Constantinople was the hub of the Roman Empire: when the shift of power from west to east became established the city became the capital of Byzantium, the eastern empire. Constantine had appreciated the advantages of the site of the existing small settlement of Byzantium as well as those of the natural harbour within the Horn. Here he built a metropolis which excited the admiration of every traveller. In addition to being an imperial capital with a population of perhaps 700,000, it was the focal point of world-wide trading. It was also a holy city, the first Christian metropolis, in which shrines and relics abounded and in which pilgrims were as important as merchants. The Christian patriarch was second only to the head of the Church in Rome—and he is still the head of the Orthodox Church following an eleventh-century schism which completely separated it from the Roman Catholic Church. But this was a tolerant society which welcomed all comers, and one in which Jews became a very influential element. In spite of this it became an Islamic city after the Turkish conquest of 1453. From that time its churches became mosques; but its greater splendour was then long past.

To travellers in the sixth century Byzantium was a stunning city. A plentiful water-supply and a plethora of aqueducts together with good drainage provided a sound basis for its growth. As its population increased there was a considerable degree of planning control; for example, side streets were nominally 4 metres wide, outside staircases were banned, and balconies had to be 3 metres away from other balconies. There were conscious efforts at creating a city of grandeur: its main streets were adorned with statues. There was an admixture of very prosperous streets lined with splendid houses and small palaces, and meaner streets for the less rich. Many of its mansions were in the suburbs, some lining the attractive waterfront, intermingling with fishing villages, others in the market-garden areas which flourished beyond the walls. The most striking monumental features of the city were its churches, of which twenty-five still remain. The gem among them was—and is—the Hagia Sophia. Rebuilt in the sixth century this church has what many consider the most beautiful dome in the world; 32 metres across and 55 metres high, it seems to float above the vast floor. When the church became a mosque minarets were added to the corners of the building to give its unmistakable silhouette.

The population of Constantinople was cosmopolitan, as the very circumstances of its foundation guaranteed. Much of its trade was in the hands of foreign merchants who formed very considerable communities, particularly, later, the Italians, who were allowed enclaves of their own, and the Jews. There were also merchant communities from Russia and Persia. Most of these diverse peoples were bound together by Orthodox Christianity. The city was a good example of a fusion of cultures, Christian in religion, Roman in organization, and Greek in language. Socially it had a rigid hierarchical structure. Below the emperor was an aristocracy, then came the Church and then the merchants; there was a broad base of artisans and the poor. As in most pre-industrial cities today rich and poor often lived side by side, and there must have been a considerable part of the outskirts which had the equivalent of today's shanties.

vi

The examples I have dealt with so far have revealed characteristics of the early metropolis which are fairly familiar, because in many ways these cities were forerunners of our own. They stand well within the tradition of the Western city, and the civilizations they represent are also those from which we have inherited so much. There were other metropolitan cities which were the products of other civilizations, and a brief glimpse of three examples will be sufficient to point to the similarities and to the contrasts. This will enable me to broaden the base on which more universal concepts can be tested before looking in more detail at more recent Western examples.

The first of these non-Western examples is Ch'ang-an. Since before the Christian era there was a city on this site on the Wei river with easy access to the Yellow River valley, Szechwan, Yunan, and Kansu. It was a trading centre with a very wide hinterland. The city grew massively during the T'ang dynasty as the capital of a province, and it was rebuilt in about AD 660. For the next three hundred years or so it was possibly the largest city in the world, with a population conservatively estimated at 750,000 with possibly as many more in its metropolitan region. It was primarily a centre of power and administration, a consumer city controlling and absorbing enormous wealth. Planned on a magnificent scale its walls, which were built first, defined a regular rectangle, 9.53 kilometres from east to west and 8.48 kilometres from north to south. The 6-metre-high wall was pierced by eleven gates of which the most important was the central gate in the south wall. Inside were two virtually separate cities, the Palace City where the emperor lived and the Imperial City which was the office and home of the administrators. A great processional way led from the central southern gate to the Imperial City, dividing the city into two parts, each of which had a market, east and west, which served as a focus for the mass of the city's people, artisans, and merchants (Tyrwhitt).

The plan is of particular interest because it accords so well with the idealized pattern which underlay all Chinese cities. The regular rectangle, the cardinal orientation, and the great processional axes were all typical of the ideal model. Symbolism reigned supreme. Even the walls were symbolic of the mountains which were thought to surround the world, for the city was a microcosm of the Chinese universe. Orientation was strictly adhered to even in the major buildings, which always faced south. The gates had symbolic ties with the seasons and their use was restricted to certain classes in the society and to specific occasions.

The size and richness of the Palace City in Ch'ang-an was an indication of the almost unlimited resources under the control of the élite. The society as a whole was the epitome of a sophisticated service society. It was strongly hierarchical (Wright). The emperor had supreme control, and beneath him was an imperial bureaucracy which formed the élite. This bureaucracy had its own hierarchy, and every year between five and seven thousand young men were examined for places in this administrative structure. Below the élite were the religious communities, both monks and nuns, and the merchants, many of whom belonged to small foreign communities. Lowest of the classes were those of shopkeepers, pedlars, artisans, grooms, sweepers, and gardeners. Social divisions were implicit in the plan, as we have seen, and it is probable that this was not only a separation of function, but some kind of social segregation. We are told elsewhere that the city 'was divided into two parts' (i.e. outside the Palace and Imperial Cities) 'by a very long, broad street . . . all those belonging to the imperial household live on that part on the right, eastward. The part on the left, westward, is inhabited by the people and the merchants, where there are also squares and markets for the necessities of life' (Tuan, p. 224). Foreign merchants may well have been relegated to areas outside the wall, for Marco Polo tells us that 'Lombards, Germans and French, were all given specific places to lodge in the suburbs' (p. 172).

These characteristics of life in the great cities of China are found again and again in a series of metropolises as the centre of civilization shifted, for example to Hangchow and Peking. By the twelfth and thirteenth centuries Hangchow was the seat of the Sung dynasty and capital of central and southern China. Later the focus swung north to the new Tartar city of Taidu, attached to an earlier city called Yenking. Together they formed Peiping (Peking), which left Marco Polo almost bereft of suitable adjectives:

Everything in the world that is rare and precious finds its way into this city, and this is specially true of precious stones, pearls and spices which come from India. All the valuable products of the Chinese provinces are brought here, to satisfy the needs of the masses of people who take up residence in the vicinity of the court. The volume of goods sold here exceeds trading in all other places, for no less than 1,000 waggons and packhorses carrying nothing but raw silk enter the city daily: and the gold-encrusted materials and silks of all kinds are manufactured here in staggering quantities. (Lathum, p. 107)

vii

Throughout these glimpses of the earliest metropolitan cities there has been an assumption that there is a congruence, a fit, between the city as an artefact, as a built environment, and the city as a community which, although an integral part of society as a whole, is differentiated from the rest by virtue of its function in that society. The city, both buildings and people, is contained, encompassable: and there was, more often than not, a wall to make the point clear.

Of course it is equally evident that the metropolis was nothing without the territory beyond, which supported it and provided the resources on which it lived. The metropolis was like the hub of a wheel whose radial spokes were lines of communication, trade routes, government links. The interdependence of the centre and the territory it controlled is the most vital element in the system. The city itself is an expression of processes within this larger community.

That the city is, in this way, a dependent variable is very apparent in its demography. The population of a rapidly growing city is mainly made up of people coming in from elsewhere. Until the last century it is doubtful if any city grew on its own natural increase. There are complex reasons for this, but put simply the city was a devourer of people. Growth came from immigration, and that movement from the countryside, almost like the movement of iron filings towards a magnet, is paralleled by an inward movement of food, raw materials, and resources of all kinds. City dynamics involve the entire region and its society. The city's success depends on the degree of its control and the efficiency of the organization with which it commands the region.

But we must also consider two aspects of urbanization which are not sufficiently dealt with in the simple model of economic-political dependency. The first of these is religion. Ch'ang-an was a powerful reminder that even at this scale of construction the religio-magical element can dominate the built environment as well as providing major social dimensions for its functioning. I have said that the layout was a microcosm of the universe; the entire structure was imbued with symbolism to the extent that a foremost authority on the eastern city refers to city planning as 'cosmosising the landscape' (Wheatley 1967), a means of demarcating a 'sacred' place in a 'secular' landscape. So much can be said about these cities that accords with our own Western view of the overwhelming importance of economics that the introduction of another value system—particularly one which lies outside the so-called 'rational'—seems superfluous. But there are great cities in which the religious element reigns supreme: Jerusalem, Mecca, and Benares come to mind immediately, and they demand some consideration in any analysis which seeks to understand the metropolis.

The holy city of Mecca is considerable by any standards; with about 300,000 inhabitants it is second only to the capital of Arabia, Riyadh. But during the season of pilgrimage its population approximates a million, as people pour in from every part of the world to fulfil one of the fundamental obligations of Islam. Islam alone has made this city. Extremely restricted arable land and an acute shortage of water mean that all food must be imported. There is very little industry, no water transport, no railway, no airport. The *raison d'être* of the city lies in the great al-Haram mosque where the Kaabah shrine rests; it can accommodate 800,000 people. Mecca is a cosmopolitan city because Islam has spread to every part of the world, but it is virtually a giant mosque, serviced by those whose job it is to look after the pilgrims.

The fluctuating population of Mecca is a reminder that such religious centres can be periodic in the sense that they serve a seasonal demand. There is a parallel here with the great fairs of medieval Europe which periodically attracted hordes of merchants. Their significance relates to a world quite different from that associated with Western economic exchange. And it forces us to ask the question whether the permanence of a city is a necessary condition of urban life. This certainly becomes relevant to a consideration of contemporary trends, as we shall see later, but an interesting example of an ancient metropolitan community which prompts a similar query is found in Cambodia.

From the ninth to the thirteenth century the dynasty of Khmer chose as their royal centre the city of Angkor. The resources on which their fortunes depended were the outcome of an elaborate irrigation system engineered in the late ninth century. By marshalling these resources, and using vast armies of workmen, they built themselves a marvellous city which must have been one of the most magnificently monumental in all Asia. Like the Chinese city the plan was based on religio-magic precepts, this time a microcosm of the Indian universe. In the centre and representing a mountain were the colossal pyramidic temples, the Buddhist Bayon of the eleventh century being the greatest. Around these were enormous enclosed palaces, and around the entire city was a wall nearly 30 kilometres in circumference. The dominant feature of the landscape around the temples and palaces was the system of irrigation channels, also representing the oceans which surrounded the central mountain of the cosmos. In the mid-twelfth century Angkor Wat was built, the most famous of all the temples, a microcosm within a microcosm. The entire complex was a religious and administrative centre, and it would be impossible to separate one function from the other. The dominant cult was that of a god-king: the king identified himself with a sovereign deity. On the king's death his temple became his mausoleum.

It is difficult to see Angkor as anything but a vast ceremonial stage. True, it—and its actors—had to be supported. It is calculated that it needed the efforts of at least 300,000 people to sustain it and to provide labour and services. Most of these lived outside the enclosure in villages. Food producers though they were, they were an essential part of the life of the city. In addition pilgrims provided links with the most distant parts of the Khmer kingdom. With the exception of Angkor Wat all this disappeared after the fifteenth century, leaving intriguing problems for the archaeologists of today. The metropolis may have decayed because of a change in religious practices, perhaps because of the decline of the Khmer kingdom. Angkor, then, was nothing but a colossal shrine, a monument to religious belief, albeit inextricably combined with secular conquest and empire-building. So much was invested in the monuments of the élite, so little in supporting the population, that the shrine-palace became the city. And there may well have been a periodic pattern in the inward movement of pilgrims which emphasized this function.

viii

There are many parallels to this emphasis on religio-magic ceremonial in some of the protohistoric cities of the New World; so much so that formerly some scholars thought they were derived from the Old World. By now diffusion has been discounted as an explanation. What we can safely say is that urban civilizations here, as in the Old World, arose from changes which were part and parcel of a food-producing revolution. Before the New World cities were built settled communities of farmers arose which could supply a very considerable surplus of food, and this became the necessary condition for urbanization. Within this economic and social context religio-magic beliefs and organizational genius provided an outcome not unlike that in South-East Asia, though later in time. Pre-Columbian civilization is a feature of the first millenium AD, coming to a climax just before its destruction by the Spaniards in the sixteenth century.

The evidence of the invaders leaves little doubt about the greatness of some of these cities and it has been more than confirmed by archaeologists. In central Mexico the city of Teotihuacan, which flourished between AD 200 and 750, must have had a population of about 200,000 at its peak. Here was a precisely planned grid of great avenues crossed by equally geometrically designed canals, covering about 2,072 hectares (20.6 square kilometres), greater in area than imperial Rome. At the crossings of the immense east–west and north–south processional ways was the ceremonial centre. Here was the citadel, two principal pyramids (not unlike the ziggurats of Mesopotamia), temples and other public buildings, and the palaces of the nobles. It is known that in addition to being a 'capital' and a religious centre this city had considerable manufacturing capacity in about 500 workshops, and that in its population there were colonies of 'foreign' Meso-American merchants.

It was Aztec power that destroyed Teotihuacan, and in its place they built another city, only 32 kilometres away. This was Tenochtitlan, the precursor of modern Mexico City. The Aztecs' became a dominant culture in the fifteenth century, not very long before it was destroyed in its turn by the Spanish in 1521. Tenochtitlan covered an area of 13 square kilometres, but its unique character was in its site, an island in a once very considerable lake. Much of its foundations were on artificial islands or on land created by draining the surrounding swamp. It was truly a New-World Venice, with a grid of canals and connections to the mainland by causeways. A contemporary observer tells us that 'the principal streets are entirely of water, and all travel is by bark and canoe, without which they could neither leave their houses nor return to them' (Swanson *et al.*, p. 107). But the most striking feature of all was the walled precinct at the heart of the city. Here was a ceremonial centre on a breath-taking scale consisting of vast pyramids, temples, a palace, and an administrative complex housing 3,000 servants. An estimated population of 80,000 is probably conservative, for outside the centre the city was divided into semi-autonomous 'wards' based on the clan system of the founders; they were landowning units and may have numbered between eighty and ninety. These were generally food-producing communities—thus strongly resembling the pattern in Angkor—and this reinforces the difficulties of identifying the urban as opposed to the rural segments. One could argue against the need to distinguish this separation, except in a functional sense; it is an academic debate aimed at academic ends. The division between the food-producing economy on the one hand and the magnificent superstructure of ceremony and administration on the other is sharp enough, yet their propinquity stresses interdependence: they were functionally complementary.

A last example confirms the problem of separation of functions. While the Aztec civilization was raising its monuments in central Mexico the Maya were also building an urban civilization in Yucatan, where cities like Tikal and Chichen Itza flourished between the ninth and the sixteenth century. The population of these cities has been variously estimated at up to 200,000, but again archaeologists have found the greatest difficulty in knowing where the city ends and agricultural communities begin.

Even the ceremonial centres tend to be rather diffuse, and beyond these the residential areas grade quite imperceptibly into farming plots. Even here the densities are quite high—*milpa* agriculture is a very intensive form of production, sometimes referred to as 'gardening'—but such densities can persist over a ten-mile radius. If we classify the entire periphery as rural we are left with a relatively small centre, very sharply focused on ceremonial. Even so there is no mistaking the monumentality of this climax. In Tikal this area alone covered 2.6 square kilometres and contained five stepped pyramids. Around them were processional avenues, colonnades, temples, courts, and an observatory. The quality and size of houses was highest near this centre, suggesting they belonged to an élite, both religious and secular. Further away standards diminish until we reach the houses of the poorest farmers.

The evidence of prehistoric and early historic cities across the world shows that social changes made possible by the increased productivity of settled agricultural communities produced rather similar results, whether in the Far East, Middle East, or Middle America. Differentiation within society, linked with specialization and division of labour, gave rise to social stratification, the élitist element of which was closely bound up with religio-magical beliefs, the ability to organize economic and human resources, and to create power structures of great efficiency. All these are common elements. The high degree of centralization implicit in political control led to the emergence of great cities which also expressed the non-material elements of the cultures which gave them birth—numeracy, literacy, science, architecture, art, and philosophy. Metropolitanism did not produce identical forms of cities: some had walls (albeit symbolic), some merged imperceptibly with farming land. What they all had was a ceremonial centre which was the climax of the whole city: the need for monumental architecture was universal and it universally expressed divinity, power, and wealth. In one way or another these will be continuing elements in the following chapters on historic and contemporary metropolitan cities.

3

Pre-Industrial Metropolis

Ships, towers, domes, theatres and temples . . .
WORDSWORTH

i

While so much of our speculation about the nature of the early metropolis is based on the interpretation of fragmentary evidence, most of it archaeological, ideas about the historic cities of Europe rest on more abundant information. There will always be debate about the relative greatness of these cities and what contributed most towards it, but there are few uncertainties about what they looked like, what the basis of their economy was, and how their societies lived and worked.

In his classic study *Medieval Cities* the French historian Pirenne was mainly concerned with the very big cities of that period, cities whose influence extended far beyond the city-state and which elevated themselves into a rather special class. His argument was that the urban tradition of the Roman world was not completely extinguished between the empire's dissolution and the early medieval period: but that following a period of comparative quiescence which had allowed freedom to move and to trade across the whole of Europe, the city re-emerged. He maintained that it was the great fairs which gave rise to cities: and although their power base was at first small they increased their wealth and influence largely in proportion to their ability to exploit free trading and so become leaders in world commerce.

A later French historian, Fernand Braudel, takes us a step further in his classic work *Civilization and Capitalism from the Fifteenth to the Eighteenth Century*. He uses a concept of 'world cities' which is not unlike that of Peter Hall. But whereas the latter's view is global Braudel confines himself to the world of medieval Europe. There were lands beyond which eventually came into this orbit, but knowledge of them was added to the world only during and after medieval times. At the beginning of the period the world was Europe together with north Africa and the Levant, and a vague penumbra of northern lands and Asiatic deserts. Braudel defines his field as being the 'world economy' (*Weltwirtschaft*) of the time, a 'fragment of the world, economically autonomous and able to provide for most of its needs, an organic unity'. It was the world perceived by those who lived in it and were responsible for its running—and for building one metropolis after another. If this world were indeed an organic unity then it must have at its centre a dominant city, a centre of economic power. But its economic integration was not that complete. What held it together socially and culturally was the Church. It was a Christian civilization.

Earlier, Islam had made its own sweeping inroads into this world, at one time dominating much of the Iberian peninsula. It was here that the Muslims had established their own metropolis at Cordoba. By the tenth century this provincial capital had become a semi-autonomous Ummayyad princedom with a population variously estimated at between 100,000 and 500,000. It was certainly a cosmopolitan city, the centre of a glittering court and a rich cultural life. Its ruler, Caliph de Hakam II, had a library of 400,000 items. But the Islamic world withdrew to north Africa and the Levant, leaving Christianity supreme with Rome at its heart.

Rome, the spiritual centre, was also the pivot of a 'universal' system of social control through its bishops and priests. It was the centre of pilgrimages. It was a seat of power. Following the decline of the classical city Rome had endured eight hundred years of strife during which it emerged as a commune but failed to exploit its religious ascendancy. During the early fourteenth century the popes had even moved their seat of power to Avignon. In spite of claims to primacy the city probably had never more than 30,000 population during this period. It was from the fifteenth century that, for the second time in its history, the foundations of greatness were laid. In a physical sense these came to fruition in the grand designs of Pope Sixtus V (1585–90), who initiated a series of magnificent avenues connecting the pilgrimage churches of the city (Bacon, pp. 71 ff.). The processional aspects of religious ceremony in all its pomp and splendour were etched on the landscape, and this became the framework of the Renaissance city. The transformation of a rather chaotic assemblage of churches and shrines into an orderly pattern combined symbolism and rationality, and accords well with what I have already referred to as conferring sacred values to the design of a city; and at the same time it reflected the age's concern with perspective, the making of vistas, and even met the new demands arising from the increasing use of wheeled carriages. The city flourished, and by 1600 it was a bustling metropolis of 100,000 persons, with a grandeur to match its significance in Christendom.

During this period many cities vied for economic supremacy in Europe, and all of them can justly claim to be of metropolitan status. According to Braudel a 'world-city' resembled other cities in most respects but it also 'stood apart from them'; 'the metropolis was a super-city'. 'Exceptional and enigmatic', this handful of cities dazzled observers. 'Venice,' said Philippe de Commyns in 1495, 'was the most triumphant city I have ever seen' (Braudel, ch. 1). Amsterdam, in Descartes's view, was a 'sort of inventory of the possible'. 'What place on earth could one choose,' he wrote in 1631, 'where all the commodities and all the curiosities one could wish for are as easy to find as in this city?' (Braudel, p. 30). Another feature they had in common was again shared by the previous examples: 'their precocious and pronounced social diversification'. They had a proletariat, a bourgeoisie, and a patriciate, the last controlling the wealth and power. And wealth there certainly was. In 1587 a Spanish historian commented that 'with the treasure imported into Amsterdam every street could have been paved with gold and silver' (Braudel, p. 31). Hyperbole perhaps, an echo of Marco Polo, but a perception based on the real accumulation of riches.

Braudel sees as metropolitan those cities which controlled for a time the economic life of the world of medieval Europe. Within this realm leadership, primacy, and power could—and did— switch from one city to another, much as they did in China in the first millennium or among the Maya in Yucatan. The switch in Europe reflected a bipolarity which has been a constant feature in its history as well as its geography, namely the Mediterranean and the North. Even the great fairs of the Champagne illustrated not only linkages but constant interplay between the two regions. Primacy in economic life was held first by Venice then by Bruges, by Genoa then by Antwerp. Eventually Amsterdam replaced Antwerp as the North finally took over economic control, only to lose it to London. Thereafter, says Braudel, we can see New York taking over from London as Atlantic links create a new axis. Perhaps the economic vicissitudes he deals with are more dramatic and more easily highlighted than the cultural continuity which these cities maintained. But by any standards here is a clutch of metropolitan cities which are worth examining because they display not only peaks of the medieval civilization which this whole world shared, but also the individual genius which makes one city different from another and gives a metropolis its distinctiveness, its claim to be the expression of a particular society with its own view of life, its own contribution to the whole.

Braudel's masterly panorama of late medieval civilization is based on the primacy of economic forces, and he sees the rise of civilization, the flourishing of cities, and the shifts of power purely in terms of commerce and the rise of capitalism. Rome does not figure in his story, nor does medieval Paris. But aspects of culture other than trade—religion in particular—were extremely important in medieval life. It may well be that by the late medieval period secular forces had partly supplanted the religious, but the sum total of social forces promoting metropolitan life were certainly more than the economic and the rational. Medieval Paris from the twelfth to the fourteenth century achieved its pre-eminence in Europe as a royal city and the home of the greatest university in western Christendom. It owed its position to political and cultural forces, and 'no view of the historic process which is exclusively economic will explain the importance of Paris in the medieval world or the influence that it exercised over the minds and imaginations of European men' (Douglas, p. 192). The University of the Sorbonne, based on even earlier colleges of 1235, was founded in 1257. It was the embodiment of European culture and became the centre of a renaissance of learning. By the late thirteenth century Paris was a city of 150,000 people. Its economic life was no different from that of any other very large town of the period: its crafts and trade were important but not distinctive enough to warrant either the growth of the city or its fame. The university, however was the embodiment of Latin culture and represented Christendom at its peak.

ii

Venice was the first European city to establish a primacy based largely on commerce, and the first to prove that a tiny city-state could develop into a 'world city'. It established its autonomy in the ninth century and grew in the unique environment of lagoons, a setting which has given it a continuing distinctiveness. Venice was wedded to the sea and soon proved able to exploit the trade routes between the eastern and western Mediterranean. On the strength of emerging as a middle-man *par excellence*, by the fourteenth century the city controlled this entire trade, having within its orbit not just the Adriatic and the Mediterranean but the Levant, Persia, India, and North Africa. By 1420 the city had a population of 190,000 and it was the undisputed master of the sea routes. Although it commanded considerable resources in its own hinterland, such as grain and wine from the lower Po valley, it can be truly said that it was the first city to live by commerce. This depended on its fleet of 3,000 vessels for coastal trade and 300 long-distance vessels; the first employed 17,000 sailors, the second 8,000. In addition the city had 45 galleys deploying 11,000 sailors and soldiers. One of the most striking features of Venice was the extensive arsenal where these boats were built and which must have employed thousands of carpenters and caulkers.

Venice also evolved a unique system of government based on a Grand Council representing the élite—its two hundred greatest families. This body had an elective role and produced a Senate which was legislative in function. The executive was a college, or cabinet, which had six ministers, responsible for war, finance, land forces, state ceremonies, and so on. The ultimate responsibility lay with the Doge, who presided over the Grand Council.

This sophisticated system served Venice well for nearly a millennium, and it was its tight control of resources and power that underlay the city's enormous success from the fourteenth to the sixteenth century.

While the economic functions of Venice were the foundation of its wealth they did not overshadow its achievements in other activities, many of which depended on the wealth it generated. Venice was a centre of art, music, and learning. It had prolific printing-presses. In the last decade of the fifteenth century alone these produced 1,491 works, compared with 460 in Rome, 288 in Milan, and 179 in Florence. Patronage was of immense importance even during the gradual decline of the city after the fifteenth century. Veronese, Tintoretto, and Palladio were still to come. Commerce produced a brilliant penumbra of cultural achievement which was a notable contribution to the mainstream of European civilization.

iii

Not far to the south of Venice another small city-state became a dazzling metropolis. On a bridging point on the Arno river where merchants brought foodstuffs from the north to the south and traded wool in the opposite direction, Florence, too, based its early fortunes on commerce. But this was limited by the fact that the city had no access to the sea, and its continuing prosperity in the twelfth and thirteenth centuries grew on woollen manufacturing, a highly developed industry closely controlled by guilds. By the fifteenth century silk had taken pride of place: there were eighty-three silk factories in the city, many specializing in satins, velvets, and brocades. But the wealth produced in this way soon became the basis of an even richer source of wealth—banking. The first 'florin' was issued as early as the thirteenth century, and it soon became the standard currency throughout all Europe. The Florentines were extremely successful bankers and dominated the money-markets of the time, and on this success they built a splendid cultural heritage. More than anything, Florence was the heart of the Renaissance. It was the home of Dante, Petrarch, and Boccaccio: it produced Cimabue and Giotto. Under the powerful patronage of the Medici family, at its height in the late fifteenth century, it had no rival in Europe. Even in its comparative decline it could still sustain artists like Alberti, Brunelleschi, and Donatello.

It is extraordinarily difficult to quantify the significance of cities like Venice and Florence. Some of the figures I have quoted are a hint of the material wealth and the resources on which they flourished. We know that in the fifteenth century Venice's budget was equal to that of France and greater than that of England or Spain. The return on trade has been calculated at around 40 per cent, but much of this was translated into beautiful buildings and the arts. The two cities set the pace not only as leaders of the European economy, but as leaders of the Renaissance as well. On the other hand, we should remember that it was a Venetian, Marco Polo, who only a little earlier was overwhelmed by the magnificence of the cities of China; his awe and wonder are the best measurement of the opulence he witnessed. This puts into perspective what was happening in Europe. But it does not diminish the brilliance of the city-states. All the ingredients of metropolis were there, put together by the initiative and genius of an élite to produce new levels of achievement.

iv

The 'world economy' of medieval Europe was not an exclusively Mediterranean phenomenon. At a very early stage northern Europe was drawn into the network of commercial activities, partly through the activities of the great fairs. Europe had been traversed by the routes of itinerant merchants from time immemorial. Their transactions were now being crystallized, given permanence in a series of cities at the ends of axes of communication, and here wealth was accumulating in the emerging metropolises of the thirteenth and fourteenth centuries. By this time Bruges, for example, was in contention for a place among the super-cities.

Bruges was the centre of the Flanders weaving industry, and even as early as the twelfth century had flourishing fairs. Its food resources were drawn from a very wide area—grain from

Normandy, wine from Bordeaux and the Rhine, and luxuries from further afield. A breakthrough in commerce came as early as 1134, when the dredging of a silted river channel gave it direct access to the sea. The channel became a harbour, and from here a series of canals fed the entire city. Incidentally, subsequent silting of this channel during the fifteenth century did much to discourage trade and contribute to the city's decline. In the period of growth, however, Bruges had a monopoly of English wool and a secure base for its manufactures. In addition, its links with the Hanseatic League of commercial cities in the Baltic considerably strengthened its role as a commercial centre, adding to the existing Mediterranean trade. The latter began in 1277 when a ship from Genoa arrived in Bruges, to be followed soon by many Italian merchants. Within a short time the city dominated the north's trade with southern Europe and the Levant.

By the fifteenth century the population of Bruges was probably around 100,000. It was now a financial as well as a commercial centre. Its role was symbolized by the great market square and hall, the belfry of which was well over 100 metres high. The famous Bourse had been opened in 1309. Guild houses adorned the fine streets and graceful stone bridges abounded in a city whose very name meant 'bridges'. As in all metropolitan cities communities of foreign merchants settled there in considerable numbers. The English, for example, had their own quarters, their own church, and even their own inn: it was in Bruges that Caxton printed his first English book. A Spaniard described Bruges in 1430 as having fine houses and streets and noted that 'the inhabitants were very extravagant in their food and much given to all kinds of luxury' (Jones and van Zandt, p. 52). Much of the city's opulence arose from the fact that it was the court of the Dukes of Burgundy. It was also the centre of Flemish art, where Memling and Van Eyck flourished. Braudel is rather reluctant to give Bruges the same status as Venice: it was not quite a 'world-city' but rather a 'world market' (p. 101). Nevertheless it had metropolitan characteristics and it was a pivotal city in the world of medieval Europe, the first city to register a swing from the south to the north, and in this way the precursor of Antwerp, Amsterdam, and London.

Not that the Mediterranean story ends with Venice. Genoa emerges as a major port in several historic epochs, Etruscan and Greek, Roman and Byzantine. After the Crusades the city re-emerged as a trading centre for the Mediterranean and beyond, as well as a centre for innovations in shipbuilding, navigation, and, eventually, in banking techniques. I have already referred to the arrival of the first vessel from Genoa in Bruges: this was a pre-cursor to trade with the whole of northern Europe; by this time Genoa already had several links with Asia as well. Now a city of some 100,000 inhabitants, Genoa was bound to clash with Venice in an endeavour to capture more trade. In fact its fleets were des-troyed by Venice in 1380, virtually eliminating the city from trade in the Adriatic and eastward. But the city's triumphs were still to come when it allied itself with Spain in 1557. For the next seventy years it was virtually a broker for New World gold and silver, and its merchants, dominating financial life in the chief cities of Spain as well as Italy, gave Genoa an 'empire' of its own. This dramatic rise in its fortunes was followed by a decline which paralleled that of Spain, and although it can claim to have been briefly the leader of European commerce and finance it never really supplanted the control of northern Europe which was by then in the hands of Amsterdam. Genoa was to expand again in the nineteenth century as a major city in a newly united Italy: but this was within a very different economic and political context, and its role, how-ever important, was local and national rather than as a competi-tor for world status.

The story of successive metropolitan leaders in Europe swings to the north again as Antwerp's fortunes flourish. In some ways it was a successor to Bruges. As a port it offered much better oppor-tunities for development and it exploited them brilliantly. Antwerp was the first port to look westward across the Atlantic, giving the first indication of the radical expansion of the world of medieval Europe. It became the successor of Venice and Genoa. Its rise indicated a firm and final shift in the centre of gravity of commerce from the Mediterranean to the north. Even so, political factors played a strong part as the shift responded to Atlantic trade and the bringing of the New World into the orbit of the Old. The fact that Spain had political control in the early sixteenth century meant that Antwerp was being used by Spain as a point of exchange in its own trading interests. There had been no tradition of commerce in Antwerp before 1500; it possessed only a small fleet. Braudel sees the beginning of commerce as being so dramatic that 'the city woke one morning to find itself at the pinnacle of the world' (p. 145). It is true that Antwerp had previously imported English wool and had dealings in German trade, but there was no hint of interest in the world beyond until the Portuguese introduced the spice trade in 1501. Thereafter the city found itself a supreme role as a redistribution centre. Not only did it control wholesaling of exotic goods from beyond Europe, but as a result of trading grain, timber, ships, and even men for New World silver from the Spanish it became the principal financial centre of Europe, reaching the peak of its prosperity in the mid-sixteenth century. At that time, with a rapidly growing population, Antwerp had all the trappings of a 'world city'. In addition to cloth manufacturing there were salt and sugar refineries and dye works, and by the end of that century it was a thriving industrial city specializing in cloth, linen, and tapestry. But by this time, too, much of the financial impetus had evaporated, some for a period going, as we have seen, to a Genoa that was exploiting its Spanish connections.

V

It was Amsterdam which took up the leadership of European economic activity in the seventeenth century; and it was on a sound basis of familiarity with the sea and sea trading on the one hand and a highly developed urban economy on the other. These traits were common to all the seven small states that made up the Netherlands. Since 1500 sea fishing had played an increasingly important role in their economy, based partly on the location of herring shoals in the North Sea and partly on whaling from much further afield (Lambert, p. 176). Although the Netherlands could not be thought of as a single state until the Peace of Munster in 1648, these component states boasted twelve independent towns. Half the population could be classed as urban, and so much of the countryside was commercialized or urbanized that wheat had to be imported. There was a great measure of interdependence between the towns and this allowed a high degree of specialization, in a way not very dissimilar to the activities of the cities making up Randstad-Holland today. For example, industry prospered in Leyden, Harlem, and Delft, shipbuilding at Brill and Rotterdam; Dordrecht depended heavily on Rhine traffic, and the Hague became a political centre.

At the top of the hierarchy of Netherland towns was Amsterdam. By the mid-seventeenth century it was dominating European trade. It had initially taken over Baltic trade from the Hanseatic League; it controlled trade in the Levant, where Mediterranean control had slipped away once and for all; it was in touch with the Far East; and, most important of all, it was in control of Atlantic trade, particularly from Brazil and North America. For a brief period it seemed as if it would establish more than a territorial foothold in the latter, but Nieuw Amsterdam was lost to Britain in 1667 to become New York, and there was no further attempt at colonizing the western hemisphere. The Dutch were much too busy expanding in South-East Asia. By 1650 Amsterdam had a fleet of between 14,000 and 15,000 vessels, 60 per cent of the entire European fleet, manned by nearly 50,000 sailors. The city was also a hive of industry, beginning with fish-curing, beer manufacturing, and wool; the last developed into a linen industry, and then into silk. Shipbuilding became a major activity, and of course there were those industries based on oriental commerce: tobacco, tea, coffee, sugar, oils, pigments, cocoa, and diamonds.

As in all the metropolitan cities I have dealt with the population was cosmopolitan. Not only did the Asiatic links ensure oriental communities, but Amsterdam was a magnet for fine craftsmen from all parts of Europe, for refugees of all kinds, and for Jews. Moreover, this city of 200,000 people was a centre for learning and the arts, familiar to Spinoza and Grotius, of Hals and Rembrandt, Vermeer and Steen. In 1699 a traveller reports:

Amsterdam I compare to a fair where many merchants from many parts bring their merchandise which is sure to find a customer; as in ordinary fairs the residents do not use the things they sell, so the Dutch, who collect goods from every corner in Europe, keep for their own use only what is strictly necessary for life and sell to other nations the produce they consider superfluous and which are always more expensive. (Braudel, p. 236)

On such exchange is wealth accumulated.

On the whole Braudel's thesis of a 'world economy' controlled by a series of 'world-cities' has proved a most useful framework for examining the metropolitan city in late medieval Europe. One of its merits is that it relates the emerging great city to the activities of society in the widest sense. In these activities he gives absolute priority to economics, relegating social and cultural elements to subsidiary roles. One must accept the dramatic changes that were implicit in the new economic order which emerged in Europe between 1200 and 1600, but without necessarily accepting the assertion that they determined the political and cultural situation (de Vries). The dynamics of an emerging European civilization, based partly on a surge in population, increasing technical skill, and the cohesion of a Christian-Latin culture, certainly facilitated the rise of the merchants to a new eminence, and from them a class of financiers who would control the wealth of the continent in a new way. The simple activity of exchanging goods by transferring them from one place to another became a very specialized affair—wholesaling, retailing, transport, insurance, banking. A plethora of new techniques and new institutions rose to deal with transactions of all kinds. Most important from our point of view was the location of these activities. The actual transportation of goods diminished to be one aspect in many, and a menial one at that. Control lay in the hands of the merchant who did not have to leave his home base. It was the concentration of families of such merchants which laid the foundation of metropolis. Europe had always had its markets and fairs and its prosperous towns, but these cities were 'like the peaks of a mountain range'.

They were all enormously attractive cities, a magnet to tens of thousands of people and consequently very large indeed by European standards in late medieval times. Looked at from a broader historical perspective the size becomes relative. Hall refers to the 'smallness' of Amsterdam before the nineteenth-century exploitation of its situation as an outlet of the Rhine led to massive growth in the industrial era. But this was a response to another civilization and another set of circumstances. In pre-industrial medieval Europe these cities were giants. More than that, they were centres of wealth and power, controllers of world commerce, and consumer cities which also gave rise to great cultural institutions, nurturing learning and the arts. The world revolved around them.

vi

There were other worlds. Through travellers and merchants like Marco Polo, Europe was well aware of 'world economies' beyond its own system of exchange. Islam was very near home. Here was an economy which laid the foundation of another great urban civilization. Important though sea routes must have been in its development this economy relied on quite a different system of transportation—the overland route with the camel as a beast of burden. Caravan routes were a Muslim monopoly and played a major part in an Islamic realm which extended from Tangier to Delhi.

The names alone of two cities are sufficient to remind us of the wealth and power of the urban population being generated by Islam in the late medieval period, just as Cordoba did in an earlier period: they are Isfahan and Delhi. In 1598 Shah Abbas of Persia moved his capital to a new site and created the city of Isfahan. Estimates of its population are highly speculative, but according to some it could have been approaching half a million by the late seventeenth century, far outstripping all the European cities I have dealt with. Isfahan had all the characteristics of a great metropolis, including being cosmopolitan with its communities of Armenians, Christians, and Jews. The richness of its architecture was only one symbol of its wealth. Even more arresting was the accumulation of wealth and power at Delhi and Agra in Mogul India. We usually think of Delhi as the seat of power, but in fact Agra and Fatelpur Sikri were brought within the orbit of its military and political control, and the combined population of the three cities could well have approached a million. Delhi at the height of its power in the later seventeenth century was a magnificent city of vast proportions, sharing the characteristics of other Muslim cities, of which it was the most easterly.

Beyond Islam were two further realms. I have already referred to China with its well-organized system of metropolitan cities. By the sixteenth century an appendage to the European realm was beginning to establish a system of cities in South-East Asia, based on the exploitation of all those exotic resources which added richness and variety to life in temperate Europe. Although the Portuguese, Dutch, French, and British were busy exploiting these resources, the seeds of empire were beginning to grow which would eventually create a new generation of super-cities.

A word about scale, for population was still an important criterion in assessing metropolitan cities, at least in the eyes of contemporary observers. 'The greatness of a city,' said Botero, 'is not the largeness of site or the circuit of the walls, but the multitude of the inhabitants and their power' (Peterson, p. 227). The medieval European metropolis, very large by the standards of the time, had between 100,000 and 200,000 inhabitants. Cities like Venice and Bruges were jumped-up versions of the city-state with a comparatively limited resource base of men and food from which to extend their mercantile and financial activities. But there were signs of consolidation of territories—as in the Netherlands—into states which were to become the standard national units, and some of these further expanded into empires. As far as metropolis is concerned we are entering the era of capital cities, i.e. cities which headed a whole system of cities within the state. Mumford considers this a very distinctive stage in the urban history of Europe. We leave the medieval city and turn our attention to what he calls the 'baroque' city, a term which signifies the kind of society as well as the formal elements of design.

The key to the new order was the consolidation of increasing political power in the capital city of the state, and its expression in the court and the administration of the head of the state. This coincides with a swing from the sacred to the secular, as the Church ceased to be the focus of social ceremony and grandeur to give way to the court and its attendant splendour. The kingdom that mattered was definitely the material one. The increasing role of the capital city meant that it attracted people as never before. There is a quantum leap in population and many cities attain numbers rarely realized in medieval Europe; some, like Naples, Paris, and London began to soar to the half-million mark. The gap between the capital city in each state—the primate city—and other cities widened, a measure of the degree of concentration of resources and power; the capital city must be unchallenged, the only centre of political control. The sheer numbers of the standing armies in some capitals was a significant proportion of the total population. By the beginning of the eighteenth century, in a consolidated Britain which had successfully absorbed Wales, Scotland, and Ireland, London, with half a million people, represented 1 in 10 of the total population of the United Kingdom.

vii

London is a good example of the new metropolis as well as of the old, because almost by accident of history the two components had been enshrined in two cities which still exist; the City of London and the City of Westminster. The first is the old commercial centre, the medieval European 'world city'. It had grown as a trading point, gradually developed as a port, and finally taken over financial control of north-west Europe from the Hanseatic League and the merchants of Lombardy. The consolidation of the United Kingdom gave it a home market unmatched by most cities, and it eventually wrested the initiative from Amsterdam as the leader of the 'world' economy. When Gresham opened his Royal Exchange on Cornhill (1566–8) it was a symbol of London's supremacy in the national and international market. Nearby was St Paul's cathedral, a centre for the exchange of information and trading intelligence, its precinct soon to become the cradle of the printing and publishing trades. Together these activities heralded London's supremacy in world commerce.

A little more than a mile upstream was the other city, growing around three institutions which enshrined state power. The first was a shrine, Westminster Abbey, where all English monarchs were crowned and most of them buried. The second was

Westminster Hall, which saw the birth of parliamentary government, the seat of political power. The third was Whitehall Palace, the residence of the sovereign in London. Together they formed a powerful symbolic base for a thriving nation, and it was the residential and institutional growth around them that was the nucleus of baroque London. From the beginning of the seventeenth century royalty became less peripatetic and more closely associated with Whitehall. It was there that Inigo Jones planned a magnificent palace which would have dwarfed Versailles: but only the banqueting hall was built (1619) and this remains as one of the finest Palladian gems in the country.

All the appurtenances of court now sprang up in and around Whitehall and Westminster—foreign envoys and their staff, courtiers and diplomats, all swelled the growing bureaucracy which erupted from the business of running the state. And there were those whose business it was to have the king's ear and to be near enough to benefit from the royal exchequer. The northern bank of the Thames which linked the cities of London and Westminster—the Strand—was lined with mansions, formerly of the princes of the church, now of the aristocracy, who had to maintain their own courts as near the centre of national power as possible. Gradually the baroque city was to lure more and more prosperous people to the new streets and squares, a salubrious environment near the royal parks, the heart of what would later be known as the West End. This was the area of conspicuous consumption, planned in the new style of handsome, classical squares parading the wealth of a leisured class. Money was made in the City: here it was spent! Masques, theatres, music abounded; luxury shops lined the avenues. Some of the atmosphere of this glittering city was captured by a German visitor in the 1770s in his description of Fleet Street, which led from the old city to the new:

Buildings with plate-glass windows line both sides of the street. On the street floors there are shops which seem to be built completely of glass, thousands of lights illuminate silver-ware shops, stores with engravings on display, book stores, stores where one may see watches, glass, pewter, paintings, ladies' dresses and finery in good and poor taste, gold, jewels and steel ornaments, and next to them coffee shops and no end of offices

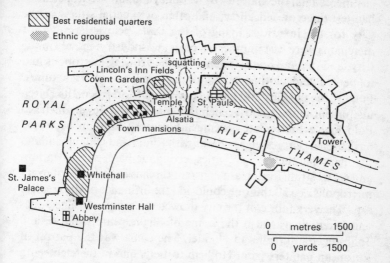

FIG. 3. Main social areas of seventeenth-century London.

selling lottery tickets. The confectioners' displays blind one's eyes and tickle one's nose with their brilliant candelabra. In the centre of the street, chaise after chaise, cab after cab, cart after cart. Mingling with this din and the hum and sound of a thousand voices and feet are heard the bells of many church steeples and the tinkle of the milkman's bells. (Schneider, p. 230)

Of course there was another side, the dens of vice in Alsatia, the rookeries and slums, the gin alleys (George). Seventeenth- and eighteenth-century London was a city of great social diversity and sharp class-differences (Fig. 3). Westminster was the outward expression of the upper strata. The monarch reigned supreme and his court dominated much of the social activity of this part of the city. Below this was an aristocracy which felt obliged to keep a London mansion in addition to their country estates. They lived in London for 'the season'. Then came those who governed and those who administered the law, who commanded the national purse. Samuel Pepys was a good example of a high-ranking official in a new and expanding bureaucracy. Lower still, and jostling for recognition, were the city merchants, the majority of whom by the seventeenth century had left the crowded, dirty, and often pestilential streets of the City for the luxurious living of the west. Below the ranks of merchants were vast numbers in craft and industry, mainly in the City, and in retail and servicing, for the growing metropolis had to be fed and clothed and groomed and served its luxuries. Finally, the old City still had its enclaves of foreigners, its Dutch instrument-makers and French lace-makers and Jews. If Marco Polo had come to late seventeenth-century London he would have been as impressed as he was with Kinsai and Ch'ang-an, and the many parallels, in activities, economic base, specialization, and social stratification are constant threads in the story of every metropolis. To all this one could add the brilliance of the creative arts. The very fabric of the city showed the genius of Inigo Jones and Wren. It was also the home of Shakespeare, Milton, and Johnson, of Purcell and Handel. The court was the patron of European painters from Holbein to Lely, and in the eighteenth century, partly through its Royal Academy, London become the centre of a native tradition in art. By this time too the Royal Society was reflecting a surge of activity in science and philosophy.

There is little doubt that London had taken the commercial lead in Europe and was already engaged in an overseas expansion in trade and territory which would give it a lead in the world. But across the English Channel another metropolis was proving an equal competitor for greatness. Paris may well have been considered a more handsome city than London until the eighteenth century. It was a long-established metropolis and had even been a 'national' capital since the tenth century; and I have already described its cultural domination of Europe in the thirteenth century and its massive population at that time. By 1500 its population was probably 300,000. But its apogee is firmly linked with the reign of Louis XIV (1643–1715), when it epitomized the splendour of a capital city and all that this implied. This was the Paris of Descartes and Pascal, of Racine and Molière; when French was accepted as the international language—the 'lingua franca'—a status it would maintain until the First World War.

A Paris which had grown haphazardly, retaining many of its

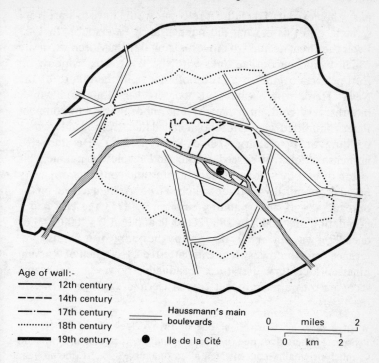

Age of wall:-
——— 12th century
– – – 14th century
–·–·– 17th century
·········· 18th century
▬▬▬ 19th century

═══ Haussmann's main boulevards

● Ile de la Cité

0 miles 2
0 km 2

FIG. 4. Paris: successive walls and Haussmann's main boulevards.

medieval features within walls rebuilt more than once, was no place for a Sun King to build a new palace. Versailles, symbolizing the wealth and power of the monarchy, was built outside the city, and it was one of the great achievements of baroque planning. The city itself had to wait another century and a half for a similar grandeur, when Haussmann razed much of medieval Paris to the ground and replaced it with nearly a hundred kilometres of splendid boulevards (Fig. 4). London never achieved this overall monumentality, for once it had turned its back on Wren's plan for rebuilding after the fire of 1666 the city was content to pursue a domestic scale of building which became its most distinctive characteristic, and which underlies much of its individuality today.

London did not attempt the true baroque vision; Paris only

partly achieved it. To realise it fully one would have to start from scratch, and this is what did happen in St Petersburg. In 1703 Peter the Great decided to move his capital from Moscow to a site which would encourage links with the West. His 'window on Europe' was begun on a group of islands in the mouth of the Neva. Here, where winter nights were very long and winter months very cold, in a marshy and inhospitable environment Peter committed what one scholar called the 'irresponsible act' of building St Petersburg (Talbot-Rice, p. 253). He imported immense armies of forced labour and resolutely pursued his vision of baroque monumental planning and construction, a city based economically on trade switched from Archangel and on the bureaucracy of an expanding empire. By 1753 the city had a population of 80,000, by 1800 200,000, and by 1875 400,000. For decades it was universally detested by the bourgeoisie, whose preference for Moscow is eloquently attested in so much of Russian nineteenth-century literature. Gradually, however, it became recognized as a magnificent city. A German diplomat writes in the 1850s:

What a pleasure to stroll at one or two o'clock along the Nevsky Prospect! Where does one find such splendour, such colourful life and so much originality concentrated all in one place? . . . If one ploughs ahead past the rows of handsome houses and throngs of pedestrians from many countries, in colourful uniforms or folk-costumes, past the many street vendors who from behind their copper samovars recommend their tea and *priskuska*, one readily forgets the Boulevards, the Rue de Rivoli, the Linden, the Jungfernstieg. This is unique. (Schneider, p. 244)

So an 'artificial' capital became a metropolis. Not often does such a project start on a virgin site. Philip II of Spain, with an eye to centralizing his power, moved his court to a small town in 1561 and transformed it into his new capital, Madrid. But more recent examples are better known: Washington, chosen by Congress to symbolize the union of the thirteen states, Canberra to avoid the difficulties of choosing between the existing state capitals, and Brasilia to counter the attractions of the peripheral state capitals of Brazil. Each one faced immense political problems initially; but for the moment let me pursue some of the implications of investing such cities with the significance of their capital function, and how idealized planning becomes an essential part of this exercise.

viii

The symbolic element has been a recurring theme in the history of metropolitan cities. Monumental expression was given to religious ideas by building pyramids, ziggurats, temples, and cathedrals: political control and the accumulation of wealth was made explicit in palaces, ritual and ceremony in processional ways. The Chinese city was seen in terms of formal elements reflecting the cosmos. The great expansion of population in Western countries in post-medieval times, and in particular the growth of cities, gave planning a tremendous impetus, and the results inevitably reflected the ideas and values of the day: secular control and rational, scientific thinking imposed a pattern no less distinctive than religious beliefs.

The new rationality, a return to the order of the Greek world, contrasted sharply with the 'organic' and rather haphazard growth which characterized the medieval world. I have already referred to late sixteenth-century Rome in which Sixtus V built a number of grand avenues which introduced order in what had been the rather aimless meandering of pilgrims for centuries. These avenues were the framework on which baroque Rome was built. The churches and the obelisks and squares which provided the nodes, together with the processional ways, arose from a need to express religious values, but used the language of the Renaissance to do so.

A sacred space was created in Rome, but the word 'sacred' need not always mean religious in the narrow sense of the word. Sixtus' Rome brought together religious and rational thinking, uniting the values of a receding medieval Europe with those of an emerging renaissance era. The impact of the new was even more conspicuous in Paris, where Versailles enshrined the primacy of a secular state. In Wren's proposal for a new London after the Great Fire the main focal point of the avenues and processional ways was not St Paul's but a new stock exchange. St Petersburg was a monument to a tsar and to the bureaucracy that kept his state in being. And the most clearly symbolic of all these cities was Washington. Like St Petersburg it had the advantage of being built on virgin territory; the plan could be translated directly on to the environment. Perhaps it was a disadvantage to have no *raison d'être* but that of government, but at least it allowed that function to be uniquely expressed in its plan.

The site of Washington was a compromise solution aimed at satisfying the aspirations of the northern and the southern groups of states. The precise location was chosen by Washington himself, and only his personal hope that this spot would eventually be the gateway to the interior could possibly have justified the choice of a low-lying, swampy, and malarial stretch of the Potomac estuary. A Frenchman, L'Enfant, was asked by Jefferson, Washington's successor, to prepare a plan for the new capital; a clear invitation for the introduction of the current European baroque fashion which also accorded with Jefferson's aspirations that Greek rationality should permeate the new city as it should underlie the new constitution. He asked for a grid, but what L'Enfant superimposed on the grid was quite ingenious. His original plan shows three nodal points (shades of Sixtus' Rome)—Capitol, White House, and Supreme Court, occupying what small 'hills' there were in the landscape. These represented the three arms of government: legislature, executive, and judiciary (Fig. 5). The first, making the most of a gentle eminence of 30 metres above sea level, was at the head of a great processional avenue—the Mall—leading down to the banks of the Potomac; this was the prime axis, the other two being at right angles and leading to the White House and the Supreme Court. Traversing the checker-board of streets were thirteen avenues, one for each state in the Union. L'Enfant had cleverly etched the new constitution on the face of the proposed city.

Most of the plan survived the rather piecemeal and sporadic building of the following hundred years. The judiciary axis disappeared, but monumentality triumphed in the Capitol. And the symbolism was confirmed in the Mall where an immense obelisk was raised in memory of Washington on the axis of the White House, and the Mall itself closed at the river end in a temple

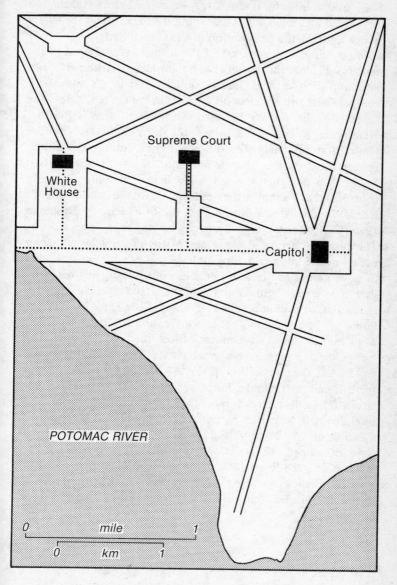

Fig. 5. The three axes of L'Enfant's Washington.

memorial to Lincoln. It took a very long time before Washington developed into any kind of a city, but it still enshrines the values which underlie the constitution of the United States.

Washington's was the last of the formal layouts born of the renaissance. Whether the city can be considered a true metropolis is doubtful; its role is purely political, and in no way can it compete with other metropolitan cities in the United States. The nearest parallel outside the States in modern times is Brasilia. Here again the conception is new, the site a virgin one. Like the United States Brazil is a federation of States, but its population is concentrated on the Atlantic seaboard in giant cities like São Paulo, Rio de Janeiro, Recife, and Belo Horizonte. To unify control and to symbolize the need to open up the interior Brazil's federal functions were moved from Rio de Janeiro to Brasilia in 1960. Lucio Costa designed the city in the shape of an airliner. The fuselage, arranged along one of the greatest avenues ever built—over 6 kilometres long and 350 metres wide—is delegated to government institutions. Brazil's constitution was based on that of its great neighbour to the north, so the great concourse at the end of the avenue is called the Plaza of the Three Powers, the home of the legislature, the executive, and the judiciary. Next come ministries and government offices, then the cathedral. The 'wings' of the plane, on a great curved axis, form residential sectors. At the intersection of the two axes are the cultural and recreational centres and a downtown business quarter. The population of Brasilia is already more than 1.5 million if we include the satellite towns which are part of the metropolitan area. However magnificent its plan and its architecture the city is too young to have developed the traditional features of metropolitanism. What it is is the latest example of the expression of a society's political ideology in asphalt and concrete, avenues and monumental buildings which will clearly tell the future what its values are today.

4

Industrial Metropolis

The monster called . . . the metropolis of empire.

COBBETT

i

One of the first generalizations I made about the primate city was
that it was usually a feature of pre-industrial society. A comparatively simple economy tended to produce one dominant city, and
when some of these societies expanded, when city-states became
nation-states and then the centres of empire, then a true metropolis might emerge which towered over its contemporary cities.
This happened relatively few times in history, producing cities
like Babylon, Rome, Constantinople, and Ch'ang-an; and later
the great cities of medieval Europe and then of the baroque
period. When societies became more complex the dominance of
the primary city decreased as other cities within the same society
played increasingly prominent roles in national life. Industrialization and the introduction of major technological changes
gave rise to new activities often tied to the location of new
resources. For this period we need a more sophisticated explanation of why people congregated in large numbers and at a variety
of locations.

The dramatic increase in numbers of large cities which characterized the nineteenth century and laid the basis of our modern
Western systems was an outcome of industrialization, though the
link was not a simple causal one. The redistribution of population in the last two hundred years must be seen against the background of an upsurge in the population as a whole in the Western
world. World population in 1650 is estimated at between 470 and
545 million. In 1950 it was 3,500 million. Whereas the standard
increase before 1650, based on a birth rate of 35/40 per thousand

and a death rate of 30/35 per thousand, was probably between 2.5 and 5 per cent a century, in the next four hundred years it was 65 per cent, and in the century 1850–1950 it was 100 per cent. This change was peculiar to Western civilization (we shall see later how radically this picture has changed). The great increase in 1650–1950 was due primarily to a decrease in death rates. A much more efficient agriculture, an enormous extension of food-producing regions, and a more varied diet, together with more trade and better distribution, had all contributed to decrease in famine and epidemics; this coincided with improved hygiene, innoculation and vaccination, and better medical care generally. By the middle of this century the death rate in North America was 11 per thousand and in Europe 12, whereas it was still high in non-Western countries: Africa, 36; Asia, 32–3; and Latin America, 24.

The nineteenth century also saw a structural shift in Western economic activities as the technological innovations in food production and processing enabled fewer and fewer people to feed the ever-increasing population. Most of the slack was taken up by the new technology based on coal, steel, textiles, and manufacturing of all kinds. People left the countryside. They swelled the numbers in existing cities and they created cities where none had existed before. Some of the industrial cities of Britain grew from the smallest beginnings, often in novel locations best favoured to exploit minerals or import raw materials. Agglomeration was inevitable. Whereas pre-industrial technology focused on the workshop, the water-mill, or the windmill, on small units widely spread, the new was geared to power whose efficiency increased with size and with the ability to use it continuously, day and night. By the 1830s a single cotton mill might employ 600 workers. A few mills could absorb the population of a potential city.

Even so, as Weber points out in his classic work on nineteenth-century urbanization, larger cities grew more rapidly than smaller (p. 451): 'Urban growth is essentially great city growth.' Using a cut-off point of 100,000 to define a city, he demonstrated what happened in Europe (Table 1).

To a large extent growth of city population was by migration.

TABLE 1. *Growth of the large city in the nineteenth century*

	Number of cities	Aggregate population (millions)	Ratio to total population (%)
1850	42	9	3.80
1870	70	20	6.66
1890	120	120	10.00

Previously cities had always depended on immigration to grow. Paris was beginning to show a very slight natural increase in the eighteenth century, and so was London by the beginning of the nineteenth. But on the whole 'in Europe cities do not sustain themselves' (Weber, p. 244). Even at the end of the nineteenth century Marseilles and Lyons were unable to replenish their numbers naturally. In the second half of the century London's natural increase was unusual in accounting for 84 per cent of its growth, and this was largely due to the immense improvement in sanitation in mid-century.

Technological innovation and its accompanying demographic changes were affecting the whole of Western life. The second half of the nineteenth century saw unprecedented movements, not just from country to town, but from country to country and from one continent to another. And so often the latter movements also ended in urbanization as peasants left the poverty of their native soil for the attractions of cities far beyond their horizons. Their freedom to move was itself made possible by the new technology—railways and steamships. Traditionally migrants travelled short distances; now there was no limit, as distance and time of travel were drastically reduced. Between 1841 and 1881 2 million people left Europe in each decade for the United States alone: in 1881–90 the figure was 4.7 million; 1891–1900, 3.6 million; and 1900–10, 8.1 million. It was by this and similar movements that the Irish peasant became a London labourer, the Italian and Polish peasant a New York hand or a Chicago railworker. Both in Britain and in America foreign arrivals augmented internal migrants, the English moving to London in great numbers and the American rural poor swelling the ranks in their own great cities. But the percentage foreign-born in the cities of America in mid-century was particularly high—over 50 per cent in St Louis and Chicago, 45 per cent in Cincinatti, and 47 per cent in New York. This was a new facet of cosmopolitanism. In the past small communities of foreigners were a typical feature of metropolis, and some of these groups had made unique contributions to the life of the city, whether as merchants, diplomats, or craftsmen with highly prized skills like the Huguenot silk-weavers and Dutch instrument-makers in seventeenth-century London. The migrants of the nineteenth century, however, represent a major displacement and a restructuring of society. Theirs was a movement of the least skilled as far as cities were concerned, and of the poorest. When they arrived in New York, for example, they were so many 'hands' to be put to the machinery of the new era, units of labour which would, nevertheless, build a new society.

The social changes, the emergence of a large middle class of entrepreneurs, the consolidation of a great working class, together with an unprecedented change of scale, all tend to overshadow other features of the nineteenth-century metropolis. There were certainly changes in the urban fabric which were easily identifiable. Those which Mumford stresses may well be the most negative—the imposition of a mechanical order in housing instead of the 'organic' growth of medievalism or the rationality of the designs of state capitals. The mass building of houses in Britain which seemed to echo machine production resulted in endless rows of near-identical designs, their repetitiveness guaranteed by an adherence to minimal standards of building (Fig. 6a). In the United States there was no apparent break between the Greek grid, which Jefferson had seen as enlightenment and which predetermined land apportionment from the Atlantic to the Pacific, and its universal application in all cities (Fig. 6b). The classicism of the eighteenth century became the mechanical reproducing system of the nineteenth simply because it was the most convenient way of handling real estate.

In Britain in particular in the nineteenth century the new

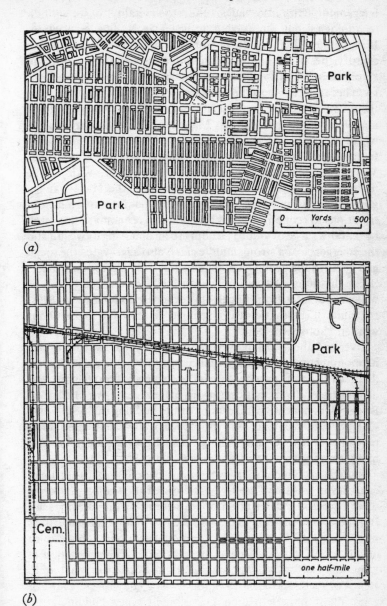

FIG. 6. The industrial city: (a) London; (b) Chicago.

burgeoning cities also had an enormous vitality, based on new technologies but embodying a belief in a new civilization. Birmingham, the centre of innovation from the eighteenth century, became a cradle of the industrial revolution. With an emphasis on small and medium manufacturing and engineering it soon became known as the workshop of the world. By the end of the nineteenth century it was also a model of municipal reform and planning. In the same way Manchester, by mid-century a city of 300,000 people, reached a golden age based on cotton manufacturing. And over and above this it became a centre of Victorian intellectual and cultural achievement, with a fine national newspaper, a first-class orchestra (the Hallé), and a great municipal university, in addition to making important contributions to economic theory and political economy. It may well be that this surge of vitality, leading to an amassing of wealth and the emergence of a strong middle class, also aggravated the social gap between the owning and managerial class and the remainder. Social divisions were certainly enshrined in the urban fabric, as we shall see later from Engels' historic description in the 1840s, for much of these cities was given over to drab and monotonous workers' houses (p. 193).

Over and above this, however, the new city had its symbols and its monumentality. The emergence of a new civic pride, largely divorced from the past because of its strong egalitarian base, was demonstrated from mid-century in magnificent town halls. Asa Briggs gives a most vivid account of the building of Leeds Town Hall between 1851 and 1858 (pp. 157 ff.). Its main feature was a magnificent hall, 49 metres long, 22 metres wide, and 23 metres high; it was bigger than London's Guildhall!

Railways produced their own monuments. The very functional canopies of glass and steel which covered the station platforms often earned the description of 'cathedrals of the railway age'. But these were often hidden behind equally monumental efforts which expressed the more traditional notion, romantic or nostalgic, of what was meant by grandeur. The new station at London's Euston was approached by a Doric triumphal arch. New York's Grand Central Station was a copy of the Baths of Caracalla in imperial Rome. Occasionally a new building arose which achieved real monumentality in the new idiom. Such was the Crystal Palace in London, a symbol not only of the new technology but of the market-place at its apogee, the market-place of an empire and of the whole world. Very different but equally dramatic was the tower that Eiffel constructed in Paris, with no function but to proclaim the city's greatness and to show what the new technology could achieve.

The Eiffel Tower indicated a new dimension in city building. Pressure of population had forced many cities in the past to grow upwards, not least imperial Rome. In medieval Italy prestige and status had given new meaning to building upwards as in the towers of San Gimignano, the only challenge to the hundreds of cathedrals which were reaching for the sky and unwittingly challenging pyramids and ziggurats. But by the end of the nineteenth century building high reached a new scale via new means. Much of the impetus came from Chicago, a metropolis which in many ways is the best example of the effects of the new technology and of the expansion of Western civilization into the New World.

ii

Chicago literally did not exist until the nineteenth century. A trading post, Fort Dearborn, was built in 1803 where the Chicago river entered Lake Michigan, but this grew very little until the penetration of the continent from the east was made possible by the building of the Erie Canal in 1824. Thereafter it became a centre for outfitting people moving further west and a collecting point for hunters wishing to send their pelts back east. When it became incorporated as a city in 1837 its population was still only 4,200. Its growth was the result of a canal network which linked it with the Great Lakes and with the Mississippi, followed almost immediately in mid-century by two rail links with the east coast. By 1850 Chicago was the chief rail centre in the United States. At the same time the exploitation of the Lake Superior iron ores initiated its great iron and steel industry, and it also became a collecting point for northern timber to be shipped to the house-building market of the east. As the west was opened up Chicago became the focus of the cattle, sheep, and hogs industry, the animals being brought in from the west to be slaughtered and packed there. One of the fundamental technical innovations of modern industry was the conveyer-belt method (1870), and this was first used in slaughtering in Chicago.

Although a fire destroyed the city in 1871, by 1880 its population was around half a million. In its rebuilding Chicago retained the mechanical grid, broken only by a few radial streets which had once been Indian trails. But there was now an impetus to build high. Chicago began building skyscrapers. The first was the Home Insurance Building of 1885, and it was seventeen stories high. The fundamental breakthrough was the use of a steel frame on which the non-supporting walls were no more than a cladding. Even this would not have produced the skyscraper had it not been for the previous invention of the 'elevator' in the 1850s. Together they led to 'vertical building'. In the decade 1885–95 the city acquired twenty-one skyscrapers and set the pattern for the downtown silhouette which was to become standard in every American city, and which reached its most dramatic in the Manhattan skyline. Nearly a century later Chicago was still vying with New York for the highest building, the 100-storey John Hancock Centre of 1970 and the later 110-storey Sears Building each being the tallest for its time. The concentration of downtown office blocks, neatly contained in Chicago by the loop of the elevated railway, proved self-perpetuating. The concentration of buildings meant a rise in land values and this in turn prompted people to build higher to get greater returns. Even in 1880 land inside the loop was half a million dollars an acre: ten years later it was three and a half million, demanding an ever-increasing intensity of use. We shall see that this is a common feature of the modern city.

The downtown high-rise area was a visible symbol of prosperity, of wealth grounded on industry and commerce. Chicago was the major steel-producing city in the States and first in the ranks of metal manufacturing, machine making, and the chemical industry. It was first in food processing and packaging. It was second only to New York in publishing. It was also the venue for fairs and conventions of all kinds, culminating in the World Columbian Exposition of 1893. In some ways this fair was the peak of the city's fortunes. Its population had swelled enormously, mainly through a second wave of European immigrants—Italians, Poles, and Russians in particular. By 1890 nearly three-quarters of its population was foreign born. There were the beginnings, too, of an influx of Black people from the southern States (who today account for a third of its citizens). In 1890 Chicago annexed extensive areas of adjacent land and became the second city in the United States, with a population of 1.1 million. This was the year its university was founded, for the metropolitan superstructure that was erected on its industry and wealth saw the rise of a communications industry and the beginning of a tradition in learning and especially in music.

Not that all was light and enlightenment. Like all great cities of that period—or of any period—Chicago had its unsavoury aspects. In the 1890s Jane Addams, one of the founders of a movement to salvage some of the debris of industrial progress, wrote: 'The streets are inexpressibly dirty, the number of schools inadequate, sanitary legislation unenforced, the street lighting is bad and altogether lacking in the alleys and smaller streets, and the stables foul beyond description' (p. 98).

With a dominant position between east and west, Chicago represented the ideals and aspirations of a vast hinterland which for half a century was reluctant to be embroiled in the doings of either the east coast or the west, and has retained more than hints of isolationism. In some ways it is a city of the past, although it is still a thriving city which looks into the future. Although Exposition 1893 took refuge in a safe neoclassicism many of its buildings were looking to the twentieth century. This was the city that produced Louis Sullivan and Frank Lloyd Wright and was home to Mies van der Rohe.

iii

Industrialization alone was not enough to produce metropolitan cities in the nineteenth century. The mining of coal had certainly produced large settlements, but at one end of the spectrum the mining city could well be transitory, particularly if resources were depleted rapidly. Many such settlements lacked real urban substance, and few acquired the range of activities associated with major cities. Sometimes a combination of industrial activities built up a complex of settlements which together bore more resemblance to metropolis. This happened in the industrial area of the Rhine-Ruhr, which is why Peter Hall put it in the first edition of his book *World Cities*, though to the layman the concept may well be unfamiliar. This area was not devoid of medieval market towns and cities, but its development into the present scale is a product of coal mining, coking, and steel manufacturing. What was a network of smallish towns in the 1870s suddenly took off, largely as the result of the enterprise of industrial giants like Krupp in Essen, Horter and Holsch in Dortmund, and Thyssen in Mulheim. A decade or so later chemical industries were introduced by Bayer in Leverkusen. The coalfield's population grew from less than a million in 1871 to 3.5 million in 1910 and continued to expand to 4.3 million by 1939. One could question the true metropolitan nature of this polycentric complex, though its cultural wealth and diversity are considerably enhanced by Cologne and Dusseldorf: but this particular form may well be a forerunner of a more dispersed kind of metropolis in the twenty-first century.

Meanwhile the giant of the nineteenth century, and the world's greatest city at the end of it, was undoubtedly London, and we must now see how this growth came about and to what extent it was the product of industrialization.

iv

London was a million city soon after the nineteenth century had begun, and we have seen how this was an outcome of its mercantile activities coupled with its being the political heart of the United Kingdom and of a growing empire. During the century London grew disproportionately even in an industrializing Britain: to 2.5 million by mid-century, representing 14.9 per cent of the total population, and to 8 million by 1900, or 18.7 per cent of the total. In addition to its own activities it controlled the resources of the entire country and fashioned its economy. It also commanded the resources of the largest empire ever to exist.

Britain's wealth was based on cotton as well as coal and iron, and on a world market in the true sense of the word. Agriculture, transformed by two centuries of improvement, produced more with much fewer workers, and the surplus was rapidly absorbed by industry and by the cities. The background to structural change was one of high technical ability, a number of basic inventions and discoveries, and the ability to organize these advantages into a changing economy.

Increasing prosperity was by no means evenly spread, and there was much that was not on the credit side. The 'dark Satanic Mills' cast a long shadow. Visitors were struck by the repetitive nature of industrial quarters. In 1828 Heine comments:

This tremendous uniformity, this mechanical movement, this negation of joy, this exaggerated egregious London crushes the imagination and tears the heart assunder . . . I expected great palaces and saw only small houses. But their uniformity and their endless number are tremendously impressive. (Schneider, p. 237)

To the romantics this was food for an anti-urban feeling which would grow and gradually dominate the feelings of most. 'Hell,' said Shelley, 'is a city, just like London.' From now on people's reaction to the city was polarized; no epithet could be too bad for some, nor any extravagance in describing its achievements to others. From a more objective, statistical point of view which tries to eschew value-judgements, London was an unprecedented concentration of trade, industry, wealth, administration, and people.

First the people. They flowed in from the countryside near and far. From further afield the railways fed the capital, from further still, the steamship. The first major influx of an ethnically distinct people came from Ireland following the famine years of the late 1840s. Almost immediately 100,000 made their way to London. Their poverty, their strange language, and their Roman Catholicism made them highly visible and evoked a stereotype which has never really been erased. From the 1880s the Jews, mainly from eastern Europe and Russia, provided the perceived alien element. In 1883 it was estimated that there were 44,000 Jews in London and they increased very considerably in the next two decades. In 1901 one person in three in the East End of London was an alien.

There was commensurate growth in area. As the immigrants crowded into the slums and rookeries of an already decaying city centre, so a growing middle class moved outwards into the salubrious fringes of London. This suburban extension had a distinctive characteristic which would stamp London as 'the unique city' (Rassmussen). People fled the city, but not so far as to cut themselves off. Two centuries before, in the green squares of Westminster the Englishman had brought the countryside into the town—*rus in urbe*: now he tried to take the town into the countryside—*urbs in rure*. Unlike most European cities, where high densities are accepted as part of urban living, London's expansion was an ever-increasing spread of detached and semi-detached houses. This was made possible by the growth of suburban railways, first to serve the white-collar workers, but soon to serve the blue, as cheap workmen's tickets became common from the 1860s. Finally electricity saw the establishment of an urban network of trams and underground trains which bound together the whole of the city. Political expression was given to the expansion by the creation of the London County Council in 1888, though by then suburban growth was pushing even deeper into the countryside.

Even a cursory glance at the structure of London's economy during this period is revealing. It would not be correct to relate the growth of the city simply to the effects of industrialization. London was still a trading city without rival. In 1800 it had dealt with 800,000 tons of shipping, in 1880 with 8 million—considerably more than a major port like Liverpool. The Pool of London had long since become inadequate to deal with commerce and new wharves and quays were continually being built downstream; the West India Docks in 1802, London Docks in 1805, East India Docks in 1806, Surrey Docks in 1855, Royal Docks in 1880, and Tilbury Docks in 1886. Warehousing was a major function. Baedeker states in 1880 that 'nothing will convey to the stranger a better idea of the vast activity and stupendous wealth of London than a visit to the warehouses, filled to overflowing with interminable stores of every kind of foreign and colonial products'

(Briggs, p. 329). London was first and foremost a market whose imports were twice her exports. City financial dealings were carried out in a series of specialized exchanges—Corn, Coal, Rubber, Tea, and Diamonds. Nowhere was the importance of trade shown more clearly than in the Great Exhibition of 1851. This vast emporium of Britain's wealth dealt with the produce of the whole world as well as that of Britain. The exhibition was visited by 6 million people, and one cannot help but see the parallel here with the movement of pilgrims to a most prestigious shrine.

This is not to deny London's place as the first industrial city in Britain. But on examination its industries were not predominantly those of the nineteenth century. Because of location difficulties heavy industry, shipbuilding, and textiles moved out of the city, and by 1861 the emphasis was on clothing, wood products and furniture, printing and stationery, scientific instruments, and finished goods. Even metal and engineering works were concerned mainly with repair. The emphasis was on high-value low-bulk, and it was geared to consumption in the city itself. The size of firms is significant. In 1851 74.6 per cent of all industrial workers were in units of five or less; only 1.6 per cent were in units of over fifty (G.S. Jones, p. 374). This is a pattern of activity much more reminiscent of a pre-industrial city, a city of workshops rather than of mills. The work was done by an immense pool of labour—about a million and a half in mid-century—of whom about a third were fully employed, a third worked on a temporary basis, and a third were casual hands or unemployed. Casual workers lived very precariously, their labour depending on how much shipping there was in the Thames, or whether their skills were needed in a particular season. During 'the season' (from April to November) there was great demand for tailors, milliners, and boot and shoe makers; but very little for gas workers and coal and wood merchants.

As well as being a market and a manufacturing centre London was responsible for governing a thriving industrial Britain and an immense empire. Whitehall was the centre of an overseas domain without parallel in history. Political power lay where it had lain for five hundred years, and here in Whitehall, with a growing army of bureaucrats, it constituted a small but extremely rich and important sector of London's life. It was this group, combined with the traditional landowning aristocracy, that provided society's élite. Although, as one observer put it, 'the élite sojourned in London and were never fastened to it exclusively. Nevertheless at the season's height society gathered there in a concentrated force that was unique . . . 500 members would be a generous estimate of London's society then' (Waller, p. 37). This is confirmed by Heine: 'Above the mob that is glued to the ground hovers England's nobility like beings of a different world, who look upon England as a temporary abode, who consider Italy their summer garden, Paris their ballroom, and the whole world as their property' (Schneider, p. 237).

Clustering as near the court as possible, it was this class that built palaces in London's West End to complement its country mansions. Below these aristocrats in social status were the governing classes: members of parliament, senior administrators, and the upper echelons of the Church and the law. Then came those who had prospered in commerce. Together these made up the first socio-economic class, about 7.2 per cent of the male population (Table 2). The second class consisted of tradesmen, teachers, and bureaucrats, but the largest number of men were in the third class, artisans, skilled workers, and small traders; the fourth included semi-skilled workers and minor local-government officials. But one in five was in class V: the base of the socio-economic structure was very broad, made up of unskilled workers and municipal workers swollen by an army of street vendors so well described by Mayhew in 1850.

There was a geographical separation between these classes, though the terms 'West End' and 'East End' did not come into use until the very end of the century. Nevertheless the polarity was of long standing. Nash recognized it, and in a way he gave it permanence, by designing Regent Street as a grand parade which would separate the rich squares of the west from the poorer streets in the east. The separation is still there. Compare the opulence of Bond Street on the one side with the open-air market of Berwick Street on the other: or the exclusiveness of clothing in Saville Row with the mass productions of Carnaby Street.

TABLE 2. *Socio-economic classification of persons over 10 years old in London, 1861*

Class	Male (%)	Female (%)
I	7.20	3.52
II	16.30	3.85
III	31.66	7.73
IV	11.30	25.88
V	20.12	2.09
TOTALS	86.58	43.05

Note: Total London population over 10 years old in 1861: males 977,553; females 1,163,881.

After his massive survey at the end of the century Booth was more inclined to think of three Londons, a rich west, a poor east, and a 'comfortable London' in between. This does not diminish the enormous gap between the luxury and wealth of the West End and the abject poverty of so many areas north and east of the old City. Outside the unmistakable slum areas nearest the city centre there extended an interminable number of 'respectable' houses, which Besant in 1901 thought of as a city within the city, a one-class city of 2 million people (Waller, p. 40). We hear little of this. Most writers, like Dickens, have given chilling accounts of the worst aspects of city life, partly because they were making a conscious attack against poverty and partly because they were writing within a general consensus of anti-urbanism. Nevertheless, some of the descriptions of the most squalid slums are quite horrifying. Charles Kingsley, for instance, gives this vignette in 1850:

Fish stalls and fruit stalls lined the edge of the greasy pavement, sending up odours as foul as the language of the sellers and the buyers. Blood and sewage water crawled from under the doors and out of spouts and reeked down the gutters amid offal, animal and vegetable, in every stage of putrefaction. Foul vapours arose from the cowsheds and slaughter-houses and the doorways of undrained alleys . . . while above, hanging cliff-like over the streets—those narrow, brawling torrents of filth and poverty and sin—the houses with their teeming load of life were piled into the dingy, choking night. (Ch. 8)

This was the city of the cholera outbreaks of 1832 and 1849, which had prompted the Chadwick report on sanitation in 1842 and which was gradually transformed in the years following the establishment of the Metropolitan Water Board in 1855. But the slums survived. In spite of experiments in rehousing, the building of model dwellings and of Peabody tenements was only a small amelioration of the condition. Road improvements and the building of railways actually aggravated the problem by demolishing the worst of the slums without providing alternative shelter for the destitute. Beyond the squalid rookeries London spread in its more orderly way, north and east; here poverty was replaced by neat respectability, though this too was barren in its way. This was Besant's one-class city in which there were no public buildings or libraries or public schools, no hotels and no restaurants. It was dull and monotonous (Waller, p. 40).

In the West End luxury piled on luxury, pleasure on leisure. Theatres multiplied as the less respectable music-hall was banished elsewhere. There were shops and restaurants galore. The Tate Gallery was opened to augment the National. South Kensington erupted in a host of museums and colleges and a vast concert-hall. A zoo was opened in Regent's Park. The University flourished, and so did many other institutions dedicated to the arts and sciences. This was the London described in the New Century Magazine in New York in 1885: 'Here is, and will remain for generations, the centre of the commercial and political world, the focus of intellectual activity and the mint of thought' (Briggs, p. 328). Its vastness was taken for granted. As Henry James said, 'A small London would be an abomination' (p. 5).

Whatever contribution the industrial revolution was making to this great metropolis its character had not changed radically from the commercial and political centre it had been for four hundred years. It was the old city writ large.

V

My main treatment of New York deals with it as a contemporary metropolis, and this must wait until the next chapter: but it is interesting to look at some of its features now to see what parallels there are with nineteenth-century London. New York had been a commercial centre since its founding by the Dutch, and it continued so under the British after 1664. For a brief period it was the federal capital (1789–90), and with 30,000 people it was then the largest city in the Union. Then it grew rapidly, doubling its population by 1800 and benefiting enormously from the opening of the Erie Canal in 1824. This established the Hudson–Mohawk routeway as a highway to the interior and gave the city a head start over its Atlantic rivals. Now it could exploit its harbour and confirm its links with the Old World. By the end of the century its population was 3.5 million. It was the mouth of a funnel that drew in millions of Europeans. The waves of migrants were so great that they gave the city a successive series of ethnic characteristics; it was an Irish city until the late century, then an Italian city, a Jewish city, and later Negro and then Puerto Rican. It was the prototypical ethnic city, and the newcomers contributed their labour and skills to building a number of industries. Whatever colour or creed they were, they were first and foremost 'hands'.

But, as with London, New York's growth was not the outcome of massive industrialization. It, too, thrived on hundreds of small manufactures and workshops. Even today the average number of workers in a factory is only twenty-seven, and in a business only seventeen. Garment-making and printing and a host of food-processing plants were typical. Commerce reigned supreme in a mass of small enterprises. Like London, New York was a consumer city. Like London, it had two parts:

> From Eighth Street down the men are coining it:
> From Eighth Street up the women are spending it.

By 1900 New York was still a comparatively low-profile city with no building higher than 20 stories. It did have steel-framed buildings and the lift was a way of life, so technically it did have skyscrapers but they had not yet made an impact on the skyline. There was an elevated railway to ease the lot of an increasing work-force. This was the period when the foundations were being laid for the twentieth-century metropolis. In 1898, ten years after London's reorganization of municipal government, Greater New York was created from the five boroughs—Manhattan, Brooklyn, Bronx, Queen's, and Staten Island. The building of the Brooklyn Bridge (1883) was the final link which made this feasible. Nevertheless, Manhattan remained the core of the city, the incipient skyscraper island, the prototype of every future central business district. Multiracial, prosperous, innovative, New York was about to become the greatest metropolis in the world.

vi

Both London and New York suggest that while the combination of exploding population and exploding technology typical of the industrial revolution gave rise to 'the second urban revolution', nevertheless those cities which towered over the rest were products of commerce and financial and political power. Their wealth was a product of exchange, their influence a reflection of financial power. They represented the centralization of vast resources and the ability to capitalize on them: England from an overseas empire, the United States from a continent waiting to be exploited.

In this exploitation the seeds of future metropolises were being sown. Several European powers made a contribution to the growth of great cities in the tropics by establishing outposts, first as means of regulating trade and later as centres of political control. The colonial city figured very prominently in later nineteenth-century commerce, and some of them became the giants of this century.

The transference of the trappings of the European city to civilizations in the tropics gave rise to all kinds of amalgams of culture. When there was a great disparity of cultural levels it often meant the transposition of Western urban life with very little residual evidence of the indigenous. At the other extreme

European merchants attached themselves to cities, or formed enclaves in what were already advanced cities, as in China and Japan. India provides examples of both kinds of development, Delhi being the latest in a long succession of imperial capitals and Calcutta being a city initiated by colonial traders.

Delhi was a frontier capital for several centuries, the furthest point to which successive waves of Islamic invaders pushed towards the Ganges valley. I have already referred to the peripatetic element in the primacy of this Islamic capital, which more than once gave pride of place to Agra. For this reason, and partly because of its frequent sacking, Delhi was the site of at least six successive capitals between the twelfth and sixteenth centuries, intermittently revelling in the wealth and power of the Mogul emperors. It became British in 1803 and from that time flourished on its present site until 1912 when it was chosen as capital of British India in preference to Calcutta. Old Delhi was itself a considerable city, but now was a time to symbolize the Raj on a massive scale in a New Delhi which was to encapsulate the greatness of empire at its peak. The result was a classically laid out city whose spaciousness could not have been in greater contrast to the overcrowded old city. It was dominated by the monumental creations of Lutyens—a Secretariat, a Parliament House, and the Viceroy's Palace, now the residence of the President of India. This was baroque planning at its most expansive, and echoed every symbolic and religio-magic grandeur of the city from Babylon to Alexandria, from Rome to Peking.

Whereas New Delhi was the last in a series of imperial capitals, the genesis of Calcutta was totally novel. When Joe Charnock established a trading post here in 1690 he saw only the possibilities of exploiting the location on the Hooghly river for trading between England and India: and the site, in the narrow sense, as one easy to defend and suitable for settlement. Such a point of exchange is a classic example of the intrusion of a maritime power into a land-based culture. Some years later, in 1700, Fort William was established, and by 1717 the East India Company was given trading rights. The fort became a focus for Indian merchants and the headquarters of British entrepreneurs, and its population grew from 10,000 in the first decade of the eighteenth century to

118,000 by mid-century, and 300,000 by 1822. It was by now a major entrepôt and its status was enhanced by its becoming the capital of British India in 1772. Its wealth was derived from its control of jute production in the immediate hinterland and of the tea of north-east India. Jute was also the basis of its early industrialization, though this soon expanded into the production of consumer goods, iron and steel, and, later, food, vehicles, and many other products. Superimposed on this was a financial city, and beyond that its administrative functions as capital until 1912. Economically it is above all a mercantile city. Today it handles a quarter of India's imports and 40 per cent of its exports. Financially it still has a third of all the foreign banks in India.

In the Calcutta of the late nineteenth century the world saw two very different aspects of colonial society. On the one hand it was 'the city of palaces', with all the residential splendour of a great capital. On the other hand there was abject poverty, for ever summed up by Rudyard Kipling in his 'Tale of Two Cities':

> As the fungus sprouts chaotic from its bed
> So it spread—
> Chance directed, chance erected, laid and built
> On the silt—
> Palace, byre, hovel—poverty and pride
> Side by side—
> And above the packed and pestilential town,
> Death looked down.

It was the intrusive civilization which gave it the trappings of glory and those institutions which still give the city a metropolitan quality. It was studded with enormous buildings of pseudo-European style. Classical elements vied with neo-gothic, and the whole was mixed with Indian influences. Many of the institutions have survived, for the city is still the capital of West Bengal and it has retained those institutions which could not be duplicated elsewhere in India. It still has the National Library, a magnificent collection of 10 million volumes; it has the National Museum, the Geological Survey of India, the Meteorological Service, the Statistical Institute, and many centres of research. It has three universities and many learned academies. It would have been an interesting exercise to see how far these still represent an alien culture and to what extent there has been an acceptance of Westernization and a fusion of cultures.

The 'other' Calcutta shares few of the benefits of Western civilization. This is the city of the Indian masses who have been attracted to it. Some have flourished in exercising a native entrepreneurial genius, and some have become industrial and financial leaders. The mass has remained the mass. At least half a million have no shelter at all: they are the street-sleepers. It is almost impossible to calculate the size of the underclass or its place in the structure of the urban society, a dilemma which we encounter again and again when dealing with the metropolis in the developing world.

The 'two-city' problem is particularly characteristic of South-East Asia. A Western-type city is grafted on to an indigenous settlement, whether this be small or large. The new city grows to accommodate the needs of the colonist culture, but its population is fed by native people as great hordes are attracted by the promise of better living standards. The result is often a grossly enlarged city totally incapable of coping with the problems of its growth, and at best left to prove its viability after the colonial power has been withdrawn. Economically these cities are extensions of the Western system, controlled by it, financially sustained by it. In terms of the local economy they have been called 'parasitic' by some because their local resources have been drained for shipment elsewhere, with precious little being put back into the local economy.

South-East Asia has a cluster of such cities. Seven of them have exceeded the million population: Singapore (2.5), Djakarta (6.5), Surabaya (2), Semarang (1), Manila (1.7), Bangkok (4.7), and Rangoon (2.4). Their growth was a direct result of European demands in the nineteenth century. European powers had already established themselves in these tropical regions from the sixteenth century; but the industrial revolution set up new conditions, a need for raw materials on the one hand and for developing new markets on the other. Moreover improvements in shipping with the introduction of steam and particularly with the opening of the Suez Canal made the region accessible to Europe as it had never been before. Most of the new ports and centres of commerce were grafted on to existing settlements: Singapore and Saigon were the only two purely nineteenth-century settlements (McGee, pp. 52–75). The growing cities were known by their warehousing and shipping, by their concentration of banks, insurance companies, and Western agencies of all kinds. The largest economic sector was that of the service industries. These cities rapidly became primate. Comparing their population with that of the second-ranking in each state, by the mid-century Singapore had a primary index of 3.4 (that is, it was 3.4 times the size of the second city), Manila 5.9, Rangoon 3.9, and Bangkok 25. Socially and culturally all was in the hands of the colonial élite aided by a small number of indigenous élite, but served by an immense and very poor population, either indigenous or immigrant, often transitory, and always predominantly male. Singapore, for example, was essentially a Chinese city with a large admixture of Indians and a very small number of English who controlled the city and its hinterland both economically and politically.

These cities were to set the stage for the massive urbanization and the city growth which have transformed the tropical world in the last half-century, and given the lead to scores of indigenous cities whose expansion has created new economic, political, and social conditions which have brought with them a host of problems. Some of these will be the subject of a later chapter.

5

Metropolis Today

We all dwell together
To make money from each other.

THOMPSON

i

If we were looking for a contemporary equivalent to the seven
wonders of the ancient world we could do worse than nominate
some of the office blocks that are now soaring above so many of
the world's metropolitan cities. Not only do they represent the
ethos of the West in the twentieth century, embody its values, and
express its wealth; they are also monumental structures which
dominate the city and which vie with the megastructures of the
past—pyramids, or temples, or palaces. A half-dozen come to
mind at once: Tour Montparnasse in Paris, the NatWest tower in
London, the Sears tower in Chicago, the Trade Centre in New
York, and the Bank of Hong Kong. Never did individual
buildings indicate such a concentration of resources, and their
height is part of a world game of status-seeking which dwarfs the
efforts of the merchants of San Gimignano.

The office block is also partly the outcome of yet another structural change in the economic activities of advanced urban
societies, a shift from manufacturing activities to service
industries. Bertrand Russell once wrote:

Work is of two kinds: first, altering the position of matter at or near the
earth's surface relatively to other such matter; second, telling people to
do so. The first is unpleasant and ill-paid; the second is pleasant and
highly paid. The second is capable of indefinite expansion; there are not
only those who give orders, but those who give advice as to what orders
should be given. (p. 94)

Today we are seeing a proliferation of the second kind of work.

Technical innovations have progressively enabled less people to be involved in the first activity. The most basic of all activities—producing food—we can call 'primary'. Manufacturing things we can call 'secondary'. It was the shift of labour from primary to secondary which created the necessary conditions for the growth of cities in the first place. Now technology has allowed fewer people to manufacture the goods we need and made room for the growth of 'tertiary', or service, activities. Tertiary work was always an important sector of urban activity, which produced its full share of people who either served the producers or, as Russell says, told people what to do and how to do it. The élite in every society has been nurtured in this particular category. The proportion of people in the tertiary sector may now be reaching a peak, but a fourth category of activity is emerging as increasingly important in contemporary society. This could be called 'quaternary' and it deals mainly with information and its transmission and distribution. Our modern world is being geared to collecting and transacting information (Bayliss, p. 175) (Fig. 7).

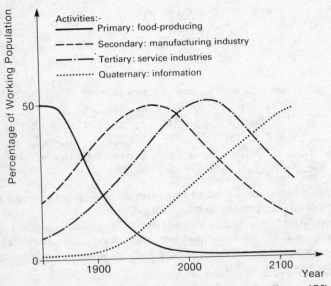

FIG. 7. Changes in economic activities (based on Bayliss, p. 175).

As with service activities some elements of quaternary work have been with us a long time. Underlying the very notion of a city is the need to exchange information and ideas. Hence the significance of the Greek agora, the Roman forum, and the medieval market-place in times when face-to-face meetings were the only means of communication. This feature has not entirely disappeared, for Trafalgar Square and Hyde Park Corner serve a similar function. The need to congregate was always associated with some particular part of the city, the more central the better. In medieval London it was St Paul's Cross, an open area immediately north of the cathedral: here proclamations were made and crowds were harangued. When the spoken word was partly replaced by the written it is not surprising that printing became associated with the same location. Wynkyn de Worde, Caxton's assistant and successor, moved his printing works from Westminster to St Paul's, and this could be regarded as the genesis of the printing and publishing activity which, until the last two decades, was centred on Fleet Street. 'Intelligence' about trading vessels, weather at sea, wars and calamities was exchanged at coffee houses in the same location in the seventeenth century; one of these was Lloyd's coffee shop, the precursor of what is now the greatest network of information on shipping and insurance.

Quaternary activities also encompass the world of education, of amassing, analysing, and disseminating information. This has exploded in this century with radio and television. We live in a society where more and more people are concerned with information, and technology is obsessed with means of collecting more data by miniaturizing its storage and increasing the speed of its handling. The microchip and the floppy disc are a long way from St Paul's Cross and seventeenth-century coffee houses, but there is a direct line of descent and the process of evolution has drawn in a greatly increasing number of people.

Between them tertiary and quaternary activities now dominate the work of the city, and naturally this is reflected in the fabric, in the hardware of city life. Up to the end of the eighteenth century business—even the business of running the country—occupied only a small niche in city life. Louis XIV housed the entire government of France in one wing of Versailles. In 1793 the British Treasury employed only 37 people. In London the East India Company operated from a private house for the first 126 years of its existence until a specially built headquarters was opened in 1760. The general separation of office from house did not get into its stride until the early years of the nineteenth century. Merchants lived over their business, almost literally sitting on their money. An expansion in business and pressure on the very restricted living space in the City saw a gradual migration of businessmen and their families westward and to the detached villas of expanding suburbs. What was left was a concentration of offices.

Thereafter specialization and growth went hand in hand; in London, first in a series of new exchanges—Coal (1849), Stock (1854), Wool (1874)—and then in entire streets of offices—Victoria Street (1871), Queen Street (1871), Shaftesbury Avenue (1886), Kingsway (1904)—to accommodate a growing army of businessmen and clerks. In 1851 there were 16,420 clerks in London: in 1891 there were 78,180. And during this time a revolution was quietly taking place as the proportion of women increased dramatically. In 1881 there were about 7,000 woman clerks in London: in 1911 there were 146,000. These changes went hand in hand with new inventions in communications, the telephone (1876) and in particular the typewriter (1867). Other innovations which increased speed and efficiency were the telegraph, the stock-exchange tape-machine, the dictating machine, carbon paper, and the basic techniques which led to photoreproduction.

Together with new sources of power and the invention of electric transport, the car, and later the radio, these changes have been seen by some as a second industrial revolution. Theoretically these innovations gave people a freedom to locate which was previously impossible. The businessman was no longer tied to the source of his information, nor even to the clerks who worked for him. Fast transit and telecommunications made nonsense of a 'market-place' as a necessary location for his activities. Paradoxically what actually happened was that in spite of these changes there was a reinforcement of the centralization and agglomeration which had always characterized the city. Its position was confirmed rather than destroyed.

Before considering the most dramatic of the physical and cultural changes which have affected the modern metropolis it is necessary to remind ourselves of the activity which has persisted throughout urban history, that of being a market-place. The original exchange of goods became progressively more sophisticated as their variety increased and as the spending power of the population grew. Even in the eighteenth century shops in cities like London had become extremely attractive (see above, ch. 3, sect. vii). In the nineteenth century there was not only an increase in their number but also in their size and the range of their products. By the mid-nineteenth century the department store had arrived, Bon Marché in Paris leading the way, followed closely in the 1860s by Marshall Field in Chicago; they depended on massive growth in the number of customers, electricity to light and run the store, and the beginnings of the art of advertising. In 1909 a former employee of Marshall Field built London's Selfridge's, a massive monument to the new way of retail shopping. Harrod's, though established much earlier, reached its peak two decades later than this, employing 5,000 people by the 1920s. The enormous attraction of these stores was their sheer diversity and the comprehensiveness of the services which they could offer.

In the centre of every metropolitan city today the luxury shopping quarter is a counterpart to the central business district: London's West End, Paris's rue de Rivoli, New York's Fifth Avenue. However many parts of this retail function have become dispersed—as they have in the establishment of suburban shopping centres and out-of-town superstores—the association of high-quality shopping with the centre persists, and accounts for much of the daily ebb and flow of people. To some extent the monumentality of the department store is now giving way to the shopping mall, often an exercise in infilling or redevelopment, having little of the unity of the department store but giving an opportunity for scores of small businesses to share the intimacy of an enclosed location. They are more like exploding arcades than disintegrating department stores.

ii

Although our concern in this chapter is with the contemporary city we must go back to the nineteenth century to see the genesis of the greatest transformation which took place later; for at the heart of the matter is the development of the skyscraper. Whether New York or Chicago has the better claim to be first in the field is immaterial (Weisman). The essence of the skyscraper was that its structural strength lay in a steel frame, leaving the wall a thin envelope. Secondly, the ability to build high, which was inherent in this method, was only practicable because of the invention of the elevator in the 1850s and its perfection in the 1860s. Both elements came together in the Equitable Life Assurance Company building in New York in 1870. Not that it looked like a skyscraper. It was only 5 stories, 39.6 metres high; but it was steel framed and had a 'lift'. By 1895 the first 'tower' (i.e. an unbroken sheer envelope) appeared in New York—the American Surety building, 22 stories and 95 metres high. By 1909 the Metropolitan Tower had reached 52 stories and 214 metres. The skyscraper had arrived. The familiar outlines and the famous names now followed, each building higher than the last; Woolworth (1913), Chrysler (1929–30), and Empire State (1931). The last was 102 stories and over 381 metres high. New York's upward growth culminated in the World Trade Centre, twin blocks of 412 metres (1970).

Chicago has gone one better than this with the Sears Tower, 443 metres. But now New York is planning a block of about 470 metres, while Skidmore partners have plans for one in Chicago which will be 476 metres! European efforts look very small in comparison. London's NatWest building is a mere 183 metres, the Post Office Tower marginally higher at 188 metres. In Paris the Tour Montparnasse is 200 metres, the highest in Europe. But it may soon give way to the Fair Tower at Frankfurt which is planned for 254 metres (Fig. 8).

Nor are these mere utilitarian containers of people. From the very beginning they have had all the trappings of wealth that one associates with monuments. A New Yorker writing in *Harper's Magazine* in 1893 describes a new office block in Chicago: 'floors

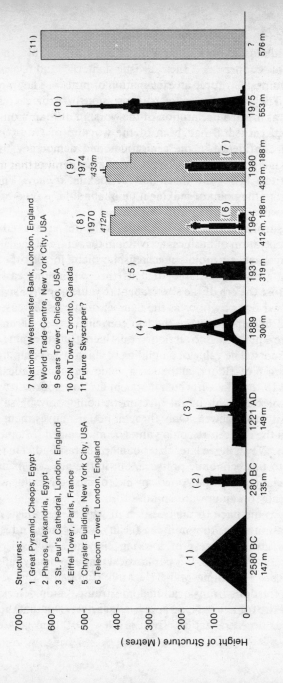

Structures:

1 Great Pyramid, Cheops, Egypt
2 Pharos, Alexandria, Egypt
3 St. Paul's Cathedral, London, England
4 Eiffel Tower, Paris, France
5 Chrysler Building, New York City, USA
6 Telecom Tower, London, England
7 National Westminster Bank, London, England
8 World Trade Centre, New York City, USA
9 Sears Tower, Chicago, USA
10 CN Tower, Toronto, Canada
11 Future Skyscraper?

FIG. 8. Monumental structures in history.

of deftly laid mosaic work, their walls of onyx and marble, their balconies of copper . . . their artistic lanterns and elegant electrical fittings . . . force an exclamation of praise'. They were meant to. They were the outward expression of progress and prosperity, as much a declaration of the worship of Mammon as the medieval cathedral had been of the worship of God. 'An emblem of confidence in the aspirations and democracy that underlie American society. They are status symbols,' says another writer. 'They are machines for making money. They exploit land to the point of making it uninhabitable,' says a contemporary writer, 'but they still work.'

It is not surprising that the skyscraper is the universal symbol of the concentration of business activities in the centre of the city. Indeed they have an inbuilt mechanism which, in retrospect, made their growth inevitable, tied as this was to increasing profits. Before the era of the skyscraper the value of office space had decreased floor by floor as the number of stories increased, because the higher they were the less convenient they became. The lift gave equal access to all floors, thus increasing the value of the upper floors. The value of a building could now be computed by the number of floors, and such a value was automatically transferred to the plot on which it was built. So important was this to become that an initial investment could only be safeguarded if it was renewed. Only through major reinvestment in and around the city centre could values be maintained (Manners 1974, p. 95). We shall see later that not all cities responded in the same way to this economic pressure, but in the absence of any kind of social control the American metropolis, certainly, was almost literally on an upward spiral.

This brings me back to the question of why the emphasis on central location seems to ignore the facility which modern technology has given business of locating elsewhere—indeed, of locating almost anywhere. It is paradoxical that a company called the American Telephone and Telegraph Company, the very essence of freedom from locational constraints, should seek a Manhattan site for a new skyscraper headquarters. Not that there has been no decentralization. Even in New York the greatest increase in office space in the last two decades has been outside the central business district; the percentage is as high as 63 in Dallas, 59 in Houston, and 45 in Boston. Business concerns are not unaware of the advantages of suburban locations, where investment is smaller in scale, where they can expand easily and incrementally, where their staff can avoid the pressure of journeys to work, and where the environment is pleasant. Where newer firms have no traditional commitment to the centre there is much to be said for moving out. In London a Location of Offices Bureau was set up in the 1960s and 1970s to encourage this movement, and it helped to decentralize 2,000 firms and 150,000 people. But there was a reluctance to go far. Many relocated within Greater London in office concentrations in the outer suburban belt like Watford and Croydon. Only 24 per cent of the firms advised by the Bureau relocated further than 80 kilometres from the centre of London.

In spite of this rather hesitant dispersal, and although most observers think it will increase in response to congestion, the fact remains that the office boom of the last three decades has been a feature of the centre of the metropolis. Between 1960 and 1972 Manhattan office space increased by 74 per cent to 244 million square metres, Chicago's by over 50 per cent to 73 million square metres. These are the central business districts (CBD) of the popular image, massive blocks rising suddenly from an otherwise low profile in the residential areas. It gives the metropolis a climax that is always dramatic and sometimes awe-inspiring. In this orchestrated form it is very much an American phenomenon. Planning controls in London prevented such a concentration of high buildings in the centre, and Paris fought strenuously against it. But in both these cities, like those in the United States, tertiary and quaternary activities are nevertheless crowded in the centre which seems to have a fatal attraction in spite of the difficulties of congestion. The élite has chosen to stay. Inertia, prestige, and competitiveness have seen to that. In the last resort face-to-face communication between executives of companies has proved sacrosanct. This doesn't explain why firms choose to have their entire organizations crowded on to a central site, although it is known that second-tier management and even the lower ranks are prepared to suffer inconvenience to be in the city centre. Above all, headquarters buildings must make a visual impact.

iii

So far I have considered the office block as a focus of activity within the city, within a local or national network. The metropolis must now be related to its wider network—the entire globe. The ability to move rapidly from one metropolis to another is essential to the élite of the business world; so is instant communication. This is where technology has really come into its own. An international airport is the first necessity:

The nature of modern white-collar workers makes it essential for them to rush around gathering more data and more advice. Hence the constant trips between transactional cities, the professional meetings, committees, symposia, conventions, congresses, with all the hardware these require from planes to convention halls, and all the soft-ware they generate. (Gottmann 1978, p. 6)

In any one metropolis these may have a precise location, but they are all points in an international network which often acts like a single entity although it is dispersed in all the metropolises of the world. So face-to-face communication is still considered an essential part of transacting information. There are times, of course, when not even the speed of a jet is sufficient and instant communication is considered essential, particularly in finance markets and for news items which demand an immediate response. The financial world in particular depends on telecommunication via satellite.

The effect of internationalizing the communication network is that some features of the metropolis are shared by every other metropolis. 'All international airports are the same international airport.' It would be extremely difficult for a traveller to identify his location by an airport interior. The ancillary services are also identical—the hotel bedroom, the rented car awaiting the executive; even the language is likely to be the lingua franca, English. A business man can move from one metropolis to another without being perturbed by unfamiliarity. He can be forgiven for not knowing whether he is in London or New York, or even in Hong Kong. He will eat from an international cuisine and enjoy an international cabaret.

This is not to say that the metropolis itself will lose its identity. Rather that each metropolis has within it a capsule of transnational character to meet the needs of the jet set, a comparatively small number of people with international expectations. I must repeat that the cultural identity is, nevertheless, extremely important, and this will be stressed again and again. To Gottmann the cultural variation is one of the main elements of metropolitan life. In some ways it is the most obvious, but it is also most difficult to define. But there is no mistaking the quality of life or even the environment which makes New York or Paris or London; it is a matter of perception. The twentieth-century metropolis expresses the culture from which it arose and of which it is the highest achievement. It shows itself, according to Gottmann, not only in 'poetical or volatile ways' but rather in variations which are 'the basic pillars of urban stability'. He refers to the 'French set of values that makes Parisians prefer to live in apartments, in compact blocks in the city centre if they can manage to do so. . . . A very different set of values underlies the American metropolitan lifestyle which prefers rambling structures in the outer suburban ring' (Gottmann 1978, p. 7). You will remember that Rassmussen's description of London's uniqueness was based on something similar. Not even a rash of residential slabs built by local authorities after the war has fundamentally disturbed this trait or altered Rassmussen's London. Indeed the slabs have been recognized as social aberrations and are now being replaced by the ubiquitous terrace.

One feature which contributes so much to the character and 'feel' of a metropolis is the fact that buildings survive and long outlive the social processes which gave rise to them. Inertia has seen to it that most twentieth-century Londoners live in nineteenth-century London, and their idea of housing is still dominated by the small-scale domestic tradition of building which was firmly established in the Georgian city.

Moreover, in spite of the cosmopolitanism which has

encouraged a mixture of cultures—and my historical examples
gave plenty of evidence of foreign enclaves in cities of any consequence—the basic population of a metropolis is the indigenous
society, sharing one culture and one set of values. In other words
the modern metropolis is made up of a large national 'body' with
its own unique social milieu, and a small international 'head'
which shares features of its economic and cultural life with élites
in other metropolitan cities. The 'body' is inward-looking, traditional, conserving values, reflecting the past, tied to place. The
'head' is 'plugged in' to a world community, is highly dependent
on advanced technology; in a sense it is aspatial. Its life comes not
through roots but through networks, intercommunications which
transcend cultural and national boundaries. Its economic
strength lies in supranational companies, its political strength in
international groupings.

The global view is an attractive one. As we saw in the first
chapter, it sees the peak of the urban hierarchy as a group of
'world cities'. It is certainly possible to identify such a group, as
Hall does; and the way I have used the word 'metropolis' pre-
supposes a loose grouping, sometimes smaller, sometimes larger,
always difficult to define. But more than anything 'world cities'
is a class of convenience to highlight certain contemporary
trends. It should not hide the individuality of each metropolis, its
cultural identity. This transcends the supranational features. Let
me illustrate this by looking at three contemporary metropolitan
cities mainly in terms of the structural changes with which this
chapter began.

iv

Developments in the last four decades in London reflect a structural change of considerable magnitude which is part of a transformation of the entire British economy. London has shed the
role of leading port and major manufacturing centre and can now
be regarded as a business metropolis. Between 1971 and 1981 the
number of people engaged in manufacturing decreased dramatically from 1.05 million to 0.65 million. Since 1945 there has been
a massive boom in office building (Jones 1988, p. 110). Even

allowing for replacement and improvement following enormous losses from intensive bombing in World War II, the annual addition of 38,000 square metres of office space is impressive. Dealing in property itself became a major activity. Before the war the city had 20 property companies: by the 1960s it had 150. The best efforts of the Location of Offices Bureau were brushed aside by increasing growth in the city. In the first half of 1983, for example, 300,000 square metres of office space was added and the total under construction was 1 million square metres. In Greater London in 1983 more than half the working population—1.175 million—worked in offices, and there is no sign of diminution in the trend.

London is still enormously attractive for business activities from all over Britain. Of the thousand largest companies one in three has its headquarters in London; of the hundred largest, seventy. Even more important to its international status is the number of world-wide activities which have links with the city. Of the world's hundred largest banks all but four have a branch in London. In 1961 there were 100 foreign banks: in 1983 there were 460, representing seventy countries and accounting for 38,000 jobs. These firms varied in size from 50 to 400 employees, though the Bank of America accounted for 1,000 (King, p. 5).

The pressure on these firms is not only to be in London, but to be in a very specific part of London. Their concentration in the 'city' (that is, the square mile which is more or less the historic City of London) is largely due to inertia. But this has been interpreted as prestige and value by association which defies any rationale in terms of today's technology. The 'prime' banking area is in the immediate vicinity of the Bank of England, around Threadneedle Street, and this extends to an 'acceptable' banking area a few hundred metres away at the southern end of Moorgate Street. Away from these explicit poles of desirability prestige values diminish considerably.

In spite of this there has been only a comparatively modest move towards high-rise blocks. Post-war planning policy advocated a scattering of high-rise throughout the city, partly to avoid overwhelming the historic centre which includes St Paul's cathedral. As a result much of the war-devastated area was rebuilt as medium-height blocks, whose lack of character is now the centre of intense criticism and which will be partly replaced in the near future. They will not be replaced by skyscrapers. The highest building, the NatWest tower, is a modest 183 metres high but still eye-catching in a low-profile city. The most prestigious building in the business district is Lloyd's Bank; it makes no effort to dwarf its neighbours, but its total commitment to high technology makes it unique in this traditional environment.

London, then, eschewed the Manhattan look. It met the demands of tertiary growth by lateral expansion and by replacing more traditional uses in other parts of the city (Wood). For example, there has been considerable movement into the former residential streets of the West End. Shops and hotels had already replaced the rich merchants who first occupied this area; and they were followed by small businesses, particularly those which wanted to exploit the social kudos of having an exclusive address. Recently there has been an expansion in publishing, advertising, and travel bureaux; and hotel accommodation has exploded and is now extending further west in response to traffic from Heathrow.

None of this activity has radically altered the environment it has taken over. Upper-class houses add distinction to so many professional services! Spectacular changes are, however, taking place to the east of the business City. Here the waste lands of the former docks, long deserted as shipping moved further and further downstream, are being reclaimed for both office accommodation and residential blocks. The most dramatic move has been from Fleet Street which has seen the departure of all but one of its newspapers, marking the end of a very long tradition and the demise of one of the most colourful and distinctive specialist quarters in London. Some of these plants moved to Wapping, on the river and just east of the old city walls; others went further to the Isle of Dogs. Here, in and around those basins which were the centre of nineteenth-century London's trade, derelict land was taken over under the Docklands Development Scheme (1981) by a corporation which has been given the special dispensations of a Free Enterprise Zone, free from bureaucratic constraints and from many financial burdens. It already has a rail link with the City and an airstrip with direct flights to several European capitals. Plans for the future include tower blocks which, at 244 metres, will be by far the tallest in London.

All this confirms London's role as a world centre for transacting business and handling information. Not only is it a trade, financial, and insurance centre, but it has all the ancillary activities, particularly those linked with the developing world. The last are largely an outcome of its own history as a colonial power only recently withdrawn from many former possessions overseas. It now specializes in data collecting, policy making, and professional advice in planning, engineering, architecture, and transport for the Third World. Finally, London has maintained its position as a prime centre for education, research, learning, and the arts. That it is a centre for foreign students in particular is evident from its 80 schools teaching English as a foreign language.

In this latest phase of development the metropolis is a leader too in handling information. The largest sector in manufacturing is printing and publishing; one of the most rapidly growing industries is radio and television. Recently Reuters decided to establish a new billion-pound centre for global information services in London, the last step in an unbroken tradition which began in Lloyd's coffee shop in the City.

In spite of all this prosperity London has a strong element of nostalgia. London exploits its history. About 8 million people visit London annually, an industry that accounts for a £2 billion income, 8 per cent of the capital's gross domestic product. Directly and indirectly tourism supports 250,000 jobs. London has much to offer the tourist, and it pays to preserve the past, as the transformation of Covent Garden into a shopping and restaurant precinct has proved. The business élite may be attracted by its international character, but the mass of visitors are attracted by its unique heritage. The fact that the more distant past is also part of the heritage of North America is an added bonus.

In many ways London's metropolitan greatness peaked before the First World War, when it might have justly claimed to be the greatest city in the world. Today, having shed most of the territory which contributed to that greatness, it has successfully transformed itself into one of the 'world cities' which operate on a supranational network.

V

Whereas London is poised between its past greatness and a challenging future, New York is the archetypal twentieth-century metropolis. The famous Manhattan skyline proclaims its complete commitment to the technology which has produced the greatest massing of megastructures ever seen, and to the economic system which made it possible.

I have already referred to the paradox of the concentration of those activities which no longer have to depend on propinquity, though this is partly explained by the spiral of land values. What Mumford calls the neo-technic—electricity, oil technology, radio—could have led to dispersion. Instead they led to implosion. The aim seemed to be to express power in concrete, and where better to do that than in the next block to your rival for power? Increase in size and complexity was also a result of organizational changes, in particular the development of joint-stock companies. In this century the production of goods and services entered a new phase, with most decisions being taken by financiers rather than by the producers of goods themselves. Marketing, and the creation of new markets, became a major occupation as did advertising, as the United States in particular witnessed the emergence of the consumer society.

Therefore, important though trade and manufacturing was, it was banking and insurance that gave the impetus to the growth of downtown New York. And when this very limited area proved too restricting, businesses moved to mid-town. This luxury shopping-cum-residential sector gave way to skyscrapers between the wars, as exemplified by the Rockefeller Centre (1930–40), a group of skyscraper slabs which combined offices, shops, and radio headquarters. Mid-town growth reflected the explosion of quaternary activities, of information transactions, research institutions, foundations, trade-union headquarters, and professional bodies; all of which still allowed some admixture of luxury shopping. Monumentalism came in too. The Pan-Am building contains 240,000 square metres and houses 25,000 people.

It would be no exaggeration to classify the whole of Manhattan south of Central Park (Sixty-First Street) as being the central business district. In this 24 square kilometres there is a working population of 1.9 million. It is a concentration of offices second only to Tokyo. At what point does this kind of concentration stop? Even half a century ago it was thought that the attraction of so many workers to so restricted a region and their disgorging into the streets at the end of a working day would cause complete chaos. Intolerable though the crowding is at times, it has not yet paralysed the city. Skyscrapers still work. The balance is a delicate one, but so far the success of these immense buildings compensates for any problems they have created.

vi

The freedom Americans have of attempting almost anything in steel and concrete is unique. In London, as we have seen, planning laws exercise strict controls. One would expect Paris to be even more conservative. Here was a city that had undergone a radical transformation in the nineteenth century to produce a series of renaissance-style avenues, boulevards, and squares which were to determine its character for a very long time. An essential part of the plan for a unified, dignified centre which also allowed a considerable concentration of people was building to a standard height. If the Parisian was smug, he had a lot to be smug about. Paris's one concession to the new age was the Eiffel Tower.

But Paris could not escape the growing pressure on the central area which was very evident after the Second World War. The 'centre' can be defined roughly as that area bounded by the major railway termini. Almost exactly as in London, such an area neatly contains the 1850 city. This is the heart of the metropolis, and all that is in it seems worth preserving. Within this area are employed over a million people. It contains the city's financial quarter, its administrative sector, its luxury shopping, and its university. In the Seventh Arrondissement, between the Seine and the Eiffel Tower, lies a 'quartier des ministères', where ten government departments are based in addition to the Prefecture of Paris. The congestion here is very marked, with departments crowded into old buildings which are often ill suited to the work. The economy has undergone the same kind of structural changes as London and New York. Paris, too, has become part of the supranational network and it has had its quaternary explosion. It is the home of international bodies like UNESCO. To the dismay of many the almost inevitable response of high-rise building began to appear in the 1970s, but the controls have ensured a result more like London than New York. Concentration is avoided at all cost by planning a series of scattered nodes where some skyscrapers are allowed (P. Hall 1984, pp. 75–7).

Five kilometres west of the Arc de Triomphe, La Défense was built in the 1970s, a great complex of thirty towers each 30 storeys high. Together they provide offices, exhibition space, shops, and apartments. The entire complex has a pedestrian platform linking the units and segregating traffic. Nearby is a campus of various new schools of the university. La Défense has the air of shelving a problem, or rather of accepting an unpalatable solution and setting it to one side where one hopes it will not be noticed. Its sole aim seems to be to keep the inner city inviolate. Yet five 'poles of attraction' have been planned which will have 40-storey blocks; most of them will avoid the centre by being grouped near the railway termini. But the most significant new building, and the highest, is unashamedly central, and the centre of bitter controversy. The Tour Montparnasse is a massive slab of 56 storeys, 200 metres high. This is now the highest block in Europe, where such skyscrapers are always a threat to carefully preserved historic monuments and traditions and a sense of continuity with the past.

Paris has been the subject of comprehensive planning since the 1960s, and most of the relief for the centre will come not just from minor concentrations of high-rise blocks immediately around the centre, but from encouraging major nodes further out in the suburbs (Fig. 9). La Défense is in fact one of eight such nodes ringing the city at about 12 kilometres' distance from the centre. A further and complementary part of the plan is the establishing of five new towns beyond the continuously built-up area

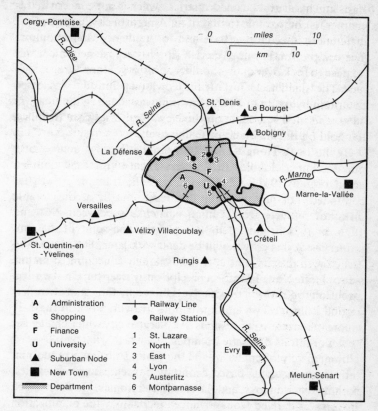

FIG. 9. Post-war planning in Paris.

though, unlike London's new towns, they are intended as an integral part of the metropolis.

vii

Any comparison of contemporary metropolitan cities and their responses to similar structural changes must include one outside the Western cultural orbit, though it is one with direct European antecedents. For Hong Kong is a Western implantation in the Far

East, and its central business district, which is our concern in this chapter, is comparable to that of an American city in spite of the differences in economic base and in the demographic context. The comparison is with America simply because here there was no need to look over one's shoulder at history. Hong Kong is very new. The island itself, just off the Kowloon peninsula, was leased to Britain by treaty in 1842. Kowloon was added to the treaty in 1860, and in 1890 a lease on the New Territories gave Britain a toe-hold on the mainland of China itself.

By the 1890s Hong Kong had a population of a quarter of a million, but it doubled in the next twenty years and doubled again, until by 1941 it was 1.64 million. The dramatic growth has continued, not just by natural increase, but by a considerable influx of refugees from China, particularly between 1961 and 1971. In 1981 it had 5.1 million people, and some of the consequences of this growth will be dealt with later. Here I am concerned with the city centre, which is largely concentrated on one side of Hong Kong Island—a precipitously steep terrain—with an extension to Kowloon to which it is linked by ferry and an underground railway. Two million people live and work in these 87 square kilometres. The result is a skyscraper city which challenges New York in its dramatic qualities.

Immediately after the war Hong Kong still had a predominantly manufacturing-based economy concentrating on textiles, clothing, later on toys, and, later still, electronics. However much the last was derived from advanced technology the organization was very much a pre-industrial one. The city was a mass of small firms, 90 per cent employing less than 10 persons; the economy was one of sweat-shops and home-based industries in which living-quarters and workshops were inextricably mixed. Its genius was entrepreneurship. By the 1980s, however, the manufacturing sector had declined to 40 per cent and the tertiary sector had taken over the lead. Personal services, hotels and restaurants, construction and transport figured most prominently, though trading, finance, and government were still important. In the gross domestic product manufacture now accounts for only 27 per cent, trade for 24 per cent, and commerce and finance for 20 per cent (Hong Kong is now among the twelve leading financial centres of the world). One might almost claim that a post-industrial city has been grafted on to a pre-industrial one (P. Hall 1984, p. 202).

The number of skyscrapers, and their intimate massing on the island is such that the newest of them is by no means incongruent but rather sits comfortably among its kind. Yet the Hong Kong Bank (1987) is in many ways novel and spectacular. It replaces a predecessor which in 1935, at nearly 70 metres' height, was itself the tallest building between Cairo and San Francisco. But the new bank is not only 306 metres high, and the largest bank head-quarters in the world; it is also uncompromisingly high-tech, an experiment in superimposing three immense blocks with inter-vening 'environmental areas' of gardens and open space. Above all else it is a status symbol, and its cost—£650 million—reflects the immense resources which lie behind it. And it may well be that even this building will soon be dwarfed when the new Bank of China is built nearby!

6

The Transactional Metropolis

> Melmotte had the telegraph at his command, and had been
> able to make these close enquiries as though San Francisco
> and Salt Lake City were suburbs of London
>
> TROLLOPE

i

The last chapter showed that changes taking place in the metropolis in this second half of the twentieth century are twofold.
First there is a structural change in economic activities reflecting
those in society as a whole and resulting in a marked emphasis on
business and the handling of information. Secondly there are
changes in the urban environment with a massive increase in
office blocks in the city centre, though there may be marked
differences in the way different cities respond to this demand.
The common characteristic of the new activities is the way they
transcend national interests and become part of an international
network of activities. As long as the metropolis was the centre of
a nation-state it was a faithful reflection of the culture of that
state. Now that activities have spilled over national frontiers to
such a degree the international circuit claims a higher proportion,
and those engaged in them move freely from one city to another
in an international milieu which uses a common technology and
which has created its own environment. The purpose of this
chapter is to examine in a little more detail some of those
functions which are part of a global system, and the implications
for the metropolis of today.

One striking feature about many contemporary metropolitan
transactions—and one that will be very important in discussing
future trends in the next chapter—is that they are not necessarily
tied permanently to a specific location, in the way we usually

think of great cities as having a particular 'place' geographically and fixed relationships with other 'places'. More people move more often and much more rapidly than ever before: events are transmitted to every corner of the earth as they occur: exchanges of data ignore distance: business is done across the Atlantic as easily as across a shop counter. Distance and time have so diminished that location has become much less relevant than ever before. More activities are peripatetic on a large scale, more are shared, and nearly all are accessible on the international network. Metropolises are nodes on this network.

In parenthesis we should not forget that there is nothing new in networks of activities within societies. The itinerant merchant is embodied in every market in Britain—or in China; we are familiar with the itinerant craftsman, teacher, preacher, or touring theatre company. What is new is the scale, and the fact that technology has made possible a global pattern of behaviour that was previously limited to small social groups and to small regions. The circuit is now the entire world. So let us first consider some of the activities which exploit this fact.

ii

To pursue the economics of the great multinationals which underlie so much of world business activities is far beyond the scope of this book; though they are at the heart of the matter as described by one writer:

The multinational corporation . . . transcending national boundaries, cultural specificity and political controls within a global strategy [has a] tendency towards decentralisation of the logic of the economic process and a concentration of decision-making in a few commanding heights of the international economy. (Castells, p. 103)

This sums up the two critical effects of the multinational; first the expansion of capital and of industrial activity to a number of developing countries, and second the centralization of the controlling financial complexes in a few 'world cities'. Global corporations are exploiting the cheap labour of the Third World and at the same time establishing a world-wide network of financial control (Thrift). This has resulted not only in a new geography of economic activity but also in a transnational organization of skilled labour and of managerial staff. International migrants now include a considerable proportion of highly skilled workers and executives (Frobel).

The idea of world economic exchanges is, of course, not new. We saw earlier that it underlay Braudel's concept of a 'world' economy in medieval Europe. The local market-place sometimes became the international fair. Of paramount importance in pre-industrial Europe, these fairs came into their own again in the later nineteenth century, this time truly encompassing the entire world. The re-emergence of the international fair began with London's Great Exhibition of 1851. This was not just an eloquent statement of Britain's achievements as an industrial nation: it was also an invitation to the world to visit a super market-place which displayed not only the exotic goods of an empire, but the produce of every country in Europe. And the world came. Crystal Palace had 6 million visitors, so many from overseas that it ensured Britain's dominance in world markets for several decades.

The world fair became an institution, a peripatetic get-together in which nation after nation invited the world to its own celebration of industry and trade, offering its own metropolis as a temporary world capital. New York followed closely on the heels of London in 1853, though attendance was small, a mere 1.2 million. Then Paris staged a fair in 1855, followed by London again in 1862. London repeated the experience in 1886, 1908, 1924, and 1951: Paris in 1867, 1878, 1889, 1900, 1931, and 1937: Vienna (1873), Liège (1905), Brussels (1910, 1935, and 1958) all staged world fairs. In the New World New York tried again in 1914 and 1939: Chicago held a very famous one in 1893, and again in 1933: so did Philadelphia (1876 and 1926), Buffalo (1901), St Louis (1904), San Francisco (1915), and Seattle (1962). Glasgow (1901) was the only British city outside London to have a world fair, but the Commonwealth has had three: Sydney (1879), Melbourne (1880), and Montreal (1967). Osaka (1970) took the event outside the Western world for the first time. They were all enormously attractive, particularly as improved communications enabled more people to attend the later ones. While the figures of attendance are largely a reflection of local and national interest, there is no denying that the city where the fair was held was at the centre of the world stage for a brief period. By 1900 Paris could boast an attendance of 39 million, New York in 1939 of 45 million, Montreal of 50 million, and Osaka of 64 million.

The fairs provided temporary links between societies, traditional vehicles for exchanges of all kinds, and, predominantly, a boost for the world economy. But they laid the basis for the increasing internationalization of technology. Since 1928 they have been subject to international regulation agreed by thirty-five countries, and controlled by a bureau in Paris.

A city must be of considerable status and command some wealth to host a world fair; and the event itself increases its status as well as paying dividends. The same can be said about those cities which have hosted the modern Olympic Games. Since 1896, when the first modern event was held in Athens, the host cities have been: Paris (twice), St Louis, London (twice), Stockholm, Antwerp, Amsterdam, Los Angeles, Berlin, Helsinki, Melbourne, Rome, Tokyo, Mexico City, Munich, Montreal, Moscow, and Seoul. All these cities are strong contenders for world status because they are on a world circuit of an international activity. The fact that an 'interest group' can focus its activities in such a range of cities—now including some in the developing world—points to a community which is worldwide.

iii

Fairs and Olympic Games are massive jamborees which can be held only in a metropolis. Not so the meetings of élites in the world of learning, for example. There was a time when scholars came to specific centres of learning, as indeed they still do: but Paris was the outstanding early medieval example, and other historic centres had a strong power of attraction: Cairo for the Islamic world, Bologna, Heidelberg, and Oxford and Cambridge. Such centres remain, but there is also a new freedom of movement and a new kind of access to information which enables the élite to bypass these old centres if they so wish. The academic élite can choose to be transient within the established network or it can identify with new, small centres, and incorporate them as 'nerve cells' within the metropolitan network. Let me take Aspen as an example.

Aspen is a small mountain resort in Colorado which was chosen in 1949 as a centre to celebrate Goethe's bicentenary. It immediately became a focus of international attention, intellectually and musically. It periodically mustered scholars from all over the world, but particularly from Europe and the United States. In 1964 an Aspen Society of Fellows was founded, limited to 100, a self-conscious élite of distinguished scholars. Their self-appointed task was the strengthening of the humanities. Significantly, in view of our metropolitan theme, in 1980 a headquarters was built in New York, and Aspen itself has returned to being a rather exclusive recreation centre. But over a period of thirty years this very small town became a think-tank, the Mecca of intellectuals, plugged into the international circuit; it was a transactional centre in the true sense of the word.

A similar group meets annually at the village of Alpbach in Austria, again turning a tiny ski resort into an intellectuals' debating chamber. One group which met there in 1969 is well-known even to the layman, the Club of Rome. This transnational group of economists and planners had met the year before in Rome—hence the name. Its concern was the husbanding of world resources, and it drew great attention to itself by the publication of *Limits of Growth*. This predicted future world demands on natural resources through the use of mathematical models. The Club of Rome has met in other cities since, but this description will give a little of its flavour:

The Club of Rome sounds like utopian science fiction. It is limited to a hundred members who share the conviction that the problems now facing the world are of such complexity and interrelationship that traditional policies and institutions are no longer able to cope with them. A majority of the Club is European with substantial North American input and token Japanese and Third World contingents. Almost all the members are industrialists and established intellectuals. (Davis, p. 113)

One of the founder members of the Club of Rome was the Greek planner Dinos Doxiadis. He had become the chief regional planner of Greece at the age of 25, and by the mid-1950s had a private planning organization of 700 with branches in eleven countries world-wide. In 1962 he initiated a series of ten annual meetings, the Delos Symposia, to which he invited thirty or so leading academics to pool information and ideas about settlements of all kinds on an interdisciplinary basis. Some of his own ideas about the form of future urbanization will be discussed in the next chapter; at Delos his function was to act as catalyst to ome of the world's most eminent scholars. The symposium was a transient group. It met on a cruise vessel, moving from one idyllic Aegean island to the next until its culmination at Delos, where, in the ruins of a former metropolis, programmes were formulated on the metropolises of today. These meetings, like those at Aspen and Alpbach, included a retreat from the realities of urban problems: they emphasized the need for relaxation, withdrawal, and even isolation.

These are examples only of some characteristics of supranational elements in the transactional society. Some illustrate the way in which an élite can detach itself from the metropolis, to move at will, and to maintain the comfortable standards of the city in physically remote regions. The élite already live in a 'global village'. In a lesser way the experience is repeated countless times in symposia, international meetings, and academic get-togethers. It is easy to parody, as Koestler did in *The Call Girls* or Lodge in *Small World*. There are academics who are more often in motion than at rest, just as there are business men who at times find it difficult to remember what country they are in. Agglomeration and permanence, our stock assumptions about metropolis, have been complemented by the transient and the temporary. For the moment, at least, metropolis wins. Aspen goes home to New York; the Delos Symposium returns to Athens: the executive boardroom is still a penthouse in a city block. What we have been looking at are tiny, floating, detached fragments of metropolitan life, moving here and there but always within the metropolitan network; the privilege of movement is utterly dependent on the resources of the permanent establishment.

iv

World networks serving specialized interest groups of necessity
ignore national boundaries. Much business is in the hands of
transnational companies; finance is global; the world of
information is one. Even those activities which are strictly
territorial, and subject to political control, are showing a
tendency to greater massing. There are blocs of nations,
economic, military, and ideological, which are committed to
some, at least, transnational activities and obligations: EEC,
COMECON, NATO, OPEC, SEATO. There is a vaguer
grouping which we refer to as the First, Second, and Third
Worlds. They all involve networks and great movements of
people within them and between them. Until recently heads of
governments rarely left their capital cities: summits and
conferences are now the order of the day. Nothing could better
illustrate this urge to move than the journeys of Pope John Paul
II, in an office which until now was considered to be confined
within the walls of the Vatican City.

If the network is so important, where does it leave metropolis?
We have seen already that one is the complement of the other;
and some scholars think that an increase in supranational
activities can only lead to increase in the metropolis and a further
concentration there of institutions serving the quaternary sector.
World-wide activities must have roots. So in addition to being
metropolises in the traditional sense of expressing the richness of
a specific society and culture, many have the added function of
being major international centres. The United Nations is housed
in New York, UNESCO in Paris, and the EEC in Brussels. In a
sense rather different from Hall's perhaps, these become 'world
cities'.

When there is a preponderance of activity in the tertiary and
quaternary sectors of a city's economy, the city is sometimes
referred to as 'post-industrial', but increasingly the term 'transactional' is appropriate. Let me stress again that this refers to the
preponderance of certain activities, their magnitude rather than
their presence. In a sense transacting has always been part and
parcel of exchange of goods or persons or information. But now

the stress is on the business, the negotiation and management, the prosecution; and the term is increasingly useful to describe what goes on in the quaternary sector.

No one has made a greater contribution to understanding this contemporary urban change than Professor Jean Gottmann, and he has summed up two decades of work in a book called *The Coming of the Transactional City*. He puts it very simply when he says that the transactional city is one in which the white-collar worker has ousted the blue-collar (as London and New York so well illustrated). The consequences are many, and Gottmann stresses:

(*a*) The crudest effect, and one which has caused problems in the society as a whole, is that there is simply less work, in the ordinary sense of the word, available, in spite of prolonging the period of education of the young and reducing the age of retirement for the elderly. More time, and a greater affluence, produces longer commuting, an increase in the work that can be done at home, and more leisure and recreational activities. In terms of city expansion it has meant greater freedom to live in outliers of the city, and consequently a more dispersed urban fabric.

(*b*) A second characteristic is an increased emphasis on a 'hosting' environment: that is, an increase in the range and variety of services. The international network depends on a transient élite which demands the highest standards in catering. High-quality hotels, good cuisine, and a range of entertainment are essential, in addition to specialized facilities for conferences of all kinds.

(*c*) Thirdly, there must be ease of accessibility to a flow of information. Specialist though each activity may be, it depends on a whole complex of complementary demands. There must, for example, be instant access to credit and money.

(*d*) Fourthly, and almost as a corollary to (*c*), the entire exercise seems to depend on a concentration of facilities and services in the centre of the city. This apparent contradiction will recur in subsequent discussion.

The transactional city, then, does have distinctive features, though these are usually an addition to the more traditional aspects of the industrial city (London) or even the pre-industrial city (Hong Kong and Tokyo). Gottmann emphasizes that the features are not necessarily a function of size. In the past smaller cities have become very specialized in transmitting information—university towns are good examples. In some ways these have a continuing significance because they are rooted in the past, for in them information is passed on verbally in face-to-face contacts or it is stored as the printed word. Although we are witnessing a revolution in data storage and retrieval there is no indication that it will immediately replace the printed word, and consequently we still recognize the need for vast repositories of books, like the British Library or the Library of Congress, in transactional cities. The technology is already available to revolutionize this pattern, but is only slowly breaking down traditional forms of communication. Computerization has opened up enormous possibilities, which are indeed necessary to cope with the explosion of knowledge which is taking place. Increase in information is a self-generating process. It has been calculated that scientific and technical information doubles at five-year intervals; but this rate is itself increasing, and soon it may double every two years. The future will depend upon computerization and miniaturization; a recent 'domesday' survey of Britain is contained on two discs!

Modern technology can certainly eliminate the classroom in the learning process. Teaching by radio has been in use for decades in sparsely populated areas in Australia. Now the Open University in Britain—the largest in the country in student-numbers—has virtually dispensed with the face-to-face trans-actions which were the *raison-d'être* of a university. Instead it packages its information and transmits it by radio and television. This is a pointer to the future university with no campus. For the time being, however, inertia is too strong and traditional values too entrenched, and status is too precious to envisage a rapid transformation or the disappearance of our old universities.

Perhaps more relevant to our universal well-being is the fact that the world of finance has been geared to computers. One reason for the New York stock market collapse of 1987 may well have been that programmed responses to fluctuations in the market were so geared to instant reaction that their very speed obviated human choice and so accelerated the downward trend.

The tendency to let the machine take over has had many repercussions, both in the last century and this. The last revolutionary machine, the steam engine, which ushered in the industrial era, was found to be more efficient and economical if it were to work continuously rather than be allowed to cool down each evening so that the process of building up steam began afresh each day. The result was a twenty-four-hour working day into which humans had to be slotted in a shift system. It took a long time to introduce the social controls and constraints which made man the master of the machine rather than vice versa. Now, in the transactional city, we are approaching the twenty-four-hour day again, from a different direction. Not only does it behove us to be aware of events—particularly in the money-markets—which are taking place on the other side of the world, in different time zones; but we also demand that services be available instantly and at any hour. Until recently banking hours were strictly limited, but now that personal contact with a bank clerk is no longer necessary to obtain money, the cash-dispenser provides cash at any time the customer demands it. The allocation of a few specific hours during which we were formerly able to enjoy professional drama or music has been replaced by near-continuous television, augmented by video for instant recall.

The metropolis which is gradually emerging is a highly technical machine, an artefact which serves what some scholars have called an 'artificial culture' (Davis, pp. 86 ff.): 'There is no direct production . . . Almost all the post-industrial culture brings are transactions; transactions that are increasingly dependent upon binary digital logic, computerised information.'

Some think of Los Angeles as a centre of such a culture. According to Davis:

Its life styles of short duration, its mammoth funfairs that attract greater numbers of people than natural wonders like the Grand Canyon: its unusual family attractions like Forest Lawn cemetery or the drive-in churches, cinemas and restaurants, its increasing use of artificial grass, trees and plants . . . its twenty-four hour day, seven-days-a-week shopping precincts kept at a constant and comfortable temperature irrespective of weather conditions; its freeways and surface streets on which traffic is controlled by computer and feed-back systems . . . Los Angeles is a metropolis in spite of environmental odds and social cost. The city sold itself as a sunshine city . . . It was an alternative world to the cold north-east where a mixture of industry, hard winters and a protestant work ethic called out for relief . . . (p. 90)

Los Angeles has many features which herald a break with the traditional. It had no natural harbour, so it made an artificial one; it has to bring in water from another state; it suffers extreme pollution and has 200 days of smog every year (even its sunsets are artificial!) It even seems to defy the traditional shape of a city. In this respect its history—or lack of it—helps. It never possessed the strong pull of a well-defined centre because it is made up of scores of incorporated 'cities' which have gradually coalesced into the most extensive urban sprawl in the world; it has been described as a hundred suburbs in search of a metropolis. Its 'downtown' is as attenuated as the rest of the built-up area. It was total commitment to the car that set aside so much of the central area for parking, as early as 1928; it set a standard for sterilizing about a third of the area from any other use. Beyond the centre the vast, loose, urban fabric is held together by the freeway. To Reyner Banham, who wrote so eloquently and sympathetically of this city, the freeway was a substitute for place, a monumental system for which there is no alternative, and so dominant that it becomes a way of life, a 'state of mind': a system which must be submitted to via automatic controls and signs: 'No human eye at windscreen level can unravel the complexities of an intersection fast enough for a human brain travelling at 60 m.p.h. to make the right decision in time; there is no alternative to complete surrender to instructions and signs' (p. 219). Signs, indeed, dominate the townscape: 'To deprive the city of its advertising signs would be like depriving San Gimignano of its towers or the City of London of its Wren steeples' (p. 139). To Banham this is not a city which denies culture, but one which expresses a totally new culture. For life to be tolerable those who live in Los Angeles must accept this, which is why it is described as a good city to live in but not one you would like to visit!

In the search for the characteristics of the metropolitan city we have now come to our own time, with the great city uneasily poised between an inherited past and a future which could produce forms which would surprise the traditionalist. I have been arguing that there have been common features throughout this story, and until recently even common characteristics of the built environment. Only in this century has technology made possible new patterns of life, and whether or not these will be adopted is something I will deal with in the next chapter. But for the time being we are still dealing with centralization, command of resources, and a desire to express power in monumentality.

Not all would agree that metropolitanism is a way of describing peaks of cultural and organizational achievement in the past. In a thesis on the supranational city Marion Davis argues that metropolitanism is a stage in the evolution of the urban system, and that it is historically very recent. It represents an advance on the 'city' but is in itself a mere preliminary to the single 'world city'. As a category, then, Davis regards metropolitan cities as a contemporary phenomenon. Historical examples are exceptional, unique, and belong to closed systems of the past. This means there is no significant connection between the great cities of today and those of the past. He further postulates that the common characteristic of contemporary metropolises, which sets them in a class apart, is their indeterminacy. By this he means that they are part of an open urban system, that they are often even physically linked with other cities in an amorphous manner, and that this is leading to a further evolutionary stage, the megalopolis, which will be discussed in the next chapter.

The concept of cities in history as closed systems is easily understood. The historical examples I dealt with emphasized their role as expressing a distinctive culture, and it is something which we can still appreciate. It is the closed aspect which is appealing to the tourist, not just the containment and sense of unity which one often gets in such cities but also the continuity of culture. A visitor to Florence, in spite of the noise and traffic, transposes himself to a past culture; indeed he moves within the fabric of that culture and its distinctiveness is very apparent. Yet we also saw earlier that Florence was part of a medieval world system. Davis's argument is that the 'world' today is literally the whole world, and that the metropolitan cities of today are the product of the twentieth century, sharing enough aspects to distinguish them as a class within the world system. And just as the medieval world had a pre-eminent leading city at different periods, so world leadership in this century has moved from London to New York—to Tokyo?

This simple model of a superclass based on shared pre-eminence, economically and technologically, is attractive. It means accepting a dynamic-evolutionary view of city development, a system of cities which unifies as it becomes all-embracing. But I think two aspects must be looked at further. The first is that the historical cities do share certain crucial characteristics with the metropolis of today, enough I think to warrant a common class. Even the transactional aspects which are rightly stressed so much today are functions which have always been present: I have stressed that the difference is one of degree and proportion, not of kind. The second point is that modern metropolises also share the characteristic of cultural uniqueness with every metropolis of the past. We tend to be blinded by those characteristics of the supranational city which transcend the limitations of location; they are also centres of local and national cultural networks. There is still much they owe to their geographic location, as a comparison of Toronto and Los Angeles would show. And however constant the cosmopolitan element—which has recurred constantly—each metropolis has its own distinctive social milieu which derives directly from the fact that it is first and foremost rooted in place, and that it exists within a specific social context.

To the layman it is the latter set of qualities which makes a city a metropolis, and it is a product of the closed system. Although 'world city' activities have made an immense visual impact in great skyscrapers, this after all is only one diagnostic feature (what 'tourist' in the 1850s would have insisted on seeing London's warehouses, or Manchester's mills?) Visually stunning, they take their place with history, 'atmosphere', and social awareness. In stressing the Western technological features we may be overstressing a Western view of a Western world, to the detriment of cities outside that orbit. Metropolitanism is a total experience, and the cities which share it include many in the developing world which have only a small share of transnational transactions.

There is, finally, a great measure of subjective judgement in any assessment of a metropolitan city. The application of strict criteria which include some cities and exclude others produces nothing more than an analytical tool, useful for academic discussions like those in the first chapter, but too narrow to do justice to the subject. At the other extreme there can be wide variations in our individual perception of what constitutes metropolitan. Increasing scale has not helped. Looking at the past, when urbanization was the exception and cities were small, there is no mistaking the giants that stand head and shoulders above the rest. Today the giant, at least in terms of numbers, is commonplace, which is why criteria of 'world cities' tend to be rather exclusive. More attention must be given to non-Western cities. Their powers of attraction are unparalleled, a feature which demands greater investigation. And the final chapters, dealing with the human implications of life in the metropolis, will reveal problems which are ubiquitous. In the light of this, Hall's seven examples of world cities are too narrow to cover the theme of metropolitanism. Davis has reduced the number still further, but this is because he is dealing with the tip of a hierarchy and with the uttermost point of an evolutionary process. We saw earlier that Robson and Reagan identify twenty-four great cities; but these again are examples, not a class. There are no Chinese cities in their list, presumably because data were lacking, and Moscow was omitted for practical reasons. They do include eight cities from the developing world, and we shall see in the final two chapters that this is critical in a contemporary approach which sees the metropolis more in the light of its problems rather than its outward and spectacular attractions.

In the last resort any list of great cities will vary enormously and for many good reasons, but the attributes of greatness should not be too difficult to enumerate. The essence of what I have been looking for lies in:

(*a*) The power of a city to attract people, and hence to be relatively great in size.

(*b*) Its centrality, and from this its ability to wield political power and to exercise control over territory, people, and resources.

(*c*) The accumulation of key economic activities and the amassing of wealth which results from it.

(*d*) The expression of a distinctive culture and its eminence through the growth of cultural institutions.

(*e*) Its participation in supranational systems of transacting business and information.

All these were features of the historical examples I dealt with; they are certainly characteristic of the metropolitan city of today.

7

The Future Metropolis

A city such as vision builds . . .
SHELLEY

i

In looking at the development of the Western metropolis I have
assumed a pre-industrial stage followed by an industrial one, and
then a post-industrial or transactional stage. Stages of this kind
are strongly linked with changes in technology and also with
changes in society and in ideology; and together these give rise to
easily recognizable features in the built environment which makes
up the city today. For example, the pattern of streets and open
spaces distinguishes 'pedestrian cities', in which movement of
men and animals is confined to narrow streets and an incoherent
system of alley-ways, from the 'vehicular cities' of renaissance
times with planned streets and separate pavements, and from
'automobile cities' in which traffic is entirely isolated from other
movements. The visual dominance of man's changing ideologies
can also suggest broad categories of differentiation, from soaring
cathedrals to baroque palaces to industrial mills to the
skyscrapers of a capitalist financial system. So, in a rough and
ready manner we relate the changing urban scene to a changing
society, and there is a fair measure of agreement on how these
changes came about.

What is infinitely more difficult is looking at the future, at
what the most likely outcome will be of the changes which are
taking place now, changes which are more radical and rapid than
they have ever been in the history of urban man. Moreover they
are changes against a background of ten centuries of inertia
during which each succeeding generation has been the inheritor
of the past. It is still so. The most we can see are relatively

marginal novelties, sporadic responses to change, and a trend—if any—set in a very familiar and accepted environment. We may think we are in a position to choose and fashion the future, but we are really very encumbered by the past.

The speed of change in this century has made the response of the metropolis particularly chaotic. Whereas a medieval metropolis grew, flourished, and eventually declined within the same technological system and the same social framework, thus giving a certain unity of form and a congruence between the urban fabric and the activities of the city, the modern metropolis is trying to cope with rapid change in an outmoded built environment. We adapt, we modify, and we are sometimes driven to distraction in trying to live late twentieth-century lives in nineteenth-century—or earlier—cities. The fabric of the city changes slowly, and most people are very reluctant to hasten this process. Indeed we place a particular value on age, on the styles of the past; we cherish the ancient, relish incongruence, and are prepared to pay very dearly for the outmoded and the inconvenient. Our urban environments are redolent of the past and no place for the dynamic urban society of today.

In a typical Western city two zones only are subject to any considerable and radical change. One is the very periphery of the city where suburbs are pushing into the countryside; and here at least there is an opportunity to build according to the needs of the present and of the immediate future—and even here it is often disguised in neo-Tudor or neo-Georgian wraps! The second zone is the very centre of the city, where the imperatives of centrality demand an often radical restructuring; here, as we have seen, is concentrated the thrust of modern construction technology, in skyscrapers. Between the two zones lies compromise, comparatively pleasant in the residential suburbs, and stable—or at least in equilibrium between the acceptance of the immediate past and the need for some adaptation to allow the most recent convenience. As we move from these stable areas to the centre we meet the decay and obsolescence of an increasingly ageing environment, in which social change becomes social turmoil, and age becomes dereliction. We are moving into what is known as the 'zone of transition'. On the whole, then, change is very restricted, and this is particularly so in many Western cities where there is little growth in population. We can hardly look forward to a brave new world. Rather it is too often having to put up with what we have.

One geographer put it this way:

The city of the future is already recognisable. It will be a city of suburbs, each more or less self-contained with its basic retail and public services, each with basically sound housing. There will be plenty of local, suburban jobs: an efficient highway system will provide good access to a wider variety of jobs across the city as a whole and to those services and social and recreational opportunities which cannot be obtained locally. There will be some congestion, both in the city most of the time and elsewhere at weekends. Perhaps it is not a bad future for us to look forward to. What can be wrong with it? (Wilson, p. 1)

This is what planners and 'futurologists' call a 'no-surprise future', although such a vision could be very rudely disturbed by technological and social changes which have already begun. It is a view which can also be called 'culturalist' because it embodies existing values which are part and parcel of Britain's existing urban tradition. Although many people would like to see something more novel and more exciting we must accept that such a future is continually unfolding before our eyes, mainly because it calls for the minimum of effort from us, and the minimum of accommodation and change. The metropolis, being an amalgam of all its pasts, has a certain fixed quality which is the despair of Utopian planners. Society has so lacked the imagination and energy to break the mould that I sometimes wonder if all we can look forward to is the chilling prospect of Mumford's necropolis or Max Ernst's 'Petrified City'. The ideal planning scenario, of course, is to start from scratch. No one put it better than Fitzgerald:

> . . . could thou and I with Fate conspire
> To grasp this sorry Scheme of things entire;
> Would we not shatter it to bits—and then
> Re-mould it nearer to the heart's desire!

> from *Rubáiyát of Omar Khayyam* (1st version)

Perversely, when that opportunity presented itself to many

cities after the bombing devastation of the Second World War, it was very rarely taken. A combination of vested interest, the sanctity of land values, and culturalist thinking saw to it that very little changed. Warsaw's rebuilding is a classic example of culturalism; the centre of the city was completely destroyed, and was replaced by an exact replica. All Warsaw wanted was its past. London's half-hearted attempt at reconstructing its centre proved to be a failure to come to terms with both the past and the future. So radical changes are shunned even when the opportunities arise. What we can look at now are some of the gradual changes of this century which have had an incremental effect and which can be thought of in the long term as constituting a trend; and we can then see where that trend may be leading us.

ii

The two processes which have shaped the contemporary metropolis and which are manifest in the two zones I referred to above are suburbanization and concentration in the centre. The profile of today's city is epitomized in the American model of the very extensive and very low residential area suddenly and dramatically peaking in a skyscraper core. Of course both features have a long history. Modern suburbanization was firmly established in the last century; though we must remember that even the younger Pliny resorted to commuting and boasted of the joys of his house in the country: 'It is seventeen miles from Rome, so that it is possible to spend the night there after necessary business is done, without having to cut short or limit the work.' Such commuting was exceptional! More usual was the accretion of houses as the city grew, a feature which London tried to curb even in the time of Elizabeth I.

Nineteenth-century suburbs in major industrial cities were the first response by a mass of people to the need for escape from the noise and dirt and pollution. It was a middle-class movement first, for suburbanization was a luxury for those who kept a carriage. But from the mid-nineteenth century railways increased accessibility, even for artisans, for whom special workmen's tickets were issued. Electric trains made it easier still by increasing speeds; and the bus and the car completed the process. A pattern of metropolitan life was established which was based on a daily rhythm of movement from and to the suburb. The classic description of transport as 'maker and breaker of cities' sums it up, for in a way the extension of suburbia was the first indication of the breaking down of the city as a contained corporate entity.

Suburban residential growth is so familiar a phenomenon that I shall not pursue it in any detail, but it is worth reminding ourselves of the subsequent dispersion of many of the activities which are traditionally associated with the city centre. The reason is simple: the fundamental assumption that centrality means accessibility is no longer true. In the past the services which needed to be most accessible had to be central, hence the agora and the forum and the market-place, the cathedral and the city hall. This simple fact is enshrined in a symbol for the city which goes back to Egyptian times. Their hieroglyph for 'city' was a cross inside a circle. This very simple device actually suggests the two basic characteristics of the traditional city (Lopez, pp. 27 ff.). Let the circle represent the containment of the city, the line of demarcation between what is and what is not 'city', indicating that the activities inside are very different from those outside. Historically the circle was the city wall. Today it could be a green belt. The cross represents exchange, and the centre is where transactions are at their peak, the point of interaction. Physically these lines could be the roads along which citizens went to their meeting-place to exchange skills, services, goods, and information; hence the point of greatest accessibility. Now, beyond a certain threshold this point becomes terribly congested, and eventually it loses its accessibility—at least, for face-to-face communication. Today most cities have curbs on using the centre in order to reduce congestion. Traffic may be prohibited, and certainly parking is severely taxed. As a consequence many services which we usually associate with the centre have migrated to the outskirts, where they are accessible, particularly to those with cars. For a very long time in American cities, the motel on the outskirts has replaced the hotel in the centre. (Incidentally, there is a very ancient precedent for this in the Islamic world; camel trains and their loads were usually dealt with at caravan- serais where the overland routes entered the city.) In America the automobile culture has further led to drive-in movies and cafés, away from the city centre. More recently most Western countries have seen a revolution in suburban and out-of-town shopping in localities where cars can be accommodated; the market-place is no longer necessarily in the centre.

This very generalized picture needs qualifying. The expensive hotels are still central, as are the luxury shops. When Brent Cross shopping centre was built in a north-west suburb of London in the 1970s, what was moved from the central area of the city was a fragment of Oxford Street, the popular department-store street, not the exclusive boutiques of Bond Street. Out-of-town shopping centres meet frequent and everyday needs and cater for the multitudes. They have done something to reduce the centrifugal/centripetal movements of the traditional city. However, as I pointed out above (ch. 5, sect. ii), the retail core is still an enormous attraction, department stores still occupy prime sites and are increasing in size, and the shopping mall, often an infill where decay has taken its toll, is adding interest to areas which were beginning to show signs of decline. I have already dealt with the outward movement of industry: the last chapter showed how in London, for example, the centre did not allow for restructuring or new initiatives; newer technologies flourish in suburbia. What has happened is that the increasing use of the car for work, shopping, and recreation has produced a more complex pattern of movement with more counter- commuting and lateral journeys which are binding the expanding city together in a more regional and comprehensive way than the old in–out rhythm. It has also led to a greater attenuation of the urban fabric, to a merging of suburb with suburb, and even of city with city. In England Salford was absorbed by Manchester, and Leeds merges with Bradford. As early as the first decade of the century the planning pioneer Patrick Geddes recognized the tendency for expanding cities to fuse, and he called the result a 'conurbation'.

iii

With the increasing sprawl of this century, especially in cities in the United States, what would happen if several cities merged in this way? Would the result be a different kind of city? To Jean Gottmann the answer was 'Yes'. In a seminal study of the urbanized area of the north-eastern region of the United States he described the emergence of a new urban pattern which he called 'megalopolis' (Gottmann 1961) (Fig. 10). People had long been familiar with the fact that there was some kind of urban corridor running through Boston, New York, Baltimore, and Washington. Journalists referred to it as 'Boswash'. Gottmann analysed it meticulously and came to the conclusion that it was more than a series of cities which happened to be contiguous and which might well merge in time. He saw it as a new phenomenon which could be a pointer to the future of urban development. He referred to the 'cradle of a new order in the organization of inhabited space'. The name he gave it, 'megalopolis', was justified because here was a new kind of urban structure unlike anything seen before, a realization perhaps of an ancient Greek dream of a super-city (ironically, the original Megalopolis in Greece never developed beyond the village it had always been). At first Gottmann used the name as a proper noun to describe a unique geographical and urban phenomenon. Its characteristics were:

(*a*) The unification of several conurbations by lines of rapid communication.

(*b*) A loose urban fabric of low density which included much green land interdigitating with the traditional urban environment.

(*c*) Nucleated and dense cores in traditional centres dominated by tertiary and quaternary activities.

(*d*) Qualitative features which differed from previous urban experience.

(*e*) A functional interdependence which merited a new conceptual approach.

Here then was an attempt to 'capture the expanding scale of urban life'. This last element was very difficult to measure and to

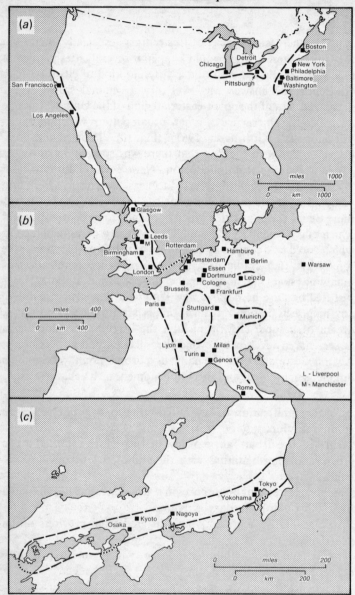

FIG. 10. Megalopolitan growth: (*a*) USA; (*b*) Europe; (*c*) Japan.

perceive as having an objective reality. The most significant outcome of Gottmann's work was the debate on the reality of megalopolis. If this was a matter of scale then it was very tempting to see it as the next stage in evolution, the next step in the hierarchy city–metropolis–conurbation–megalopolis. And we shall see in a moment how another planner saw it as a logical step to the ultimate single world city—ecumenopolis. But in that case, were there no other megalopolises? Geographers and planners began to see them everywhere.

The idea of interconnectedness based on fast communications—transport in the first instance—had been familiar for a long time in the guise of the linear city. Soria y Mata, at the end of the nineteenth century, had planned such a development around Madrid, and much of it had been built—a necklace of suburban houses strung along the line of the newfangled electric tramcar. Instant accessibility to fast transport is essential in a linear city if a very long corridor of movement is going to be exploited; hence the width may be very small. In an *ad hoc* manner ribbon development in Britain along roads and railway lines was producing something of a parallel pattern. Le Corbusier saw the future map of urban Europe as a series of linear cities. In England there seemed to be a corridor of towns from London to Liverpool via Birmingham. The American journalists who had invented 'Boswash' also knew of a 'Chipitts' (Chicago to Pittsburgh) and a 'Sansan' (San Francisco to San Diego). And at this scale they looked more like a megalopolis than a linear city. Was the proper noun really a common one? Was not 'megalopolis' a generic term?

The closest parallel to Gottmann's concept, the one approaching nearest to his criteria, was in Japan (Fig. 10c), where a series of cities lying along the axis of the Inland Sea—Tokyo, Nagoya, Kyoto, Osaka—form an integrated urban corridor—'Tokaido'—with a total population comparable to the north-eastern United States example. A Japanese Policy Plan for National Income (1960) favoured a strategy for development that would concentrate investment on this axis, in road, rail, and harbour facilities. The word 'megalopolis' was translated as *obijo-toshi*, literally a 'belt-like city'. One feature of the belt is known world-wide; this is the Bullet Train, which has an average speed of 120 m.p.h. Its split-second timing, computerized control of passenger seating, and incredible frequency are every bit as impressive as its speed. According to Japanese scholars the belt of urbanization has several distinctive features (Ito and Nagashima):

(*a*) It has a rapid and sustained urban growth.
(*b*) Its polynuclear centres have metropolitan quality.
(*c*) Economic and political power is concentrated here.
(*d*) It dominates the national economy.

To some extent the formation of this belt was aided by the natural environment, for there are no other comparable lowland areas where cities could easily grow. Here the plains of Kanto, Nobi, and Osaka merge. But it was economic and planning policies which exploited these advantages and advanced the changes. In this respect the Japanese megalopolis contrasts with the American, where the evolution has been the product of market forces, and where planning has been non-existent.

The parallels, however, are obvious. Here are two heavily urbanized belts, 740 kilometres long in the States, 500 kilometres in Japan, both with populations well over 30 million, with internal air, rail, and road links serving millions of people daily and catered for by many radio and television networks. There has been less of a tendency towards physical merging in Japan, the cities preserving their identity well, but economically the system is closely integrated.

By the 1970s Gottmann himself recognized six urbanized areas which were incipient megalopolises. Apart from the north-eastern United States and Tokaido, there was a Great Lakes belt, an English north–south corridor, an Amsterdam–Paris–Ruhr belt, and Shanghai. He considered three others as potential candidates: San Francisco–Los Angeles–San Diego, Rio de Janeiro–São Paulo, and Milan–Turin–Genoa. Some would put Toronto–Ottawa–Montreal in this class. The southern Californian example is, perhaps, nearest the public image of a continuously urbanized area, known not only as 'Sansan', but as Sun City and California Strip City. It already has some of the features of megalopolis; a vast concentration of over 20 million people, three distinct and concentrated centres, and fast communications in a narrow belt of coast country.

On a smaller scale the cities of Holland may also be candidates. They have long been described as a linear city, but one which is curved back on itself. Its spine is a circle, which is why Randstad–Holland has also been called the Greenheart City, the centre being jealously preserved as a rural area. But on the circle is a series of cities—Rotterdam, The Hague, Amsterdam, Utrecht—each a distinctive and specialized city in its own right, but each being part of an integrated whole. The scale is smaller than Gottmann would like, and he includes this area in the larger potential belt which would include Paris and the Ruhr. I wonder, too, if a channel tunnel will not provide the essential link which would bring England's urban corridor into this complex. A European or EEC new world would encourage such an outcome, but cultural divides would make it extremely difficult to realize.

On the least controversial level 'megalopolis' provides a good description of a new scale of urban growth which is easily perceived by the layman and therefore not easily dismissed as the invention of a geographer. Only one example, however, has been vigorously analysed, and not everyone would accept Gottmann's thesis that it represents a new level of organization. Certainly no administrative or organizational framework is emerging to meet needs different from those in the constituent cities of megalopolis. It is distinctive as a stage in urban growth and coalescence, but it is not easy to see the way in which the whole is greater than the sum of the parts. The most significant element is the degree of integration through fast movement and communication, but whether this demands a new and specific form remains to be seen.

The vision of a coalescing of linear cities appealed to Dinos Doxiadis, who foresaw a final stage in urban evolution as a single world urban system which he called 'ecumenopolis' (p. 217) (Fig. 11). He made certain assumptions which seemed to point in this direction; first, that the population of the world would continue to grow to about 12 billion in a century or so; and secondly that by that time urbanization would be universal. By the mid-twenty-first century a global network would have

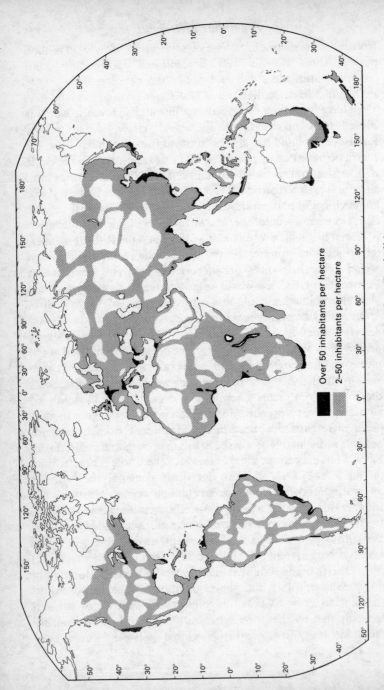

FIG. 11. Ecumenopolis (based on Doxiadis).

Over 50 inhabitants per hectare

2–50 inhabitants per hectare

subsumed all urban activities in the world. This would match the concept of 'one world' for which McLuhan coined the phase 'urban village' in 1968. Physically the extension of urban corridors would be complete, and would cover about a sixth of the land surface of the earth. Much of it would be in very attenuated urban regions, but it would also retain its great city centres. This is not quite as all-consuming as Asimov's dream in *Foundations*, where he envisaged 'all the land on the face of Trantor [the planet Earth] 75 million square miles in extent, was a single city. The population at its height was 40 billion. This enormous population was devoted almost entirely to the administrative necessities of Empire.' This is science fiction, but only an exaggerated version of the ideas of Doxiadis. Small wonder that according to one critic, 'Ecumenopolis is not a concept, but a poetic vision.'

iv

There is something frightening and abhorrent in the idea of an amorphous sprawl, an amoeboid shape thrusting its way into the countryside. It is the very antithesis of the traditional idea of the city, contained, encompassable, and ordered: 'Jerusalem is a city bounded by a wall.' Ancient walls, as we saw, were not necessarily defensive, but could also symbolize the imposition of cosmic order. Perhaps this innate desire for clarity and differentiation was strengthened in the last hundred years as the city crept more chaotically outwards until it was difficult to discern town from country; wanting both guaranteed neither. Many people yearned for the return of the circle. If not walls, why not green belts? Limitation of some kind seemed enormously attractive to planners, even by the end of the last century. It set a trend which was going to be very influential in the twentieth century, and which still looks an attractive alternative to urban corridors.

The outstanding example is London's green belt, which played a pivotal part in post-war planning and is still jealously guarded as a concept and a policy. The belt was inviolate and it was also ensured that any growth beyond it should be in discrete and relatively self-sufficient towns. Satellite towns are a widely adopted answer to sprawl—even in Tokyo and Hong Kong. Most major cities in Britain have their green belts, and this is a recognized way of maintaining the 'containment of urban growth' (Hall *et al.* 1973), safeguarding the discrete nature of individual cities even within massive belts of urbanization. This emphasizes the fact that green belts are not just interstices in an urban continuum; they imply a very deliberate and positive change of mood in the landscape which not only complements and balances the urban but also helps to safeguard traditional forms and values which are an essential prop to a society undergoing rapid change. Britain's last new town was built in the very urban corridor which may have suggested a megalopolis, but it is economically and socially quite self-sufficient. Milton Keynes is an ambitious new city but has all the elements of containment which a traditional city has, in spite of being in the long run part of a system of cities linked by fast communications.

Doxiadis looked upon what he called 'post-city' developments as the last step in an evolutionary progression. The sequence in time he matched to a sequence of scale, which he related to 'human spaces'. He looked on all these as part of a system of settlement which became known as 'ekistics' (Doxiadis 1968). His complete sequence of 'living space' was: room, dwelling, group of dwellings or neighbourhood, small town, city, metropolis, conurbation, megalopolis, urban region, urbanized continent, ecumenopolis. He thought that the problems of managing these spaces had been solved as far as the city. Beyond that were new problems, so far unsolved. The planner's task was to devise environments at this scale which would allow social intercourse, exploiting modern technology to fulfil these social aspirations.

There is more than a little contradiction in arguing the inevitability of a global urbanizing process while arguing for control of society's use of space. Doxiadis' scale is immense, and it may be more profitable to think of the extremes as meriting different approaches. The local and small-scale is dominated by face-to-face communications, is inward-looking and self-sustaining: the global scale is focused on supranational transactions and a freedom to communicate which almost defies time and space. The planner's dilemma is whether he should involve himself at both ends of this scale, and how far the socio-cultural elements will be at risk if the large-scale planning takes over.

Scale is very important, even within the metropolis. London, for example, has experienced three hundred years of control over the details of its buildings in materials, elevation, elimination of fire risk, standard of hygiene, and drainage. This was not reflected on the larger scale or on the general pattern of growth. The latter was an outcome of major social changes, sometimes reflected partially, always unevenly, and sometimes even arbitrarily: such things as the emergence of the middle class, industrialization, the effects of the railways and of cars. In Britain today there is still a reluctance to see planning at a large scale, in regional terms, for example, or at national level. At supranational level there seems to be a free interplay of market forces, particularly in technology, with no hint of policy for its control or management.

v

We have seen in megalopolis and its extension into ecumenopolis a possible future which is based on the trends of today. They are just more of what we already have, an extrapolation of Western tendencies. Already rather chaotic and by no means under control, they represent a frightening threat to some. Megalopolis embodies two diametrically opposed tendencies in settlement growth: agglomeration and partial dispersion, pronounced centralization and light-density sprawl. Now contemporary technology in communication lends itself more particularly to dispersal. It is almost a truism to say that you no longer have to live in a city to be a part of urban civilization. Some have questioned whether we need cities at all in the future. How long will we persist in overcrowding and the discomfort of physical pressure when the need to congregate is no longer there?

A few years ago a report on cities presented to the United States Congress began 'Cities are not permanent.' Not permanent? Surely cities are built for ever? They are certainly built with that in mind, but a moment's reflection reminds us that they do indeed disappear: Ur, Thebes, Ch'ang-an, Tikal, Angkor Tom.

In a thousand years, London? New York? Civilizations do pass and their cities die. But the impermanence referred to in the report was not a reference to the effects of age, but to the effects of contemporary social and technological change. The city is no longer necessarily the best expression of urban culture. So let us modify the message of doom a little.

Many western cities are losing population—or seem to be. Take London, for example. Figures are falling, but this is largely because the statistics are referring to a rather static political entity. The real London, the social realm which has grown beyond a neat political boundary, is still growing, but the growth is far beyond even the old suburbs. Location, in the simple, common-sense meaning, is losing its meaning. There was a time when the social entity known as London matched the physical reality that was London. In medieval London Skinners Street, Goldsmith Street, Silk Street, and a score of others indicated the exact location of the work of particular guilds; location was absolute. Industry today, based on computer technology, can choose its spot, free from locational constraints. This is even more true of informational transactions. Theoretically, location is irrelevant. But there are undoubtedly limits to this freedom, for few activities are created *sui generis* but rather evolve from an existing situation (Gertler). But certainly as far as informational transactions are concerned location seems less relevant than ever before.

The effect this could have on developing urban forms was very cogently argued by an American sociologist, Melvin Webber, in the 1960s. Technology has enabled us to live in what he calls a non-spatial world. If we think of urban-ness as a way of life, then this can be enjoyed without living in the confines of a city. In future we should be thinking, not of cities, but of 'urban realms', and to emphasize the point further, of a 'non-place urban realm', i.e. one that is not tied to a particular location. Another aspect of the same idea is expressed in his phrase 'community without pro-pinquity': that is, you need no longer live next door to a person to be his neighbour. This would sound very familiar indeed to a farmer living in the scattered agricultural communities of mid-Wales; or to a farmer in the mid-west of the United States, who depends on the phone and the truck for all his contacts. The stress is not on nearness but on relatedness. After all, Oxford Street may provide us with an endless number of contacts (mainly physical!) but they are socially meaningless; whereas social interaction over distance, as on a phone, may be a vital link in a network which gives cohesion to a community.

Let me return to a point I have made before: there are historical antecedents to many of these concepts, but they affected very few people. It is the fact that they are now affecting most of us which demands our discussing them. Consider, for example, one of the basic assumptions of the idea of an urban realm—that there is a very high degree of mobility. There always has been a sector of society which could take such mobility for granted, within the constraints of the period. In England the élite was always mobile. For several hundred years royalty was more or less peripatetic. Many of the massive ancestral homes which are such a feature of the countryside are explained by Elizabeth I's continual royal 'progress' during which she was lodged in almost every part of her kingdom. Her successor, James I, was the first monarch to spend at least half the year in his capital, London—and that in Westminster, not the City. And even though this location became semi-permanent, royal palaces were dispersed throughout the 'metropolitan region', from Windsor to Greenwich and Nonesuch; later further afield to Balmoral, the Isle of Wight, and Norfolk. The aristocracy was also very mobile. A town house for the 'season' and a country estate were the minimum requirements. And one can think of the country house even as representing an extension of urban values in its fine architecture, artificial landscape, grand library, music, and sophisticated society. The élite sent their sons to be educated at Harrow or Eton—neither in London; and later at Oxford or Cambridge, for the capital itself had no university until the nineteenth century. In other words, for the select section of society life was lived in an 'urban realm'.

The freedom of movement I have ascribed to royalty and the aristocracy was the outcome of wealth and leisure, and these took some time to percolate to classes below them. Gradually, however, more and more people shared in the luxury of being able to travel easily and enjoy the benefits of an increasing prosperity. Sociologists sometimes refer to 'de Tocqueville's law' which states that what the few have today the many have tomorrow. This is easily illustrated by those material things of life which begin by being scarce and costly but which eventually become commonplace and cheap. Telephones, cars, radios, and television have all followed the pattern of downward diffusion through society. This downward movement does not necessarily close the gap between the haves and the have-nots. By the time radios had diffused throughout society, 'they' had television: when television had reached almost every household, 'they' had colour sets, and so on. Diffusion does not lead to homogeneity or to the erasing of class differences; and there is always an under-class which benefits very little indeed from the increasing prosperity of the society as a whole.

We can now apply this notion to freedom of movement. It has increased immeasurably for all, but disproportionately in different classes. In Britain and elsewhere leisure was until recently the prerogative of the well-to-do, and spas like Bath and Cheltenham and watering-places like Brighton were select outposts of metropolis for spending part of the year. Later, in the industrial era, the working man's family could spend a day, or even a week, at the seaside. Blackpool vied with Brighton. But by this time the rich were relaxing in the south of France. Today, with Mediterranean resorts open to families of very modest means, the rich prefer the Bahamas or the Seychelles. Commuting patterns, too, show that the richer travel further than the poorer, partly because they have more time (i.e. their office hours are shorter), and partly because many have a *pied-à-terre* in the city centre for the working week. In the United States most commuters are still tied to freeways whereas a minority commute by plane.

Nevertheless, it can be said of Western society as a whole that the level of prosperity is such, and technical innovation so advanced, that location has become less and less important; and the outcome is that there is no necessary correlation between where we live and where we work. For a very long time greater freedom of movement has loosened the urban fabric, and activities have become more scattered. It is an extension of this process that Webber envisages as the 'urban realm' which will replace the compact city.

All the elements of dispersion are already there; Soria y Mata's linear city, ribbon development (so condemned in post-war Britain as a 'threat to the countryside'), second homes, retirement resorts, the caravan. The ideal seems to be the completely self-sufficient house, freed from all the services into which houses are normally plugged (for after all one of the main reasons for contiguity is wanting to share the main drains, the water-supply pipes, the electricity . . .) and therefore capable of being built anywhere. We are getting nearer this ideal, particularly with methods of waste disposal and of producing power from solar panels. Meanwhile the caravan will do, and is a mobile home for millions, at least for part of the year. In the United States the mobile home has become very sophisticated, but this trend can easily reach a stage which again demands immobility.

Let me sum up the necessary conditions for the 'non-place urban realm' and the social processes pointing in its direction. Telecommunications are the basis of many community networks, an extension of the telephone which has served this purpose for many years in rural areas. Electric power and technology enables dispersion in many industries, particularly in quaternary activities; even computerized shopping is now a fact of life. Recreation—sport, drama, music, and opera—is already at our fingertips on the television screen. It is estimated that by the year 2000 the average household will have invested in electronic communications the equivalent of today's investment in a car.

Changes in society are no less dramatic. First and foremost in Western society is an increase in life expectancy and a very great increase in the proportion of the lifespan not given to work. In a peasant society a boy enters the work-force at twelve or so and rarely retires. In our society the period of productive activity has been greatly reduced by increased education at one end and earlier retirement at the other. This means a higher proportion of the population is no longer tied to work location. Increasing prosperity has also given these people the means to live where they choose, where the climate is better or where living is cheaper.

Many British pensioners winter in Spain, so taking advantage of both.

vi

There is no better society in which to see these trends at work, and so witness the possible dissolution of the traditional city, than the American. Americans have always been great movers. Many of them crossed an ocean before settling; in two centuries they have peopled a continent, their frontier moving inexorably westward. Statistically every family moves once every five years, compared with once in ten in Britain. The popular interpretation of IBM is 'I've been moved', but the statement that the city was not permanent was a shock to most. It was a tardy acknowledgement that the traditional metropolitan regions were declining. Much of this is due to migration to the countryside—not just an overspill, not just statistical boundaries failing to catch up with city growth, but movements beyond the suburbs. And this rural net gain has nothing to do with farming, but rather with retirement, second homes, or recreation. In this very urban country the mystique of the countryside is still strong. Retirement is a major factor. Whereas in 1947 nearly half the men over 65 still worked, that proportion in 1980 was only 21.8 per cent.

On the national scale the change in urban/rural balance has been accompanied by a new regional balance. Horace Greely's advice in 1850 was 'Go west, young man, go west.' His advice was taken—almost too enthusiastically, according to a poster I saw many years ago on the Utah–Nevada border: it said 'Stay east, young man, stay east.' But the tide of movement continues, though it is now to the south-west and the south, and the movers are no longer young, but the middle-aged and old. In the 1970s the populations of Nevada, Arizona, and Florida were all increasing by more than 3 per cent a year. In that decade the population of the mountain states increased by a million, of Florida by 1.5 million, and of California by 800,000. The traditional industrial belt was the loser, an area bounded by a line from Portland (Massachusetts) to Milwaukee, south to St Louis, east to Baltimore, and north again to Portland. This contains megalopolis and the Great Lakes belt. It may not invalidate the concept of megalopolis, but it is a little ominous for the future. The snow belt is losing to the sun belt.

This shift is partly to do with the freeing of constraints on the individual in later life, and partly with the fact that so many post-industrial activities can take place outside the metropolis. So-called agribusiness, space-extensive manufacturing, mail-order houses, warehousing, research- and communication-based activities, insurance, and finance have a new freedom of location. Communities based on retirement, recreation, and education often use parks, forests, camps, the wilderness, and sanctuaries. Wealth often comes from sources radically different from the industrial era. In California federal funding in rocketry research and armaments, together with oil, are creating a new environment based on wealth. The sociologist Nathan Glazer said of Los Angeles in the 1960s:

It looks less like a city where people work than any other great city in the world. The gap between work and play must be narrower than in any city. It produces less than any other city of the things that, from a grim protestant way of looking at things, anyone really needs. And yet it grows like mad, while those cities that supply us with useful things like coal and steel and cloth and machinery, decline. (p. 131)

So the cities developing in the southern and south-western United States may well be pointers to a future metropolis freed from many of the constraints of the traditional city. The overwhelming impression in any of these cities is the complete absence of form, the feeling that freedom has run to licence rather than that any new form is emerging. The product of the combination of individualism and market forces is an amorphous sprawl in which even the old symbols of centrality are little more than symbolic. Phoenix, Arizona, with 1.75 million people, is three-quarters the size of Greater London, with 7 million. It is a two-dimensional city, a thin smear of residences with a central business district of only two or three high-rise blocks, a vestigial reminder of the central skyscrapers of eastern cities. Its wide streets and large opulent houses, luxuriant lawns and lush vegetation, shrubs and orange groves are all strangely at variance with the desert into which the city is steadily expanding. Its greenness only accentuates the aridity surrounding it. The desert is, of course, part of the mystique. Once it was sought for seclusion, for the contemplation of beauty. Frank Lloyd Wright had this in mind when he built Taliesin West, when the embryo Phoenix seemed very small and far away; it is now lapping at the gates of his foundation. The desert also meant relief for sufferers from respiratory complaints. More recently it has provided both space and secrecy for defence research. Wealth is a prerequisite of living here, for maintaining a water supply and air-conditioning is expensive; but everything carries the hallmark of prosperity. 'Wilderness is paradise enow.' Perhaps the greatest lack is the sense of place in this endless rich suburb. As Gertrude Stein said of Oakland, California: 'But there is no *here*, here.'

Nearby are other symbols of contemporary American society: Youngtown, which is restricted to people who have retired, and Sun City, which has no industry but over 300 business firms, 14 banks, and 16 savings and loan companies, all for a population of 35,000.

However difficult to live in, the desert did have one of the most important resources in the history of the United States—land. A moving frontier and a strong belief in individual freedom has always been linked with the acquisition of land. A real-estate hoarding reads: 'There is no greater feeling of pride and security than that which one experiences when standing on one's own property and saying: this is my land, to do as I please.'

Not surprisingly speculation is a major industry, and examples of exploitation are legion. Platting (that is, subdividing acquired land into building plots) leads to fortunes: litigation leads to more fortunes. The plans are vast. Since 1959 enough land has been subdivided in Arizona to accommodate 2.2 million people; in New Mexico, enough has been platted for a potential nine million—this in a state with a population of only one million.

A last example. Lake Havesu City in Arizona is some 50 kilometres south of Needles. The Lake is an 80-kilometre ribbon of water lying behind the Parker Dam on the Colorado river. It was a site used by an oil tycoon, Robert McCullough, to test outboard motor engines. Expanding this business in the 1960s

McCullough decided to build a new town on the shores of the lake. He bought—very cheaply—enough land to provide 40,000 building plots and zoned them for mainly residential use, with some commercial and some recreational areas. The plots sold quickly, and by the mid-seventies the city had 60,000 people. Sales were boosted when McCullough bought London Bridge in 1972 and rebuilt it over a watercourse at the side of the Colorado; it is now the centre-piece of the 'British village', a great tourist attraction.

There are aspects of this story which are the despair of all geographers who like to think in terms of rational explanations of why cities are where they are. No site could be less propitious for a future city than that at Lake Havesu. This is unrelieved desert country with forbidding summer temperatures; it is barren, dry, and hot. Its choice was so arbitrary that it brings to mind Brigham Young's selection of the site of Salt Lake City with the famous phrase, 'This is the place.' But that was divine guidance, about which geographers know little. It was the co-operation of a tightly knit community in bringing water from the mountains which made Salt Lake City possible. In Lake Havesu City the miracle arose from vast corporate resources. Salt Lake City was an earthly image of the City of God. Lake Havesu City is an offering to Mammon. The result is a two-dimensional sprawl of rampant individualism which serves only to highlight the beauty of the desert around.

I have described this one example of unplanned urbanization in the dry belt of the United States in order to show that (a) technically people can now live more or less where they want to and how they want to: and (b) that an increasing number of people are taking up this option of living outside established cities. What results by no means adds up to metropolis in the old meaning of the term, but it does point to an alternative which is acceptable to many. It points to the urban realm or the urbanized region, in which a tenuous urban fabric is sufficient for people to live a full urban life, and within which are centres of high specialization in the tertiary and quaternary sectors. Webber himself points out that the result is unlikely to be complete dispersion, but rather a polynucleated realm which will have its own balance of activities.

If the examples which come to mind most readily are all from the United States this is because that country has both the resources and the technology on the one hand and the space to experiment on the other. It is made possible because there are so few constraints in government policy or in planning ideology. This has been a constant thread through the urban development of the United States. Superficially it has some of the attributes of rational order because of the regular grid system which is the framework of development. But this does no more than lay down the rhythm governing the use of the environment. The essence of planning is having an end in view, aiming at a fixed and finite form and having a programme to achieve it. Platting (surveying the land and demarcating regular parcels) is a system which can be extended indefinitely, and sets no boundaries: it is open-ended. The platting of townships from 1780 onwards was continued mechanically until it reached the Pacific. City platting enables the city to expand indefinitely in any direction, allowing the dynamics of expansion to determine the form. The grid is an invitation to indeterminacy. Anthony Trollope was so mistaken when he wrote that the (American) 'city is laid out with intention'. Apart from the intention of making a profit, purpose is probably the last ingredient. The parcels of land in the city are not platted so that something should happen, but rather so that anything could happen. One of the most startling features of the American city is the contrast between the cool formality of the grid in two dimensions and the eruption, in the third dimension, of the often idiosyncratic buildings which are the very antithesis of order. Someone has drawn a parallel between this relationship and jazz music, in which the basic rhythm is maintained against the individual soloists who do more or less as they please. The city is spatial jazz.

Trollope's exception to his general admiration for American cities was, significantly, Washington, which, as we have seen, was the ultimate in planning. Because it was only half realized in the 1850s all he could see was the gap between the plan and what had been built. He despaired of 'this ragged, unfinished collection of unbuilt broad streets, as to the completion of which there can now, I imagine, be but little hope' (ii, p. 17).

vii

The American ethos is highly individualistic, pragmatic, and passionately anti-planning. The result is seemingly haphazard adaptation to market forces and instant response to high technology. This fluidity of ideas and open-endedness is certainly a necessary condition to produce the 'non-place urban realm'. In western Europe there is less land on which to expand and experiment, too many state boundaries to make movement easy; there is the inertia of long-established tradition, the tendency to conserve, and a belief in planning. What I have said about recent American developments contrasts sharply with, for example, new-town policies in post-war Britain.

Milton Keynes was the last and most ambitious of these new towns. Behind it lay the conviction that the future lay in discrete, self-contained settlements of 50,000 or 100,000 inhabitants: Milton Keynes was meant to be a city of 350,000, a figure later revised to 250,000. Lying between London and Birmingham it gave punctuation and identity to a location on the potential corridor of a future megalopolis. The first decisive act was to circumscribe a 'designated area', drawing a line on the map which predetermined what should be urban and what should remain rural. The parallel with the medieval city wall is tempting, and we are certainly back to the circle in our very simple model of a city. Size of territory and population were both laid down, and so, it follows, was density. Density was light, maintaining the garden-city tradition which has dominated British planning since the work of Ebenezer Howard nearly a century ago; and combining this with de Tocqueville's law it was assumed that the city of tomorrow would look like the middle-class suburb of today (the dream, it was thought, of every working class family). Net densities varied, depending on the varied architectural style of the score or so 'villages' into which the city was divided. The main-road system was more or less a grid, but very different in derivation from its American counterpart. This grid is a logical answer to accommodating the projected traffic generated, on the assumption that workplaces will be more or less dispersed throughout the city. Having tentatively reached out that far into the future the planners reverted to a highly centralized shopping core which produced one of the largest covered retail centres—and one of the handsomest—in Europe. Perhaps this compromise between past and future was as British an element as one could expect to find. British planning has always been culturalist with a nostalgia for the past. Howard wanted the civilized social life of the city to be combined with some of the physical attributes of the countryside. The classical progression in the Bible is from a garden to a New Jerusalem. In Howard's New Jerusalem each house would have its own garden.

viii

Looking into the immediate future of the metropolis I have so far emphasized only those elements which make for dispersion, whether they are technological or whether they are social changes which make for more choice in living styles. Relating this to the simple model of the cross in the circle we can see that the processes dealt with so far in this chapter have tended to eliminate the circle. Growth itself militates against the permanence of the circle. Many European cities rebuilt their walls to accommodate expansion: Paris is the classic case, the last wall being built in the nineteenth century (see Fig. 4 above). But more effective are those processes which erode the idea of a wall, which diminish containment, and which blur the differences which the circle symbolized. Suburbia has effectively erased the circle. Correspondingly the cross has increased in importance. Movement, exchange, transactions have all emphasized the cross and extended it far beyond the former circle to the furthest corner of the urban realm. It is the cross which binds the urban realm.

Now we must consider the opposite trend—towards greater concentration. Gottmann insists that the tendency to spread is balanced by the tendency for some activities at least to aggregate. Traditionally the urge to congregate has won hands down. In the past, and for most people, there was no alternative. It is still true for most of us that it pays to be as near the city as possible in order to 'plug in' to its amenities. Citizenship still means bread and circuses.

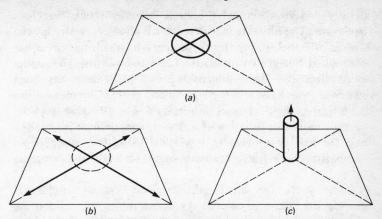

FIG. 12. The circle and the cross. (*a*) Cross in circle; extension of cross shows complementary relationships with the region. (*b*) When the circle disappears the cross takes over to give dispersion and an urban realm. (*c*) Emphasis on the circle, and movement becomes vertical; concentration in a megastructure.

There is also an assumption that the social interplay involved in physical interaction and congregation is good. This is the argument for the concentration of office activities, and it also applies to interest groups. 'Men thinly scattered,' said Dr Johnson, 'make a shift, but a bad shift, without many things; it's being concentrated that produces convenience.' And if technology has taken the need for propinquity out of community it has also enabled us to live and work more compactly than ever, as skyscrapers testify.

There have been many reasons why people have built high in the past; an effort to conserve land and to remain inside a city, as in medieval Edinburgh; social status, as in Tuscan hill towns; and most spectacularly, to express religious ideas. Megastructures like pyramids, temples, and palaces all express society's wish for prominence and permanence. Today's skyscrapers top them all, as much symbols of wealth, power, and status as any great monument in history.

How does this fit in with the symbol of the cross in the circle? The emphasis shifts to the circle again (Fig. 12). With greater density and compactness the circle becomes fixed, the cross irrelevant. The ultimate megastructure is a tower—yesterday the Tower of Babel, today the skyscraper—in which the circle has contracted but grown upwards. There is no cross. The model emphasizes the third dimension, and movement has been switched from back and forth to up and down. Communication is vertical as the lift comes into its own. The structure has now become more like the stem of a flower; containment is absolute and the axis of movement is vertical along the 'stem'; each compartment—office, workplace, home—is a cell, and density is intense.

Some years ago an English engineer called Frischmann envisaged a future city in the sky within this century. Soon, he claimed, technology will be capable of erecting two-mile-high towers. Each tower would be home for 300,000 people—a city, in fact—arranged on 850 floors. Each level would be a 'village', a small closely knit community whose living quarters would be arranged around the periphery. In the centre of the tower would be the communal activities (industry, business, services, schools, hospitals), and there would be a very efficient vertical transit channel guaranteeing fast movement and a high level of communication (not very unlike an up-ended linear city). The parallel with the plant stem is close, even to the mechanics of its strength, for there would be an extensive underground 'root' to provide parking space. The environment inside the tower would be completely controlled, thus making the contrast between inside the tower and outside absolute. Not that all would be sweetness and light outside (at least in Britain, where the cloud ceiling would be rarely high enough to allow the supposedly fabulous views). This vision may not be as outrageous as it seems at first glance. We already have buildings which are a quarter of a mile high, and we are forced to consider how far these ideas are just dreams or serious glimpses of the future.

Many architects have toyed with the idea of a megastructure city. So have many writers of science fiction. H. G. Wells was an eminent practitioner, and ideas in his *Futures* translate well into glass and concrete. Such ideas are often combined with social engineering and the desire for an ideal, planned society. Frank

Lloyd Wright found this very attractive. His Mile-High City, Illinois, conceived in the 1950s and not at all unlike Frischmann's later model, was a complement to his Broadacre City. The first freed the countryside for many people to live at a low density and close to nature. For the most part the visions of most architects and writers in this direction have gone no further than the drawing-board. This is why they remain perfect, Utopian. The wonderful drawings of the young Italian architect Sant'Elia will remain wonderful drawings:

> The city is built
> To music, therefore never built at all—
> And therefore, built for ever.
>
> Tennyson

This does not mean that the idealist, the visionary, even the mystic, has no place in shaping the city. Elements of the most abstruse ideas are preserved in metropolis, as so many cosmic plans show. But most dreams eventually come down to earth, and their realization is often a faint echo of the ideal. It is the influence of the ideal which counts. Le Corbusier was more successful than most in influencing the future. In the first place he did build his megastructure, though the scale was moderate. The *Unité d'habitation* in Marseilles was built for a community of 1,600, and it included shops, nurseries, a school, and recreation facilities. This early experiment influenced the John Hancock Centre in Chicago, a hundred-storey skyscraper which is virtually a self-contained town with offices and an hotel as well as apartments, school, and recreation areas. For the last forty years architects have thought big.

The most radical proponent of megastructures today is an Italian-American architect, Paulo Soleri. Rather than merely building upwards he has further emphasized compactness by using models of cubes, globes, and pyramids. The circle has become a complete envelope for the city; and there is no cross. Behind Soleri's models is a philosophy embracing the whole environment, one which is a reaction against the unplanned, amorphous spread of settlement which he sees as a threat to the United States. It is not so much that contemporary sprawl eschews location, but rather that it is destructive of the natural environment. The philosophy is called Arcology, a compound of architecture and ecology, which proposes solutions to building which will be ecologically acceptable.

Much of Soleri's criticism—which often becomes invective—is directed against Doxiadis' idea of ecumenopolis. He refers to the latter's map of future urban growth in the United States as 'infamous'. This is a 'map of despair, blackened by urban tissue'. One must guard against proselytizing prose and the exaggeration of propaganda. When Soleri talks of Doxiadis' map as looking like 'torn sacking' he draws his own sketch-map which looks like torn sacking, but which is in fact a travesty of the original. But he has made his point. He objects violently to the destruction of the countryside by urban blight; he is appalled by the urban realm.

To counteract contemporary trends Soleri claims that two processes are necessary: implosion and miniaturization. The tendency of cities to explode must be reversed, and in order to make this possible we must miniaturize our built environment. To illustrate this he has produced many models, the most compact of micro-universes, three-dimensional structures under complete ecological control, producing their own food, maintaining their own atmosphere, and completely cut off from the natural world. Someone once said that the entire population of London could be accommodated in a cube of one square mile. Such a model is Soleri's starting-point. The circle of our original model has become a shell, a lidded box, the skin of an orange. Inside would be a self-sufficient organism in miniaturized apartments, so compactly put together that movement would be minimal; outside would be the unblighted world of nature.

In the Arizona desert, about 50 kilometres from Phoenix and not far from Frank Lloyd Wright's Taliesin West, Soleri has begun the construction of a prototype arcological city called Arcosanti. It will eventually house about 3,000 people, a mere foretaste of the cities of a million and more which he usually plans. Arcosanti will be an élitist colony of artists, craftsmen, and idealists—one cannot help recalling Aspen. Its communal activities will take place in two vast half-domes of cast concrete, already built and orientated to get winter sun and summer shade.

Behind these there will be a mega-framework in which accommodation units, mass-produced 3-metre concrete cubes, can be plugged, with circular holes to act as doorways or windows. The structure is being built on the lip of a ravine, the slopes of which will be glass-covered and produce food.

Soleri's ideas, particularly as they are being partially realized in Arcosanti, raise some fundamental issues. The first is sociological. His scale of modelling is so large that even in his drawings human beings disappear. Even the modest Arcosanti will look rather like a gigantic beehive into which people as well as apartments will be plugged. To build so inflexible a shell and expect a community to adapt itself to it is sanguine. Secondly in no way can the city be economically self-sufficient. A specialized 'city' of this kind is the product of contemporary forces but it can only survive as part of the economic system of existing society. Like Aspen it will be no more than an offshoot of New York or Chicago. Even the construction of Arcosanti is being sustained by students and disciples who are indissolubly linked by resources to the very metropolis against which they are reacting. Perhaps the desert is the only environment in which so uncompromising a philosophy as Soleri's could show a first delicate shoot, let alone flower; but all too near are Phoenix, Sun City, Lake Havesu City . . .

ix

The concentration of people in megastructures is not a new idea, but until recently rarely tried, modest in scale, and an extension of contemporary high-rise buildings which have become multi-purpose (Fig. 13).

On paper Le Corbusier went much further, visualizing the ideal metropolis as a series of massive blocks which would leave plenty of space to counterbalance aggregation. *La Ville radieuse* went no further than the drawing-board, but the slab structure which was its basic unit had very great influence on the modern metropolis. As residential units such slabs have had a chequered history. In post-war London the idea of creating breathing-spaces on the ground by building high to a specific ratio of land

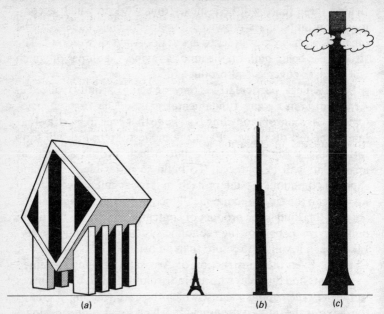

FIG. 13. Futurist cities: (*a*) Soleri model; (*b*) Frank Lloyd Wright's Illinois Tower; (*c*) Frischmann's two-mile tower; Eiffel Tower to scale.

was eagerly adopted by planners and architects, and enthusiastically backed by local authorities pledged to produce accommodation quickly. There are many reasons why they proved only partly successful, from poor construction and inadequate maintenance to lack of fitness to meet the needs of young and poor families; and in London and elsewhere in Britain many such blocks have now been demolished to make way for more traditional low-rise housing. Nevertheless high-rise blocks were a feature of the Barbican redevelopment in the City of London, combined with high-rise offices, an arts complex, school, museum, and a college of music. These very expensive blocks are successful, though we should remember that for many of the tenants this apartment is often no more than a *pied-à-terre* and complements a country home. The critical factor for success or failure seems to be the quality of life rather than the physical plan of the building. Nor has high rise been unsuccessful in Sweden, for example. And in Hong Kong new towns in the New Territories are a dramatic, exclusive use of high-rise slabs to relieve the immense pressure of population. These settlements are the nearest thing to what some science-fiction writers saw as the metropolis of the future; possibly they have no alternative in Hong Kong. Even to build these vertical cities land has often had to be created in estuarine areas or literally carved out of the hillside. High rise can not be the simple answer to all population pressures nor can it be transferred from the drawing-board to any site. Economic pressures must be considered as well as quality of life, and in particular the perceptions of society are a vital consideration. It is often tempting for an architect to put forward a building solution to a social problem which makes the most of modern technology. Kenzo Tange's solution to Tokyo's growth would be to build out over Tokyo Bay a series of megastructures connected by road and rail. On his model they look like a series of traditional Japanese houses, dominated by great curving, sweeping roofs; in fact each structure would be fifty storeys high, a small city in its own right.

X

In this chapter I have dealt mainly with examples of metropolitan growth which lie towards the extremes of possible futures, whether towards dispersion or concentration. Inevitably either trend will be changed in the metropolis of the twenty-first century for two reasons. First there will be compromise between the two visions of the future because people are torn between contradictory ideologies. There are culturalists looking to the past and wishing to emphasize tradition supported by the security felt in familiarity with the known tinged with not a little nostalgia and reverence for so much of what is thought good in the past. British planners exemplify this approach. At worst it means a slavish revival of the past and sterile imitation: at best it maintains a human element and domestic scale together with an insistence on open spaces and gardens. *Rus in urbe* may be the most distinctive contribution of the English to town planning, and the persistence of the garden-city ideal the most profound effect on post-war building. On the other hand are those who are looking to the future who wish to exploit contemporary technology to create a new order of living. They have been more successful in fields other than housing—shopping complexes, universities, factories, hospitals, museums. In the Third World there is parallel dichotomy between those who would accept, for example, many aspects of spontaneous settlement but funnel resources into improving the process and others who see the answer in municipal super-blocks. The outcome in both worlds will probably be compromise and variation.

The second reason why we are unlikely to see the emergence of a new world in the coming decades is simply that the scope for experimenting is really quite limited, particularly in the Western world. We have inherited the bulk of our urban world. Our commitment to the existing infrastructure is overwhelming; to alter it radically is unthinkable, mainly because it is economically unfeasible. Very often we can afford to do no more than tinker, even with the superstructure, and we are forced to become skilful in adaptation and rehabilitation. There may be fewer constraints than elsewhere in North America, but open-ended though their urban development may be, this is fully consonant with the prevailing spirit of individualism and enterprise; it is a response to market forces. Here lies one of the critical factors in the future development of metropolis: whether it will be under social control and guidance with a large planning component, as in Britain, or whether it will be given free rein as in the United States. In the last resort political and social consensus will determine the shape of things to come.

It may be that I have paid too much attention to the planners and the theorists and too little to those who actually create the metropolitan city by choosing to live in it—or out of it. They may not articulate their needs or their desires, but they do sometimes vote with their feet. In the Third World the metropolis is still a powerful magnet, providing so strong an attraction that its disadvantages are ignored. In the United States the desire for space and the freedom to choose an environment rather than endure it

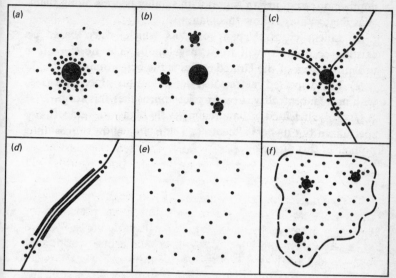

FIG. 14. Possible future forms: (*a*) core city; (*b*) compact satellite cities; (*c*) core with extension along routeways; (*d*) linear city; (*e*) complete dispersion; (*f*) urban field with centres of specialization.

is leading to a shrinking metropolis. European cities have had a diverse range of controls, as if they at least recognize a problem which demands a policy of some kind. In most sophisticated societies some planning of incremental changes keeps control on unregulated growth. All we can predict is that the metropolis of the future will offer a range of possibilities, but that most of these are forms which are already apparent. The future can only exaggerate aspects of the present.

The forms we can expect are summed up in Figure 14, which suggests six possibilities:

(*a*) The core metropolis: an extended metropolis with very high centrality and high concentration at the core.

(*b*) Satellite metropolis, with a well-developed and high-density core, but with a galaxy of planned, well-defined offshoots. London is a good example.

(*c*) Star-shaped metropolis: a strong core with a limited

number of radial urban routes with smaller centres along them. Washington may follow this plan.

(*d*) Linear cities. Urban corridors which, when based on existing core cities, will form megalopolis. The north-eastern urbanized area of the United States is the best example.

(*e*) The dispersed metropolis, dependent on super-highways, with no real centrality. Los Angeles approaches this form.

(*f*) Polynucleated urban realm, with highly developed and specialized but dispersed centres. The Ruhr region is possibly a pointer in this direction.

8

Metropolitan Problems: The Environment

Among the close and overcrowded haunts
Of cities, where the human heart is sick . . .

WORDSWORTH

i

For every person who sees the metropolis as a promised land, a city whose streets are paved with gold, there is another who would heartily agree with Shelley that 'Hell is a city—much like London.' Offsetting the attractions, the opportunities, the wealth, there have always been the opposite: at worst misery and degradation, and at best enormous difficulties and problems facing the city-dweller. And the ills of metropolis are those of the city writ large. It is all too easy to romanticize the metropolises of the past and see only their monuments and their glory; it takes more imagination to see them peopled by tens of thousands of men and women who were only too aware of the price to be paid for living there, in particular perhaps of the enormous pressures that mere numbers create: Juvenal's experience of imperial Rome has been repeated millions of times. Man is the most adaptable of animals, but it is still remarkable that he has been able to accommodate himself to an artificial environment which has so many shortcomings that a wish to be part of it is always countered by the desire to escape from it.

Until comparatively recently even advanced Western cities were consumers of men. Death rates were high and birth rates were low; the city could not have maintained itself were it not for its capacity to attract and absorb great numbers from beyond its boundaries. High mortality, overcrowding, and disease were all a high price to pay for the advantages the metropolis seemed to offer. And many of those ills were the result of large populations and high density lacking the technical or organizational ability completely to control the artefact that society itself had made. It is true, of course, that many of the problems—such as poverty—were common to the society as a whole, however much they were aggravated by urban conditions; and if there were progress in dealing with them, where could that be but in the metropolis? But one cannot escape the feeling that urban problems seem to have a dimension of their own.

Today we constantly think of metropolis in terms of its problems. No one has driven at snail's pace through London, already late for an appointment and with no guarantee of a parking place at journey's end, without fulminating at the road system; no one has approached Caracas or Rio through the awfulness of their shanty towns without wondering why they are tolerated; or seen the street-sleepers in Calcutta—or those under Charing Cross Bridge, for that matter—without being convinced that man has made his own hell. A recent international conference on the major metropolitan cities of the world was called 'The Pathology of Cities'. Pathology is 'the study of morbid or abnormal mental or moral conditions' as well as 'the study of disease'. Strong words. The organic analogy is a familiar one. Cities are seen by many as having a life cycle of growth, maturity, decay, and ultimately death—in Mumford's chilling word, 'necropolis'. Not only does time itself guarantee a process of obsolescence and decay in whatever is built, but urban society seems to contract ills which threaten its very existence. I repeat that it is mistaken to divorce these ills from society as a whole and to romanticize the countryside as the antithesis of urban misery. In our Western culture the memory—for it is nearly always in the past—of the rural idyll, of Arcadia, is never far away; the hankering for the garden, for rustic simplicity and peace which makes the English dream of garden cities and which drives the American into the desert. In a recent London poster advocating the moving of firms out of the city there was a graphic suggestion that being held up by a flock of sheep in a country lane is infinitely preferable to being held up by other cars in the city!

Nevertheless, problems seem more acute and their perception

sharpened in an urban context, possibly because they become common experience to such a large number of people in the city. And whereas in the countryside the compensations are immediate, environmental, and available to all, the benefits of metropolitan life are too often enjoyed only by the few. So what follows is a discussion of some of the problems of society in metropolis, aggravated by and often inextricably interwoven with the built environment in which they are found.

I have used the word 'problem' more than once. It is difficult objectively to say what it means in the context of the city because my observations are cross-cultural, and so much depends on how different people see the so-called problem. Let me take one small example. My immediate response to the statement that there are a million squatters in Bangkok is that that city must be suffering an immense housing problem; because I assume that squatting is an illegal, do-it-yourself response to the city's inability to provide adequate shelter for its population. I see it through Western eyes, via an expectation that housing provision is a necessary concern of municipal authorities. Local planners view it a little differently (Angel *et al.*). They have classified the housing system of Bangkok, which accommodates about 5 million people, into five categories. The first subsystem is of workers' houses, dormitories, staff housing, and all the provision enjoyed by virtue of having a certain job; the second is public housing, accounting for as little as 12,000 families; thirdly comes 'filtered housing', that is, housing occupied by successively poorer people as the rich privately build better houses for themselves; the fourth subsystem covers rural commuters; the fifth is squatting. In other words squatting is perceived as a class of housing provision, i.e. a way of providing shelter rather than an index of need. This class is further subdivided into true squatters, renting squatters, and boat people. Squatting is accepted as a solution to housing in exactly the same way as the other categories. Everyone, the planners point out, is provided for; there are no street-sleepers. Squatting is a reliable and self-working system. Some of these points are subject to debate: all I am emphasizing is that there are different views on the nature of the problem—and on whether there is a problem at all.

This reminds us that at the heart of the difficulty is the fact that many circumstances in the metropolis in developing countries are seen through Western eyes and judged by Western values. This is not to deny the existence of problems. It is just that our definition of problems relates to particular standards which we use as a measuring rod, often assuming that the only criteria which matter are those which we can quantify. Even in this country legislation which improves housing standards can literally create slums overnight by shifting certain criteria to include houses which were previously not considered slums. There is no easy way out of this difficulty. For all kinds of reasons standards and criteria are useful and necessary, but their universal application is often of doubtful validity because they preclude social criteria which are of paramount importance to other societies. In the West we are obsessed with defining things objectively by measurement, by standards, by legality, often at the expense of subjective criteria: and we also have a weakness for imposing our criteria on every culture under the sun. We transfer our problems to others rather than analyse circumstances elsewhere in the context of different societies, different expectations, and different sets of values. There may well be a common denominator, a universal bottom line, and UNESCO, through its organization Habitat, is very concerned about this. Above this basic minimum it may well be that the variety of cultural experience outside the Western world will force us to redefine 'problems' and 'solutions', and look for a more sympathetic and subjective approach to the way people accommodate themselves to living in a metropolis.

ii

We can think of the metropolis as having two component parts; the physical shell, the built environment of streets and houses on the one hand, and the people who live and work in it on the other. The interaction of society with the built environment is a very complex one, especially when we remember that the urban fabric itself is the result of many such interactions, most of them in the past. For the moment the emphasis will be on the fabric of the metropolis, not on its people.

Buildings are themselves subject to processes; they grow by being added to, they decay, and they also acquire different values in the eyes of society. The average life of a dwelling in London is about eighty years. Well constructed, traditionally of brick, they can and do last much longer, and hundreds of thousands of people are living in houses built in the last century. But generally speaking, decay and obsolescence take their toll. Obsolescence is difficult to assess. It arises from function rather than from age, a product of new demands and rising standards. It is more critical in specialist buildings where demands are more exacting. For example, modern office blocks call for air-conditioning and controlled heating, both of which are subject to rapid technical improvements, and it is likely that the 'services' of such a building will become obsolescent much more quickly than the fabric. In the same way the kitchens of middle-class houses may be replaced every twenty years. The latter can be dealt with fairly easily, but with an office block there is a case for making the whole building renewable to match its service technology. In the industrial sector of one new town in Britain, Hemel Hempstead, nearly all the buildings which were erected in the early 1950s have by now been replaced. Gone are the days when architects were expected to build to last.

Fortunately men are very adaptable creatures. Replacement is not the universal response to obsolescence. The common answer to the challenge lies in adaptation and improvization, particularly in dwellings. Garages are attached to Victorian houses, roof-spaces become studio rooms, central heating replaces the coal fire, and so the life of the original house is prolonged to meet new demands. In an almost perverse way value systems emerge which put a premium on age. To be able to live comfortably in the past is the prerogative of the upper and middle classes, for it takes greater wealth to sustain tolerable life in very old buildings. Adaptation and preservation, therefore, interrupt the normal curve of obsolescence and decay. If the fabric is not preserved then the process takes its toll and leaves decrepit structures offering the minimum of shelter and less than the minimum of services and comfort to those who live in what are collectively known as slums.

The problem of slums is a recurrent one in the metropolitan city. To appreciate the nature of the slum it must be seen as a social as well as an environmental phenomenon—I am already finding it difficult to keep these two aspects separate!—but it does have physical and locational attributes which are more or less universal. Physically the slum expresses decay and obsolescence, an outworn fabric which fails to provide efficient shelter or adequate services because of its age. It also exhibits over-use, overcrowding, insanitary conditions, and lack of resources. Slums are usually found near the centre of the metropolis. In a modern city the centre itself—the oldest part of any city—will normally have been almost totally rebuilt to accommodate offices, shops, and prestige buildings. As this new centre grows it will expand into what is by now the oldest part of the city. This means that the latest, and often the grandest, of the city's buildings are often cheek by jowl with the oldest and the meanest. In this unstable zone—the 'zone in transition'—houses which were once commodious have been abandoned by the class for which they were built, and are decaying rapidly. They are also ripe for multiple occupancy by the poorer people in society who need to be near a source of work in the centre but who cannot afford the amenities of life. Among these poor are migrant people from other countries who often set up a ghetto condition as they huddle together, grossly overcrowded.

This process of inner-city slum formation has been going on for a very long time. It emerged as a major social phenomenon in nineteenth-century London probably because of greatly accelerated growth. The poor were attracted in vast numbers to form a pool of casual labour which led to a marked localization of slum areas. For previously poverty and wealth coexisted, the poorest often living in alley-ways immediately behind the rich man's mansion. There was also an increased perception of poverty. Victorian London is often seen through the eyes of Charles Dickens. Alleviation of the problem, both by charitable institutions in the last century and by local authority rehousing in this, was based mainly on physical rehabilitation, without necessarily touching the fundamental issues of poverty which had given rise to a class of slum-dwellers. Rehousing does little more than confirm the characteristics of the zone in transition in which the environment, whether it be a Peabody Building or a municipal tower block, is often an expression of social deprivation.

Traditionally, then, slums are a problem of the metropolitan centre directly related to ageing housing stock, and characterized by overcrowding and deprivation. This is true not only of European and American cities, but also of many cities in India and Latin America. Although they share so many environmental and economic characteristics, slum-dwellers are by no means a homogeneous society. Here, in Western cities, are the 'adjusted poor' who are apathetic and cannot see a way out of their predicament; but here also are those who may be trapped by circumstances but who see their values as identical with those outside the slum, and will remain unadjusted because they hope eventually to move out. Slums are also reception areas for migrants, often desperately poor, but to whom slum conditions are possibly better than those they have left. Often slums are a temporary place of residence for people of limited resources, beginners, climbers: not the end of the road, but a place of opportunity in which every movement is upward. Finally, to some the slum is a place of refuge, an asylum, even a hiding-place (Stokes).

The concentration of such groups in the slum means social as well as physical segregation, and for some contains all the dangers of becoming a 'culture of poverty' in which social values are adjusted to internal circumstances and not to the outside world. Inequality and the uneven distribution of resources are a major problem in society as a whole, but their concentration in the urban slum poses a problem of daunting magnitude. The existence of entire districts of obsolescence in particular gives rise to an immediate perception of one aspect of urban pathology.

Charles Abrams, an American planner who did so much to awaken the world's conscience about poor living conditions in the Third World, refers to the word 'slum' as 'as distasteful a four-letter word as any in the dictionary'. Whether it was derived from 'slump' or 'swamp' is immaterial: 'slum gives its meaning the moment it is uttered' (p. 2). His definition would be that 'slums make up the worst structural and sanitary conditions and most degraded occupancy, normally by the lowest income group, in any given period'. This emphasis on living conditions is rather different from the early Victorian evaluation of slums which put all the blame on the slum-dwellers. Victorians looked upon the poorest in society as a deviant group, and consequently any improvement had to begin with moral uplift. It is true that they recognized the inadequacy of poor housing, and from the time of Chadwick's report on sanitary conditions in London (1842) they began a vast cleaning-up process. It was a combination of salvation and sanitation. But it took Booth's studies of poverty in the 1880s and 1890s to show that the dissolute and the improvident were indeed a very small minority, and that a vicious cycle of poverty and illness was trapping most slum-dwellers in conditions not of their making.

Even in this century the municipal approach tends to deal with effects rather than causes; it is concerned more with housing and environment than it is with poverty and inequality, and it is tempting to say that it is often doing no more than re-creating slums. There are two constants in the continuation of slum conditions. The first is the difficulty of dealing effectively with obsolescence, not only because ageing is inevitable but because with limited resources rehabilitation can never quite catch up with deterioration; houses that are not gentrified or replaced will continue to supply the needs of many. Secondly there is a considerable proportion of metropolitan society which has no real choice of housing. An increase in prosperity in society as a whole, a raising of the standard of living and of expectations, almost inevitably leads to an increasing gap between the haves and the have-nots, and a subproletariat is soon formed. This is a view of slums which not only recognizes that they are inevitable but sees them as a part of the functioning of society. A more radical view would decry the mere amelioration of the environment but insist on changes in society as a whole. Social change is difficult on this scale unless we envisage a revolution. In fact there is still much that can be done in planning and management. This is not to subscribe to the popular theory that social engineering begins by manipulating the environment. But there are cognate issues of ownership and tenancy, of control over limited resources, which could be resolved by legislation, and which would make life more tolerable for slum-dwellers while changes on a larger scale are being debated.

iii

To a Western visitor approaching a metropolis in a developing country, its whole structure may well seem to have turned completely inside out. The slums are on the outskirts! Or so it seems. The visitor must often pass through extensive shanty towns, pitifully inadequate as shelter and seemingly very squalid, and teeming with people. They seem the very negation of the sense of permanence and order and well-being which are the usual hallmarks of the metropolitan suburb in the West. That there should be slums is understandable, but why should they be here, on the approaches?

These 'slums' are in fact rather different from the ones I have just described; but before examining them more closely, remember that that such features were very familiar in all great cities in the past, as well as being found in some Western cities even today. This is Stow, writing on late Elizabethan London, referring to the areas outside the walls as:

streets pestered with cottages and alleyways . . . into the common field: all of which ought to be open and free for all men. But this common field is as encroached upon by buildings of filthy cottages . . . enclosures and lay-stalls (notwithstanding all proclamations and acts of Parliament made to the contrary) that in some places it scarce remaineth a sufficient highway for the meeting of carriages . . . which is no small blemish on so famous a city. (ii, p. 72)

Whereas most migrants to Western cities find their first shelter in the decaying inner city, in the developing world they usually attach themselves to the outskirts of the city. This may well have been the traditional way in which cities grew, as Stow's comment strongly suggests. It would explain the usually accepted model of the pre-industrial city as having an élite at the centre surrounded by the lower classes and then by the poor. The beggar was always at the gate. In no way can the Third World city accommodate the influx of people it attracts except by their accumulation on the outskirts. So it is not at all surprising that even very rich cities may be surrounded by do-it-yourself shanties in which the standard of existence—one can hardly call it standard of living—is so pathetically low.

Immediately we can see a crucial difference between shanty town and Western slum. The latter is the oldest part of the city, the former the most recent. It is always a shock to realize that most shanty towns are relatively new, but this is reflected in one common synonym—'spontaneous settlements'; and indeed many of them appear literally overnight. There is a classic case of one such settlement appearing on the outskirts of Lima in December 1963. It had been nothing more than a parcel of bare countryside the day before. Suddenly it was a community of 20,000 persons occupying huts and shelters in various stages of construction. This was an extreme and dramatic example, but most squatting has these elements. First there is a sudden influx of people occupying land which is not theirs—'illegal housing' is another synonym! The best way of effecting this and guaranteeing its permanence is to make the event so sudden and on such a scale that it cannot be easily overturned by the forces of law and order. This reflects a very widespread peasant belief in many parts of the world that erecting a 'house' between sunset and sunrise on what was accepted as common land conferred right of ownership. While under modern circumstances it does not confer a right it certainly demands recognition, and usually acceptance.

There are variations on this theme. In post-war Athens, for example, such land was usually bought legally, but erecting a house was illegal. So houses were built clandestinely at night, and in large numbers—again to create a problem too big for the law to deal with; often it was enough to erect concrete pillars and add a very rough, temporary roof. There were always too many for effective demolishing, and in the quarter-century after the war about half a million houses were added to Athens in this way. Once the overnight houses were established time could be taken to make them habitable, to add a storey even. Many of these squatter areas look like building sites, incomplete and lacking services. Very often an elaborate doorway surmounts marble steps which lead to nothing more than a rocky defile which one day may be a road; but the doorway is a token of the eventual aim. The authorities' response to the post-war squatting movement was to pass retrospective legislation which formally incorporated them into the city. Most of them are now so integral a part of the fabric that only historical studies can reveal their origin (Leontidou).

The second feature which is common to most squatting is a degree of social organization which seems quite at variance with the often chaotic appearance of these settlements. Whereas the slum is disorganized and fragmented, with little social cohesion, the shanty town is often a community. Indeed it is a community which very often decides to make the move into the city in the first place, and the very act of making a 'spontaneous settlement' demands a high degree of organized planning and co-operation. We may see the shanty town as a problem, but to the inhabitants it is an answer to a problem. Such dynamic, co-operative processes are the very antithesis of what we normally associate with a slum. In the words of one specialist in the field, the word 'slum' is 'no more appropriate than if it were applied to building in progress'. The shanties inevitably lack many of the rudiments of urban living and they may look like slums, but they represent a very different outlook on life.

To get a balanced perspective on Third World squatting we have to modify the perception we have of housing standards and appreciate the differences in attitudes which lie behind slums and shanties. A slum consists of houses on the way down; a shanty is a house on the way up. One is the last refuge of the city-dweller; the other is the first. One represents the fragmentation of society; the other often shows social cohesion. If both are still referred to as slums then we must distinguish between 'slums of despair' and 'slums of hope'.

On the minimal budget of the shanty-dweller housing has to fit into a flexible programme and may have a very low priority. Rent of any kind may be utterly out of the question. On the other hand, access is important—which is why the people came to the city in the first place—and so is security of ownership even if this may be deemed illegal by the host community. Investigators are always stressing the respect for ownership of plots once these have been established, and for the ownership of the shack even when the land is disputed: shanty owners sell and buy as if they owned the land anyway. What is important, and what gives these people a great psychological boost, is that they have a base for consolidation and for capital accumulation. Even erecting the shanty leads to the acquisition of some skills—houses are not just for consumption as in our society—and these will increase as improvements are made to the shanty.

So there are many positive aspects to this movement from country to town which compensate a little for the deprivation and squalor which is all the Westerner sees. Not that these aspects should be minimized. First impressions are appalling, and further investigation disheartening. Nowhere is the shanty town more characteristic of today's metropolis than in Latin America, and a few details from that region will make the picture a little clearer, though we must remember that there are very considerable variations from one continent to another. But whether it be in Rio de Janeiro, Lima, Bogotá, or Caracas, there is no mistaking the shanty town, made in the first instance from any cast-away material that the rubbish heap can provide—cardboard, hardboard, zinc sheets, or beaten-out oil drums: some shanty towns look like a scrap-heap. Caracas in the 1960s had 60,000 shanties, called *ranchos* here (Fig. 15*a*). Only one in ten had water, one in four any kind of sanitation; there were 37,000 cess-pits. Three out of five had walls of cane-palm or straw, one in five some kind of timber or zinc. Moreover, most *ranchos* are found on the most difficult terrain, where private speculators have not dared to build; on steep slopes or in precipitous ravines which are subject to flooding.

The scale of shanty building is frightening. There are half a million people in Caracas' *ranchos* (Fig. 15*b*), one and a half million in the *barriados* of Lima. 'Popular settlement' accounts for 65 per cent of the urbanized area of Mexico City. Here one of the most distinctive areas of the city is Nazahualcoytl, a settlement which grew from 65,000 inhabitants in the 1960s to 650,000 in the 1970s, and which now numbers 1.3 million. São Paulo has half a million living in *favelas*.

Turning to the old world, in Ankara about half the population lives in *gecekondu*. In Cairo 80 per cent of the building in the last decade has been illegal. Manila, Djakarta, and Hong Kong each have hundreds of thousands of squatters. The list is endless. Nor are shanties the only response to the need for shelter. In Hong Kong one harbour area is choked with boat-houses. But the most bizarre adaptations are in Cairo, firstly in the so-called Second City, which refers to roof-dwellers in the poorer part of the city, secondly in the City of the Dead. There may well be a million people in the latter, occupying the tombs in the city's main cemetery. Paradoxically these have a solidity and a permanence which is the very antithesis of shanty towns. Moreover, the orderliness of the cemetery gives the semblance of planning to the community. The city authorities supply water and electricity to this city within a city which has regular markets, mosques, street traders, and even a police station and a clinic (Khalifa and Mohieddin, pp. 248–50).

For all the mass squalor which is almost inevitable in squatting, I must sum up on a positive and hopeful note. The perception of those who live in shanty towns is that they have considerably improved their way of life. They have left an even worse situation and they are within striking distance of a chance for better living; they are more often than not part of a community; they possess something on which they can build; they are contributing to their own improvement. They are also becoming part of the metropolis and tapping its resources—sometimes literally: in Caracas 90 per cent of the *ranchos* had electricity, for here was one resource which could be tapped free! They even become part of the transactional society. In a Hong Kong shanty town, above a sea of zinc roofs rises a forest of television aerials; a woman sits at the 'door' of a shack, puts her hand inside, and brings out a bright green telephone. Perhaps communication is more important than shelter after all.

I have referred to squatting as a traditional form of metropolitan growth. There are times when this can be seen to be so,

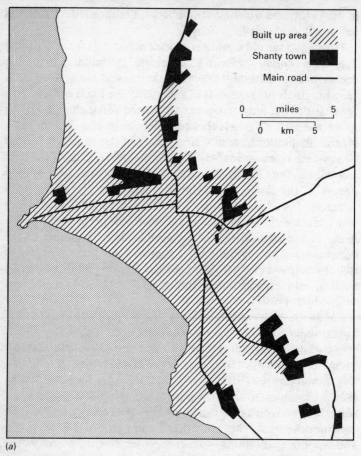

FIG. 15. Spontaneous settlements: (*a*) Lima (based on Dwyer, p. 193); (*b*) Caracas.

quite literally. In one shanty town in Caracas there are four contiguous *ranchos*. The first is extremely makeshift, a two-room affair of hardboard and palm fronds, a first crude attempt at building a shelter. Next to it is another *rancho*, no bigger, but made of sheets of zinc and boasting a verandah. Slightly above it on the steep slope is a third, in course of reconstruction, half zinc

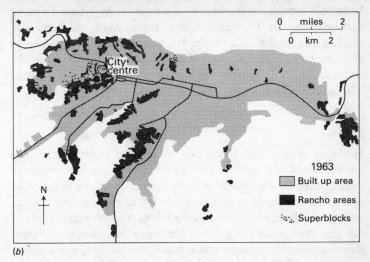

0   miles   2

0   km   2

1963

Built up area

Rancho areas

Superblocks

N

(b)

sheeting, half adobe brick. And next to this is one completely rebuilt in brick, plastered, and with a neat verandah. This last house, not *rancho*, has television, a three-piece suite, and the owner has an ancient car. The four are eloquent of the way in which rough shelters become small houses; one can literally see the city being built, for the last of the four could well be in a typical lower-class Caracas street. The family in this house has made the complete transition. They are now citizens of no mean city.

Throughout the world there is such a range of spontaneous houses that it defies a neat typology. It covers a great spectrum of complexity and sophistication. In India and Pakistan, for example, shelters rarely go beyond the first provisional stage of *ad hoc* arrangements which are only sometimes improved. The Indian *bustee* does not develop into an urban residential area. This is largely because incomes here are at the lowest possible level. In some South-East Asian countries on the other hand spontaneous settlements are acceptable as an alternative to municipal housing when this is not readily available. This is so in Bangkok where, as we saw earlier, squatting is an acceptable part of housing provision. But the economic level here is higher, and services are almost universal. There is a strong infusion of better-off people. A survey of a *kampong* in Kuala Lumpur showed that in this community there were policemen, a mechanic, a teacher, clerks, drivers, watchmen, and gardeners in addition to unskilled workers. Finally, illegal housing can be the foundation for relatively high-quality housing, as in Athens where the socio-economic level of the squatters is fairly high.

iv

However strong the functional arguments that spontaneous settlements are a traditional way of city expansion, they are usually seen as a problem in those countries where they occur, and it is a challenge to authorities to try to manage and control the lives of those who live in shanty towns. The very magnitude of the phenomenon is the greatest challenge and usually an insurmountable obstacle to proposed solutions. Nothing can stop the process, and it is almost impossible to alleviate its ills once a settlement has appeared. There is a limit to what an individual can do beyond rebuilding his own shanty, and a limit to community action when resources are so small. The really crippling element is the lack of infrastructure, which is almost impossible to install once squatting has taken place. It is a great temptation to do nothing.

At the other extreme, given the resources, could they not all be swept away and replaced by municipal housing? In the 1950s Venezuela had the wealth from oil revenue, and a dictator who had the power to act instantly. To him the *ranchos* were an affront to Caracas, an eyesore to be swept away. Bulldozers cleared the hillsides and a forest of super-blocks appeared, 85 tower blocks fifteen storeys high and capable of rehousing 100,000 people. But the problem was by no means solved. The work created in constructing the tower blocks attracted thousands of new migrants, all of whom built *ranchos*. At the end of the programme Caracas had more *ranchos* than ever before. Moreover the blocks were a social disaster. Whole communities were literally up-ended and isolated, trapped in a third dimension which they had never experienced before, dependent on lifts they could not operate. Some showed great initiative by building shanties inside the blocks under the angle of the stairway; some let their apartment and built a shanty elsewhere.

Yet this kind of solution is working in Hong Kong. There nearly half a million apartments were built between 1951 and 1971 in public and private programmes both in Victoria and in Kowloon. It was all high-rise, high-density. An even greater impact was made on the problem after 1971 when new towns were built in the New Territories. These are most spectacular clusters of very high blocks, already housing a million and a half people, a quarter of the metropolis' population; 70 per cent of this is public housing at a low and fixed rent. The advantage of these towns is that they are discrete entities, relatively self-supporting, and not too rapacious of land in the city's hinterland. Singapore, too, claims to have no squatters and to have solved housing demands by accommodating 75 per cent of its population in public housing schemes.

Such solutions require immense resources. The majority of metropolitan cities in the developing world are the products of poor economies. In no way could they meet the demand by what is essentially a Western approach. One strongly advocated alternative solution is to accept the process of squatting as a 'natural' one, but to exploit the energy, skills, and organizational abilities of the squatters by providing the infrastructure and the necessary materials (Turner). Lack of infrastructure is the most serious obstacle; it must precede occupation. Therefore basic amenities must be provided in incipient squatting areas. Taken a stage further this means preparing individual plots, or even building a 'core', the heart of a new house which has the essential services. Each squatter would build round the core of kitchen/washroom/lavatory and be guaranteed water and electricity. The house itself could then be built in stages, sometimes with materials also provided by the authorities. This would ensure an acceptable level of shelter created at a minimum of cost, as well as an orderly layout for the entire scheme. This would be adding to the fabric of the city in a much more rational and acceptable way.

Variations on this site-and-service scheme have been tried in some African cities—Lusaka, for example—with considerable success. Plots are rented in platted areas which provide the essential infrastructure, though water and sanitation may be shared on a community basis. Loans are available to enable families to build their own house, but these have frequently proved to be difficult to repay, and many peasants are reluctant to commit themselves to these schemes.

In India planners like Charles Correa, who has worked extensively in Bombay, insist that the gap between need and provision of shelter can be met if the new housing is kept simple and cheap and if some facilities are shared: 'There exist in this country solutions at a price which people can afford. There is no problem of low-cost housing; what exists is a problem of land use planning' (Wilsher and Righter, p. 139). Meanwhile two-thirds of the families of Calcutta live in one room, and the response to self-help solutions varies enormously from one place to another. It is comparatively easy to envisage the ideal stages: recognize squatting, prepare the infrastructure and core amenities, provide cheap materials, capitalize on the energy of the migrants, add social provisions to maintain health and welfare, legalize the process, and bring it within the framework of the metropolitan government. For most this remains a dream, as theorizing is overtaken by new waves of migrants.

9

Metropolitan Problems: The People

> The crowd and buzz and murmurings
> Of this great hive, the city . . .
>
> COWLEY

i

Slums and shanty towns are the most obvious, the most visible of metropolitan problems. They are both aspects of a more fundamental system, the economic base; and the problems posed by the economy of the city are very large indeed. And just as slums and shanties emerge in the city rather than being an outcome of it, so the economic crises are mainly an expression of what is happening in the country as a whole, even though there are facets that are peculiar to the city. As we have seen in previous chapters changes in metropolitan economic activities reflect larger structural changes in the economy. Many Western metropolises are struggling with the transition from an industrial stage to a post-industrial; in the Third World they are still being overwhelmed by the influx of peasant workers directly from the land.

London is a prime example of the difficulties inherent in structural change. During the period 1971–82 London lost 0.83 million jobs, almost one in five. Those in manufacturing fell from 1.09 million to 0.63 million, a drop of 42 per cent. This reflected a national trend, but there were special reasons why losses in some sectors were greater than one would expect from the national trend. For example, whereas clothing and footwear fell nationally by 10 per cent in 1966–74, they fell by 38 per cent in the capital. Electrical goods declined by 25 per cent in London but hardly at all nationally. Food and drink fell by only 3 per cent nationally, but by 28 per cent in London, paper and publishing

3 per cent nationally and 24 per cent in London (Wood, p. 65). Inner London was proving much more vulnerable to change because here industries were outmoded, restricted, unable to adapt, and using obsolescent buildings; they could not be restored *in situ*. Moreover, managerial preferences and regional policies were encouraging moves to the new towns where modern plant, a better environment, and grant aids were proving very attractive. Government aid to deprived areas elsewhere in the country was actually creating a deprived area in the inner city. Increase in office activities has not provided work for those who were engaged in the traditional industries.

In a comparable period, 1963–83, New York suffered a total loss of 11.9 per cent in employment, losing 47.7 per cent of its manufacturing jobs. In the same period transport and public utilities declined by 27.1 per cent and wholesale and retail by 18.8 per cent. As in London much of this work went to the periphery of the city. Although there has been a slight resurgence recently, structural change has left a legacy of problems in the very areas where manufacturing had attracted so many migrants. Again as in London, post-industrial activity has created a demand for very different skills and better education. In the period 1977–83 radio and television increased by 39 per cent, commercial services by 11.7 per cent, computer and data processing by 84 per cent, and technical services by 30 per cent. Small wonder that one person in seven in New York is supported by welfare and that 25 per cent are below the poverty line.

Such a down-swing in the fortunes of the inner city is dramatic in these cities whose growth was nurtured on manufacture and services. The picture is a little more complicated in newer cities where inertia and obsolescence are not conspicuous. Los Angeles has a range of activities more attuned to the twentieth century. Although manufacturing still accounts for 30 per cent of the work-force its emphasis is on aerospace work and electronics. Los Angeles has 10 per cent of all the Federal defence contracts in the United States. In 1984 one of its constituent districts, Orange County, had 1,432 computer companies and 98,800 people working in high-technology jobs. Topping a considerable table of skills, the city also has the greatest concentration in the United

States of mathematicians, engineers, and skilled technologists, and is third in scientific research after Boston and San Francisco.

This does not mean that Los Angeles has escaped entirely from the economic problems of contemporary metropolis. Its manufacturing is concentrated in the suburbs and its inner areas are open to immigration on an immense scale and in the traditional way. Migrant increase here was the most marked feature of the city's demography between the wars, and since the early 1970s it has again dominated its growth. A very large number are from Latin America and Asia, but the overwhelming majority come from neighbouring Mexico, probably between half and one million in 1970 alone. Partly as a result of this there has been a revival of more 'primitive', labour-intensive activities dependent on women and immigrants, mainly in the clothing industry, rampantly violating the sanitary and wage provisions of the labour code. The small workshops are usually run by well-educated entrepreneurs from Hong Kong, Taiwan, and Korea, replicating what goes on in their own cities. It could be that 65 per cent of the workers are undocumented. The very presence of these workshops has stimulated the growth of small retail shopping and ancillary services.

For many reasons, therefore, any broad generalizations about the effects of technological changes and the subsequent structural changes in the Western city must be applied with great caution to individual metropolitan cities. Age and tradition, the degree of economic control, and the unique circumstances of migration all contribute to a wide variety of situations. In the last century the technological changes preceded the demographic. Societies were industrial before the great surge of urbanization, and consequently the migrants could be absorbed into the labour-intensive activities. New York was a prime example of the transformation of peasants into industrial hands.

ii

Problems of employment structure are very different in the metropolitan cities of developing countries. It would be a great mistake to transfer the idea of development in the Western sense to the Third World as if it were an evolutionary process in which one stage succeeded another in some predictable way; we should not expect development here to replicate that of nineteenth- and twentieth-century Europe. There are obvious reasons why this is so, the greatest being that in the developing world urbanization has preceded industrialization. Here the surge in metropolitan growth is not a response to the demands of the city. Nor should we lose sight of the magnitude of the growth, an explosion which has no parallel in nineteenth-century European cities. London's growth from 1 million in 1810 to 2 million in 1850, to 5 million in 1900, and 8 million in 1950 looks positively sluggish compared with São Paulo, say, which in 1890 was a small town of 60,000 people, but was 2 million by 1950, nearly 5 million by 1960, over 8 million by 1970, and nearly 13 million by 1980—and projected to be 24 million by the year 2000. Mexico City had a mere million inhabitants in 1930, 5 million in 1950, 9 million in 1970, 14 million in 1980, and maybe 22 million by 1990 and 31 million by 2000.

The dilemma of absorbing such numbers into the urban economy reaches new and frightening dimensions. It represents a colossal shift from the primary sector to secondary and tertiary activities without the industrial capacity to absorb them. In Brazil, for example, a comparison of figures for 1950 and 1980 shows that the proportion in primary activities was halved, from 60 to 30 per cent of the work-force. The secondary sector increased from 14 to 24 per cent and the tertiary from 9.5 to 15.5 per cent. In the same period urbanization increased from 36.2 to 61.7 per cent. The metropolis has unlimited labour searching, not for jobs that have disappeared, but for jobs that were never there.

One difficulty in trying to assess the consequences of this situation is a tendency to see everything in the classical economic framework of the West, to use the same categories of work and the same definitions of unemployment, standard of living, and GNP. Ours is a culture in which such concepts have been quantified to the nth degree, and we are constantly looking for parallels or drawing comparisons by forcing circumstances into figures and tables which are totally inadequate to express the experience of other cultures. This difficulty will have to be overcome somehow as the economies in question are being drawn more and more into a world economy, subject to global fluctuations in demand and to international money-markets. On the behavioural level, however, in the everyday lives of millions of people in cities in the developing world, things look very different. If we in Britain find it difficult to give an accurate number of the unemployed, then it is quite impossible in the Third World, where it is as difficult to assess an individual's contribution to society as it is to measure his demands on that society.

Unemployment in the statistical sense is high enough, however inaccurate, but fringe employment, a twilight zone which defies accounting, is much higher. In Mexico City it is thought that 47 per cent of the economically active population is in the category of being not unemployed yet not having a recognized, official role in the economy. In such societies the number of so-called self-employed is truly staggering; and it is a shock to the Westerner to learn that 'self-employed' can mean selling lottery tickets on a street corner, or indeed selling anything, however small, and however obtained. One of the unexpected features of travelling by car in a Latin American city is to be accosted by a street vendor while the car is stopped at a traffic light. Traffic is so congested that the nimble vendor can keep up with a moving car even, and this kind of transaction is sometimes called 'slow-lane selling'. The vendor will proffer one article—a screwdriver, perhaps, or a hammer—in the hope of a sale. The roads are alive with such vendors whose income must be marginal in the extreme. There are some 300,000 in Lima. It is difficult to conceive how narrow the line is between existence and starvation. Together, however, the activities of these people form a very considerable part of the total urban economy. Perhaps we should remember that London in its heyday, and at the height of the industrial revolution even, had tens of thousands of street vendors too.

It is true that the activities of multinationals are having some effect on this rather crude model. I have already referred (above, ch. 6, sect. ii) to the way multinationalism creates a global class of technical and managerial people who form a growing part of migrant streams of labour. These have a leavening effect on many of the cities of the developing world, but the emphasis in the employment structure in these cities must still remain on the unskilled employed and the underemployed.

It is a matter of debate whether or not these people are productive in the usual sense of that word. The system is defended as one which allows millions to be economically active without capital and without technical skills; and it is tolerated as a method of sharing what little goods are produced by the city. One estimate is that half the population of Third World metropolitan cities ekes out an existence in this way. It even provides the means for a small number to establish themselves on the next rung of the entrepreneurial ladder, to employ other people, and gradually to amass real capital—just as the first shanty sometimes leads to a first house, to a street, to part of a city: so these activities may become first essays in the regular, accepted structure of the urban economy.

For the mass of migrants and urban poor all this is part of surviving. Again, by Western standards and Western accountancy the reckoning is abysmal. In São Paulo in 1982 it was calculated that a minimum wage had to be $90 a month, the amount needed for the survival of three persons. Yet 15.2 per cent of the population lived on less than that, 29.6 per cent had an income between $90 and $180, and 35.4 per cent between $180 and $450; only 19.7 per cent earned over $450.

iii

It would be a gross simplification to put all metropolises into only two classes of urgent economic/structural problems—former industrial cities transforming to post-industrial economies, and developing metropolitan cities largely dependent on a hidden economy. For example, some Chinese cities are struggling with problems of industrialization very reminiscent of those of nineteenth-century Britain. Shanghai is committed to heavy industry. Although there have been many political upheavals in its recent history Shanghai still maintains a premier position in industrial output. Even in 1982, before its most recent expansion, the city accounted for 11.4 per cent of China's total industrial output, and the country's biggest new steel plant is currently being built there. Having long been in the forefront of change Shanghai has built up a pool of skilled labour. In spite of the political anti-urban movements which weakened its position between 1950 and 1978, the city's advantages of site, infrastructure, traditions, and links with other cities led to enormous growth. A city of 1 million inhabitants in the early years of this century, it had grown to 4 million by 1936; by now there are probably 6.5 million in the city itself and as many as 5 million more in its rural hinterland. Most of those expelled in the anti-urban period—and they may well have numbered 600,000—have filtered back. The attractions of metropolis are as seductive in China as in the developing countries. In spite of 25 per cent unemployment there is no doubt that the city can offer a higher level of living than the countryside; it has more consumer goods, and better medical care and education. Its wages are three times the rural norm, so that a very large number of people can afford to enjoy its resources—big stores, recreation centres, and sixteen universities and colleges (Murphy).

In addition to its industries and its comparative wealth and possibilities for advancement, Shanghai has other characteristics of the Western early industrial period; in particular, overcrowding and pollution. High density is traditional and acceptable in the Chinese city; its people are used to overcrowding, lack of privacy, and generally spartan conditions of life. In Shanghai each person has to be content with three to four square metres of living space, half that of even overcrowded Japan. Even so about one in ten lives in a shanty town, and a third of all houses have no water. And pervading every aspect of life is pollution. This is partly due to China's commitment to using coal as a fuel; it is one of the few states where steam locomotives—a sure symbol of the industrial age—are still used. Not only is the use of coal universal, it is also inefficient, and because of the prevalence of industry the result is intolerable pollution. One site in the city registers a dust fall of 1,822 tons a month, all containing carcinogens. The chronic smog is known as 'Yellow dragon'. Fortunately this has not yet been augmented by traffic fumes, for this, like every city in China, is a city of bicycles and a dearth of public vehicles. Water pollution, though, is an allied problem. Less than 5 per cent of sewage is treated. The rest goes into the Huangpo river, which has been described as a 'chemical cocktail composed of raw sewage, toxic urban waste and huge amounts of industrial discharge'. The combination of explosive population growth and an economy based on palaeotechnology create a social and environmental problem of staggering proportions.

Contrasting with this picture in many ways, Hong Kong has absorbed much of its growth in a very different way to become the centre of manufacturing export in tune with the late twentieth century. Growth has been dramatic in the last few decades; 2 million in 1951, 3 million in 1961, 4 million in 1971, and over 5 million in 1981, much of the increase a reflection of the high birth rates of post-war immigrants from China. The economy seems to be able to absorb these numbers. It is based on small firms, most of them of less than ten employees, and sweat-shops which often combine living space and work-room. From the beginning the economy was geared to foreign markets, first specializing in textiles and clothing, then in toys and electronic goods, all the time increasing in sophistication and improving in organization. There has now been a swing to the tertiary sector, but in 1982 41 per cent of the working population were still engaged in manufacturing industries compared with 16 per cent in services, 19 per cent in trade, hotels, and restaurants, 8 per cent in transport and construction, and 5 per cent in finance and business (P. Hall 1984, p. 202). The last is growing rapidly and Hong Kong is now a leading financial centre in a world network. But the city has by no means lost its pre-industrial elements, as the number of street vendors and the size of the informal sector testify, as well as the fact that so much of its wealth is tied to the small family workshop. Its success comes from a combination of high productivity and low wages and expectations. The inherent weakness in its industrial base is the comparatively low technical skill which prevails, and the need now is to increase this skill and add a scientific input to increase the city's role in the electronic industry, together with a restructuring and rehousing of workshops (P. Hall 1984, p. 204). That the latter have survived and coped so well is 'nothing short of miraculous'. Whether it can continue to thrive without a conscious readjustment to the demands of the contemporary world remains to be seen.

iv

In an earlier chapter it emerged that one of the continuing characteristics of the metropolis throughout its history was the ethnic and social variety of its society. It is natural that once growth on a large scale has begun the population will reflect the incursion of peoples far beyond the metropolitan hinterland. Increasing contacts with the world beyond the city will attract merchants, ambassadors, refugees, and skilled craftsmen, and eventually these will become part of the social pattern of metropolitan life. More often than not, circumstances and the rules of the host society will not allow the complete assimilation of these 'foreign' elements. Rather they will become distinct but complementary parts of a complicated pattern. The idea of assimilation, as in the 'melting pot' of the United States, is relatively new. Traditionally metropolitan society has been a mosaic, the interlocking of parts dependent on unwritten rules and patterns of behaviour, and a delicately balanced tolerance. The medieval metropolis in the Middle East, for example, had its Christian and Jewish communities segregated and outside the Islamic core. Most immigrant groups in seventeenth-century London lived in communities outside the walls, and were not admitted to the guild system. Foreign merchants in Chinese cities had their own quarters, often in the 'suburbs'. In all these cities there was a place for everyone—and everyone knew his place. In the modern world mobility has increased considerably, group movements have become mass movements, and life is not as easily compartmentalized as the numbers of outsiders increase. Nevertheless segregation is still an important aspect of life in the metropolis and most social changes to the contrary bring tension and the danger of violent clashes.

Since the 1960s London has experienced an influx of people from its own Commonwealth countries and, since Britain's entry into the EEC, from Europe. Of London's total population of

6.6 million in 1981, 1.2 million were born outside the United Kingdom: 382,000 in Europe, 296,000 in Asia, 170,000 in Africa, 168,000 in the Caribbean, 69,000 in the Mediterranean, 22,000 in the United States, 10,000 in Canada, 30,000 in the Middle East, 27,000 in Australia, and 18,000 in Latin America or the USSR. New Commonwealth immigrants increased by 35 per cent from 465,000 in 1971 to 631,000 in 1981; within this group Pakistanis and Bangladeshis have increased by 93 per cent. These figures are striking but they are by no means a complete picture of the metropolis's racial and ethnic mix; for by now a new generation born of immigrant New Commonwealth parentage has increased the figure very considerably, though they are not registered as immigrants because they were born in Britain.

The greatest impact on the social life of the city is always made by those migrants who are highly 'visible', that is, easily recognizable because they are racially distinct or have a different language or religion. In those cities where, in the past, a mosaic of different groups was acceptable, such groups often deliberately identified themselves, made themselves more visible, and in this way ensured that conventions of behaviour and attitudes could help the smooth running of society. Modern society makes the mosaic difficult to accept in this way. It is true that many groups still identify themselves—the Sikhs by turbans, Rastafarians by a distinctive hair-style, orthodox Jews by curled locks of hair and skull-caps—but there are many aspects of life in which all groups are expected to merge. Theoretically any group can be absorbed into the work-force without discrimination, and ideologically we preach integration and equality of opportunity. Assimilation is the stated aim. But of course there are many impediments to this in the host society; prejudice and racism are very strong barriers to assimilation, and such attitudes are exacerbated by the fact that immigrant life is concentrated in well-defined districts with high visibility, and moreover almost always associated with areas of deprivation within the metropolis (Lee, ch. 5). For example, whereas the proportion of coloured people in London's total population is still relatively small, it is much higher in inner London, 19.37 per cent, than in outer, 11.81 per cent, and very much higher in some inner boroughs than in others (Brent:

33.46 per cent); and even higher in individual wards—Ealing has two wards with 71 per cent and 85.35 per cent coloured. Together the areas of greatest concentration add up to a distinctive belt within the inner area where deprivation, obsolescence, and unemployment are all high. It has been pointed out by investigators in this field that the place occupied by coloured migrants in London is determined as much by socio-economic class as by colour or ethnic origin. Take away colour and the immigrants would still be in the same location, around and fairly near the city centre; and incidentally sharing this location with a much larger number of deprived native white people. One way or another there is potential for conflict in such a zone of scarce resources and environmental and social deprivation; and it sometimes erupts as racial rioting, as it did in London's Brixton in 1983.

The problems of New York and Chicago have been those of London writ large. New York has faced these problems since the mid-nineteenth century. Even in 1861 47 per cent of its population was foreign-born. But that metropolis's greatest problems arose from the number of black Americans originating from the old slave-owning states after the emancipation of the 1860s. In 1984 only 52.9 per cent of the population was white; 25.6 per cent was black, 11.8 per cent Puerto Rican, and 9.7 per cent of other race. Changes indicate that the white population is decreasing and the black increasing. The 'melting pot', the assimilation of European ethnic groups, does not apply to racial groups. They can never become invisible, a necessary condition for assimilation. As in London, it is impossible in New York to dissociate race from social disadvantage; they are interrelated problems. Time and again a combination of poverty and race differences in a deteriorating environment has resulted in the trapping of minorities in the inner city, as in Harlem or the black belt of Chicago, giving rise to unrest. Even in the post-industrial city of Los Angeles the long-standing problem of a ghetto development of black people in Wattstown seems intractable, and the extensive immigration of Mexicans is giving rise to similar problems elsewhere in the city.

There are no strictly comparable problems of racial or ethnic tension in Latin American metropolises. Two centuries of racial mixing has blurred the physical distinctions between people of different origins and allowed a greater degree of tolerance. Whereas in the United States everyone who is not white is black, here everyone who is not black is white. Consequently the problems focus entirely on the division between the haves and the have-nots. In the Middle East and India cultural difference, and particularly religious divides, can often tear a metropolis apart, as we well know from Beirut or the Sikh problem in the Punjab. The uncompromising attitudes of orthodox Islam can cause bitter conflict, as does super-orthodoxy among the Jews in Jerusalem.

v

In the Western metropolis racial and ethnic minority problems are part of a more general social malaise, that of economic inequality. This again is a problem in society as a whole, not something unique to cities or to urbanization. But these social ills are perceived as urban problems because they are found here in extreme form; the most abject poverty is often side by side with great affluence. The social landscape one is of sudden and violent contrasts and changes. The richest, the poorest, the highest and lowest status, share the same city. It has always been so, of course, but in the Western metropolis in particular there has been an increasing awareness and a growing social conscience which have recognized the widening gulf between rich and poor, and it is no longer an acceptable facet of life. Increasingly state intervention and welfare programmes focus on these inner-city anomalies. Lazarus at the gate of Dives was always a fact of city life: today it demands a response.

In the traditional pre-industrial city disparities of wealth meant a rich city centre and a poor relegated to the outskirts. This reflected the fact that power, and all that went with it, was concentrated at the core, the point of greatest accessibility, of control, where wealth was created in the market or the bourse. The mass of people surrounded the élite; and the beggars and the outcasts were often outside the city gates. It was a plan that survived in the baroque city and beyond, particularly where industrialization had had little impact. For example, this is a description of Vienna at the turn of the century:

Vienna, through its century old traditions, was itself a clearly ordered and beautifully orchestrated city. The Imperial Palace set the tempo. The Palace was the centre, not only in the spatial sense, but also in the cultural sense. The palaces of the Austrian, the Polish, the Czech and the Hungarian nobility formed a second enclosure around the Imperial Palace. Then came the 'good society', the lesser nobility, the higher officials, industry and the old families; then the bourgeoisie and the proletariat. Each of these social strata lived in its own circle and even in its own district; the nobility in the heart of the city . . . merchants in the vicinity of the Ringstrasse, and the proletariat in the outer circle. But everyone met in the theatre and at the great festivals, such as the Flower Parade, when three hundred thousand people enthusiastically applauded the upper ten thousand in their beautifully decorated carriages. (Zweig, p. 25)

The changes brought about by industrialization transformed this pattern; it turned the city inside out. The result is nowhere better expressed than in Engels' account of Manchester in 1840:

Manchester contains at its heart a rather extended commercial district, perhaps half a mile long and about as broad, and consisting wholly of offices and warehouses. Nearly the whole district is abandoned by dwellers, and is lonely and deserted at night . . . The district is cut through by certain main thoroughfares upon which the vast traffic concentrates and which at ground level is lined with brilliant shops . . . With the exception of the commercial district all Manchester proper is unmixed working peoples' quarters, a girdle averaging a mile and a half in breadth around the commercial district. Outside, beyond the girdle, live the middle and upper bourgeoisie, the middle bourgeoisie in regularly laid out streets in the vicinity of the working quarters, the upper bourgeoisie in remoter villas with gardens, in free, wholesome country air, in fine comfortable houses, passed every half or quarter hour by omnibuses going into the city. And the finest part of the arrangement is this, that the members of the moneyed aristocracy can take the shortest route through the middle of the labouring districts without seeing that they are in the midst of the grinding misery that lurks to the left and the right. For the thoroughfares leading from the Exchange in all directions out of the city are lined on both sides with an almost unbroken series of shops . . . that suffice to conceal from the eyes of the wealthy owners of strong stomachs and weak nerves the misery and grime which form the complement of wealth. This hypocritical plan is more or less common in all great cities. (pp. 46–7)

In very general outline this is still the basic social pattern of the industrial city today throughout the Western world. In the intervening century those who could afford it have fled from the pressures and pollution of industry to the salubrious suburb, leaving those who worked in the mill to live in its shadow and under its pall. This was the genesis of today's division into inner and outer city, now more than confirmed by the ageing of the former, by the disappearance of jobs, and by the immigrant intake.

This social polarization was first measured rationally by Booth in his survey of London poverty in 1889. This was undertaken, curiously enough, to test his disbelief in a magazine article which claimed that one person in four in London was living in poverty. Rather than proving that this statement was 'a gross exaggeration', his own survey showed that the figure was really 35 per cent. Of course paupers had long been accepted as an inevitable part of city life, those people who would never be able to maintain themselves without assistance, unabsorbable products of the economic system. What Booth did was to measure poverty. He suggested a level above which a person could be well fed, and below which he was in danger of being underfed; and to be above this line demanded an income of between 18 and 21 shillings a week. Much of this was spent on food, and naturally the proportion so spent increased as the total income decreased. Engels had made the same observation a half-century before. It is still true. The average percentage of earnings spent on food in Britain today is 35; in Latin American cities it is 60, and among the urban poor can be between 70 and 80. Applying his criteria to where people lived Booth gave statistical substance to what was commonly perceived: the extreme poverty of the East End and the affluence of the West End and the suburbs.

By today the exercise has been repeated a dozen times in as many cities with data now much more easily available from official sources. Unemployment, overcrowded squalid rented accommodation, lack of amenities, ill-health, and deprivation of all kinds confirm time and time again the polarity between inner-city poor and suburban rich.

This simple model must, of course, be modified to describe particular cities at any particular time, and we must remember too that we may be dealing with a snapshot only of a very dynamic situation. In London, for example, inertia and strong historical associations have meant that some inner-city areas, like the West End, have maintained a very high social status. At the other end of the scale the rehousing of many inhabitants from inner-city slums by local authorities has taken them to new estates on the outskirts of the city. These have often been subsequently engulfed by expanding suburbia, so that there are now enclaves of rented local-authority houses in traditional owner-occupier suburbia. In the opposite direction there has been a not inconsiderable movement back to inner London of more prosperous people who can afford privately to rehabilitate communities of previously decayed middle-class nineteenth-century property. Such 'gentrification' has led to social upgrading in small pockets of streets in the inner city. On a much larger scale a massive redevelopment scheme such as that in London's former docklands has seen the transformation of derelict land into a transactional and business area which has attracted very expensive residential speculation. The social discontinuities which these changes give rise to are very apparent and only underline polarity by revealing a widening gap between sectors of society.

vi

The life of every metropolis is dependent on the movement of people. Perhaps the closest organic analogy is that between the movement of goods and people within a road system and that of the blood in veins and arteries. Both are referred to as 'circulation'. It is no accident that we refer to arterial roads. But compared with the body's system the city's regulatory function is very inefficient. One of the major problems of the metropolis is catering for the demand for movement of traffic which always seems much greater than it can reasonably accommodate.

The amount of space available for movement in a pedestrian city—a pre-industrial city not planned for vehicular traffic—is extremely limited (Fig. 16*a*); it is no more than the small spaces left over after building to a high density. In many cities in the developing countries there is just about enough room to walk, or manoeuvre a beast of burden, in a maze of unregulated alleyways. The few grand avenues and processionals of early metropolises were meant for ceremonial (Fig. 16*b*), not for day-to-day movement. Introducing wheeled vehicles led to problems, and we have seen that in imperial Rome they were prohibited except at particular times of day. The introduction of the pavement in medieval Paris was a brilliant innovation which segregated people and carriages in the same street. But it was still a long way away from planning streets which were the framework of city development rather than being accidental spaces. In London the first planned street, Great Queen Street, was built in 1680. From that time movement became more rational by being catered for. Railed transport, first drawn by horses, eventually powered by electricity, allowed fixed but fast movement within the existing framework of roads; but the steam train and its progeny demanded an exclusive route, totally segregated, which meant a system of its own.

There were problems common to all these forms of movement. First, the built environment was, inevitably, the product of a former age, and transport always had to struggle in a strait-jacket of road systems belonging to past eras. Medieval streets choked with twentieth-century traffic are a ubiquitous problem in Europe. Secondly, most movements were centrifugal/centripetal, a pattern which was part of the city's fundamental structure of the cross within the circle. Increasing traffic and greater speed has increased the inevitable congestion which arises. In any city the area of road available for traffic decreases towards the centre whereas the amount of traffic increases. Every innovation and every technical advance, as well as every improvement in living standards, has exacerbated the problem. The miracle is that life in today's metropolis has not come completely to a halt.

Finding a path through the complexities of these problems is

FIG. 16. Circulation space: (*a*) medieval Venice; (*b*) Haussmann's Paris; (*c*) down-town Los Angeles.

almost as difficult as driving through the metropolis; so I will first deal with Western cities, then with the developing world. In the West we suffer most from lack of congruence, the misfit of traffic and the built environment, because we are so eager to exploit technical improvements and the resultant prosperity. Traffic has proliferated. The twentieth century, also, has seen so effective a separation of workplace and home that it has created unprecedented movement. Commuting has become a way of life in the metropolis as our desire for private retreat has driven so many further and further from the city centre. Although there are now clear indications of a radical redistribution of some central activities, the overwhelming pattern of movement is still the daily rhythm of in and out. Our ability to tolerate travelling up to three hours a day, at times slowly and always uncomfortably, contributes to the problem.

There are two kinds of solution, public and private. Municipal attempts at transporting large numbers of people have been with us for more than a century, from trams to rail and from buses to tubes. To some extent they have succeeded, and train and tube transport can be quite fast. But they are geared to the rhythm of work and they are fixed systems, which means that easy access to them is a prerequisite of their efficient use. They are also costly to install. The great asset of the private alternative, the car, is its flexibility, its ability to penetrate the furthest recesses of the city and provide a door-to-door service. On the face of it it is relatively cheap, though the initial outlay is high; but it is wasteful, one person often using a vehicle designed for five, and it is subject to the inadequacies of an ageing road network. This last aspect discourages many drivers. For example, the percentage of commuters in New York using their cars in 1970 was only 7, only a little higher than Tokyo at 6 per cent in 1973, when even London was only 10.5 per cent and Paris 19 per cent. In contrast to these cities where the road network is very old, newer cities, more custom-built for the car, had very different figures: San Francisco and Los Angeles were about 65 per cent. Los Angeles is now a car-designed city where the freeway takes precedence over all other systems and in which the proportion of land set aside for the car is very high, about 30 per cent.

Moreover, there is no alternative transport (Fig. 16*c*).

It should not be forgotten, of course, that private transport depends upon public road-building and maintenance. Congestion is its greatest disadvantage, with the consequence that it can be very slow. The speed of movement in most metropolitan cities seems to be about 16 k.p.h., a figure which has been fairly constant for most of this century.

Most metropolitan cities have provided public alternatives to private transport. Municipal authorities alone can supply the so-called 'indivisibles'—the heavy cost of installing new roads, underground systems, or elevated trains. These are critically important in moving millions of people daily. But the more advanced the technology the more restricted the access. The economy of public transport is self-evident in the size of the units; whereas it takes 140 cars on average to transport 200 people, the same number can be accommodated on three double-decker buses. On the other hand, too big a bus loses its flexibility, and it is unable to meet the demands of some groups who cannot walk to the main thoroughfares—the old, the young, and the handicapped.

Only recently has proper consideration been given to the social aspects of movement in the city (Council for Science and Society). The movement of goods and the journey to work has dominated transport debate at the expense of an increasingly large proportion of the population who need it for shopping, recreation, or medical care. However comprehensive car ownership may be there are still many people who are excluded from driving for reasons of age, inability, or lack of access to a car. If we begin with the assumption that to be able to move freely is a right, then transport policies need considerable rethinking. Some flexibility is already evident in the use of minibuses on fixed routes, dial-a-bus systems, and the use of shared taxis (so common in developing countries). The strictly economic criteria which have dominated policies must give way to considerations of social well-being.

Possibly the most acute problem facing Western metropolitan transport today is lack of integration. Movement has several modes and occupies several networks, yet the attempt is rarely made to co-ordinate either modes or networks. Great energy goes into traffic management, and there is increasing sophistication of traffic-flow control; but in spite of this congestion and environmental deterioration are increasing. There is need for greater control and discipline. There are arguments for various methods of discouraging private transport such as higher parking costs, limiting access, or licensing certain vehicles only. But most authorities have done no more than increase traffic control and management. For example, metropolitan cities with strong and attractive centres, such as London and Paris, have tried to develop strong public transport which would prove an attractive alternative to the car. If centrality is weak, as in Los Angeles, then an incipient system of motorways is encouraged and the private car given its head at the expense of public transport. The choice between public or private dominance seems clear-cut, but in fact the issue usually ends in compromise; even London has its ring system to complement its radial, and public and private transport still fight for supremacy. New measures are introduced so gradually and so half-heartedly that the public adjusts itself to modest changes without being asked to face major issues or decide on sweeping priorities.

Problems of movement are no less acute in the metropolis in the developing world, but the level of sophistication and the input of money in corporate solutions vary enormously. Lack of resources dictates one mode which has only a limited appeal in the Western city—the bicycle. Its extreme flexibility and minimal demands on space as well as its cheapness have made it an ideal form of transport in pedestrian cities. Peking is a city of bicycles and so is Shanghai, where one person in five has one. In Asian and African cities there is also enormous pressure on public transport. This usually suffers from lack of capitalization and maintenance as well as from over-use and mismanagement. In most of these rapidly growing cities a new system—such as a metro-rail or underground, which have proved such a boon to many Western metropolitan cities—is too costly to contemplate. It is always a question of trying to improve, or even simply sustain, the existing system. In cities like Lagos, for example, the strain on the stock is aggravated by obsolescence, and the return on investment is further diminished by an erratic collection of fares in which family connections and petty transactions seem to outweigh the regular flow of cash (Hicks, p. 240). The rail transit system in Bombay is under tremendous pressure and there is continual agitation for a new system; but the cost would be too high, and city planners favour extending the existing system which is comparatively economical. This now consists of two railway lines serving parallel corridors in what is fast becoming a linear city. The trains, packed with people, particularly in the morning and evening, are more or less efficient, and the future probably lies in duplicating the pattern with two more lines. The high density of Bombay ensures fairly easy access for millions to this system.

The metropolitan cities which seem to have the gravest problems are those which have acquired considerable wealth and have tried to duplicate the complex systems of the West. Tokyo is a good example. The number of commuters in this city has grown dramatically in the last decade and by now may be in the region of 3 million. Moving this number daily is hampered by the fact that both road and rail systems are out of date. The density of building is such that the area covered by the transport systems is much less than in a comparable Western city, and only recently has Tokyo embarked on a series of freeways independent of the old street pattern. Public road transport is run by no less than seven bus companies (P. Hall 1984, p. 188). Rail travel is no easier. Nine private lines approach the centre but do not penetrate it; they stop short at a loop system which is part of the nationalized service, and this has one direct line to the centre! The pressure on this inadequate and uncoordinated service is proverbial; we are all familiar with pictures of Tokyo's army of 700 'pushers' who manage to increase the system's capacity by sheer force—at one time in 1972 it managed to reach 260 per cent capacity. The efficiency of the municipal underground is now beginning to relieve the strain. Car ownership is still relatively small at one for each seven persons, so public transport must take the burden of movement. What cars there are combine with the taxi services to choke the totally inadequate road system.

Mexico City faces dilemmas which are partly the direct result of cheap petrol and subsequent high car ownership. Again the underlying cause is the population explosion, but it has been unnecessarily exacerbated by the fact that industry is concentrated at the opposite pole to the main area of population growth; the major movements are across the city, and they have rightly been described as 'epic'. There are 2 million cars in the city, about one for every four households. Even so their use accounts for only a fifth of the journey to work, most people using buses and a modest metro system which does not go beyond the federal district. This means that most of those using it also change their mode of transport for every journey to work. The problem is further compounded by the fact that in common with other Latin American communities people go home for lunch. This means four peak periods of traffic daily, and the speed of movement—not surprisingly—is diminishing. On a saturated road system the average speed is about 8 k.p.h. Technology has reduced movement to walking pace. Caracas is another city in which the casual observer would be excused for thinking that every line of traffic has come to a halt once and for all; when it does move it is to a cacophony of horns which shatters even the normal din of a noise-polluted metropolis.

Not so in Hong Kong. Here the total commitment is to public transport, well co-ordinated and well controlled, and serving the city extremely well. Car ownership is as little as 1 per 24 persons, and space for the private car is kept strictly limited; there are no extensive car parks. Mass transit is good. Tramcars flow unceasingly, almost like 'a horizontal paternoster' (P. Hall 1984, p. 209); ferry services involve no waiting; the highway system integrating the new towns is designed for more than its flow of traffic. The emphasis on public transport in an area of high density has paid off handsomely.

vii

One overriding concern which is experienced by every metropolis and which is universally exacerbated by size is government. It can be taken as axiomatic that the larger the city the more difficult it is to govern. This does not mean that small cities are well-governed, but that the chances of efficient and acceptable government diminish with size. Aristotle was in no doubt about this: 'Experience shows that a very populous city can rarely if ever be well governed; since all cities which have a reputation for good government have a limit of population' (p. 226). Which is why I bring it in under problems!

I have no intention of defining what is 'good' and what is 'bad' government; the criteria would differ in various value systems. What we can assume is that it is meant to meet the basic needs of the people of a metropolis through a stable organization which will ensure an adequate distribution of services. This must be done 'equitably and efficiently' and 'adequately in terms of local tolerance' (Miles, ch. 8). There is also a political component which tries to recognize how individuals and groups can express their demands.

What I really mean by 'problems' in this case is the sheer size and complexity of this task and the variety of ways in which it is undertaken. There are almost as many structures of metropolitan government as there are metropolitan cities. One reason is that although some very large cities share the same system of government with other cities in the same state, so many of those we are interested in are capital cities, and these tend to have unique systems. This is so in Paris and Tokyo, in Buenos Aires and Washington (both of which lie in a special federal district), and of Delhi, which is governed by the President of India acting through an administrator. This means that quite often, and paradoxically, capital cities have less power to order their own affairs than other cities; their control often lies with central government. For nearly two centuries Washington DC was ruled by three commissioners appointed by the Federal Government. Since 1967 it has one—called a mayor—with an assistant and a council of nine, all appointed by the President. Mexico City is a federal district and its council has no elected members.

The majority of cities have an elected council, but this varies in strength from 15 in Los Angeles to 710 in Warsaw so that the ratio of representatives to the population varies enormously. One of the disadvantages of the small number is that there is so much less chance of participation, and also less direct contact between the public and its representatives. On the other hand the number of councillors in Warsaw or Moscow leads to what one writer describes as a 'mass meeting of city fathers'.

There are many ways in which power is exercised in metropolitan government. In Great Britain the city council is itself the executive, exercising control through a number of committees. In other cities, like Warsaw, Rome, and Montreal, the council appoints an executive. In the United States executive power is in the hands of an elected mayor, and this system has been adopted in countries influenced by the States—in Tokyo, Osaka, and Manila, for example.

The range of services and activities controlled by a metropolitan authority is immense. Among other things it is responsible for health and hospitals, water and sewerage, education, policing, fire-fighting, housing, amenities, social services, planning. To meet this demand it needs money, and there are various ways in which this is done. One of the commonest is the taxation of real property, well established in Britain until now but about to be radically changed to a taxation of individuals, the so-called 'poll tax'. Many cities levy a local tax on sales or entertainment; and sometimes a graduated income tax is applied. There are arguments for and against each one. Whatever the system there are marked disparities between the abilities of different cities to raise sufficient money to achieve their aims efficiently.

All I have done so far is to suggest the complexity of this topic; comparative studies are of little help and would tax anyone but the serious student of local government. The problems revolve around (a) generating the necessary revenue, (b) linking the population with the executive in such a way that control and accountability are guaranteed, and (c) in view of the size of the metropolis, finding the scale of operation appropriate to the function of government. This last is particularly interesting, again because of the wide variation in practice.

In the United States the metropolis is highly fragmented. On average the American metropolis has 87 governing bodies; Chicago has over a hundred. Within the metropolis there are municipalities, school districts, health districts, police precincts, and many others. Services are split up and so is the revenue-raising for their support. In very general terms the American metropolis has a central city and a ring of suburban municipalities, and this political separation usually coincides with many of the characteristics of inner city and outer city which I dealt with under polarization. Tax revenue has moved out with the rich, leaving those in the centre—migrants, the unemployed, the chronically poor—who not only produce very little tax but who are dependent on the support of the city. The city centre is the core of welfare provision. Here too services are more costly to provide and to administer. Fragmentation, then, leads to most wealth being produced where it is least needed and vice versa. To aggravate the difference the suburbanites, by commuting to the centre, make heavy use of the services of the centre, such as transport, to which they do not contribute. No one was very surprised in the 1970s when it looked as if New York was about to become bankrupt, or at the federal laws of 1978 which forced the city to cut jobs massively, to put an end to free tuition in its colleges, and to increase fares dramatically on its public transport.

London, on the other hand, has since 1888 tried unitary control on selected services by expanding the jurisdiction of the metropolis to keep pace with growth. A metropolitan police force was established as early as 1829. By mid-century it became clear that the necessary sewerage works could be undertaken only by a single body, the Metropolitan Board of Works (1855); similarly a Metropolitan Water Board was necessary for water supply and distribution (1904). Meanwhile public housing had become a major political issue and the subject of debate between those who wanted local control and the so-called centralists who saw the problem as too great for small local authorities. The latter won the day and this resulted in the setting up of the London County Council in 1888, the boundaries of which coincided with those of the Metropolitan Board of Works. The LCC was responsible for transport in the capital until the London Transport Board was set up in 1933. With continuing growth the LCC became anachronistic. In 1964 it was rationalized to take in all the built-up area within the green belt, a reasonable definition of London as a cohesive entity. This region was governed by the Greater London Council, which had authority over housing, transport, and planning; while 32 new and enlarged boroughs dealt with more local and less costly services. The GLC was abolished by central government in 1988, a political gesture which shifted some unitary obligations to central government and divided the others among the boroughs. There is still strong debate about the wisdom of destroying this tier of government. London is now one of the very few metropolitan cities outside the United States which has no central controlling body to deal with issues transcending local level without direct reference to central government.

Unitary or fragmented, controlled by decree or consent, by tight management or benevolent guidance, rich or poor: the permutations are endless. As far as the problems of adequate provision are concerned, resources are at the centre of most. The budgets of some metropolises are now greater than those of some sovereign states, and financial crises are common, particularly in the developing world. And there are almost as many proposed solutions as there are metropolitan cities.

Afterword

Most of the material I have drawn upon for this book was published in the last twenty years or so, from *Cities of Destiny* by Toynbee to Dogan and Kasarda's *Metropolitan Era*. The first was a celebration of the achievement of great historical cities, the latter an analysis of the pathology of the cities of today. Neither can be regarded as the basis of a balanced assessment or final judgement on metropolitan cities. The evidence we have from the past is too fragmentary to give a complete picture of historic cities as they appeared to those who lived in them. Time has made it much simpler to recognize what they created and bequeathed to the future than to recreate how the mass of their people lived. And our preoccupation with today's social urban problems may well blind us to what is praiseworthy in our own cities. The nature of the evidence encourages us to look back at all that was great and glorious. The tourist in Tikal and Chichen Itza is shown the pyramids of the monumental core and rarely glances at the foundations of the simple huts which form the mass of those cities; visitors to Egypt see the great temples of Karnak and Luxor because there is so little left of the nearby towns in which their craftsmen and labourers lived and died. So we see the relatively few great cities of the past as monuments of achievement, a fulfilment of the best in their societies, the results of great leaps forward in civilization. What lives on is the greatness of the city. The rest is shrouded by time and ignorance.

The evidence available for the last two centuries is very different. Not only have we a fairly complete and objective record of all that has been built, what city-dwellers did, how they behaved, what they thought: we also have extensive documentation of how those who lived in metropolis saw their own city. And paradoxically this last evidence does not make our own general assessment easier. What we have are perceptions of metropolis, how those who wrote about it saw it, often partial glimpses of restricted aspects—this corner of the city, that activity, this class—often to serve polemic, sometimes to catch a passing mood. To some extent the different emphases seem to come in cycles; there is a succession of perceptions as realism succeeded romanticism. For example there was a strong reaction, almost universally felt, against the worst features of the industrial city and its overcrowding and squalor; it reached a peak in the 1840s. There seemed to be another wave of critical condemnation at the end of the century. And I have drawn attention to an apparent preoccupation with social problems in contemporary metropolis, particularly in the Third World where it is a reaction against the latest wave of urbanization. There are periods when anti-urbanism is very strong indeed.

In spite of this it is true to say that reactions to the metropolis in the last century and a half have been a mixture of pro-urban and anti-urban. Not only have diametrically differing views coexisted, but the same observers have often changed their stance. This is not unexpected, because what evokes a response is not a reflective view of the city as a whole, but rather specific aspects which are often emotionally charged. A writer may well be virulent in his condemnation of urban poverty and simultaneously enjoy membership of élite societies which only a city can provide. Lastly there is that constant undercurrent of nostalgia, which Raymond Williams portrayed so well, which has always extolled rurality at the cost of urban-ness, or, as with Augustus Pugin, romanticized the cities of the past at the expense of those of the present.

There has always been a tension, therefore, between the perceived ills of metropolis and its attraction and benefits, and this has been particularly apparent since the growth of the industrial city. Whereas some of the expressions of anti-urbanism were ill defined, romantic in origin, and extreme—'Hell is a city'—by the beginning of the Victorian era the disadvantages of metropolis were being measured in cold—but no less frightening—statistics. Several rapidly expanding cities had extremely perceptive medical officers of health whose study of the incidence of diseases like cholera led to their utter condemnation of an urban environment in which sanitation was primitive, water polluted, and dwellings unfit for habitation;

they were particularly conscious of the effects of high densities, high birth rates, and poverty. The demographic facts of urban life were fully revealed in Britain after 1837 when the General Register Office began publishing its vital statistics: the worst fears of the romantics and the extreme pessimism of the medical officers were laid bare in the figures, and became facts. All this, together with official reports like that of Chadwick, was strengthened by the much more accessible, and possibly more frightening, descriptions of the plight of the urban poor by writers like Dickens and Mrs Gaskell.

In mid-century Henry Mayhew produced his graphic account of how tens of thousands of Londoners existed, in his *London Labour and the London Poor*. But to many this was no more than a statement of an aspect of life in the capital which had to be accepted along with its advantages. For the city was stoutly defended by people like Robert Vaughan in his *Age of Great Cities* of 1843. The case for metropolis was simply that this was society's source of intellectual advancement and moral health. Given that there were grave disadvantages which needed righting the city had self-regulating mechanisms which controlled these evils. Other growing industrial cities in Britain were vigorously defended and extolled, for their economic benefits outweighed their shortcomings, and indeed some of these cities were to initiate great advances in civil organization and community work, and become leaders in technical advances, the arts, and science. London's primacy in economic, intellectual, and cultural achievements spoke for itself; the Great Exhibition of 1851 was followed by the establishment of a spate of institutions like Imperial College, the Victoria and Albert Museum, art galleries, colleges of music, the Albert Hall, and eventually a score of organizations which took education and learning to the ordinary man. The Greater London Council was the culmination of local government evolution which was a model of its kind.

By the end of the century London was taking a more sober look at itself. The debit side was clear in Booth's researches on poverty. Undertaken to show that conditions were not as black as they had been painted, the studies came to the conclusion that they were even worse than had been thought, with one person in three below the poverty line. Booth continued with a monumental survey which left no one in doubt that there were two sides to metropolitan life. The highlights merely darkened the shadows; increased enlightenment revealed only greater depths of deprivation. Ebenezer Howard's solution to the overgrown city was the establishment of garden cities which would capitalize on the good aspects of metropolis—the creation of community, intellectual vigour, creativeness; but this could be preserved and encouraged only within a physical environment which had more in it of the country than the town, where density would be low and controlled and space, light, and fresh air natural commodities.

A revealing study by Lees shows how other countries experienced the same ambivalence. Germany went through a marked anti-urban phase, though later Berlin and Munich were seen as centres of progress and enlightenment. In the United States city growth was first seen as a threat, and a nostalgia for the countryside characterized many writers, though some, such as Emerson and Whitman, later became proponents of the city. Here, as in Britain, the late nineteenth century saw many studies which laid bare the bankruptcy of the city for most of those who lived in them. Perhaps this was inevitable in the fast-growing cities whose population was mainly foreign born and whose commitment was to industry and technical progress at the expense of those who supplied the labour. Several reports appeared which were critical of the housing of the poor. Workers like Jane Addams in Chicago saw that the problem went beyond mere poverty, however: hers was more a critique of city culture and its inability to control the situation. Its degradation was moral as well as physical.

Nevertheless, one has to consider side by side with this the optimism of a scholar like Weber. His was the most intensive study of city growth in the nineteenth century, and in spite of all the evidence on the negative side of the story what he was left with was its progress, its economic vitality, and its great achievements across a wide range of cultural activity. Many contemporary writers agreed and celebrated the greatness of London, Paris, and New York.

There were troughs of general despair to come in this century. After the First World War, films like 'Metropolis' and the settings of so many of Grosz's most savage paintings saw the city as harsh, demanding, and inhuman. And in the last quarter-century physical decay at the core and the redistribution of many activities, let alone the outward movement of the more prosperous people, have created an environment in the centre to which most of the ills of society seem to have drained. The inner-city problem is the result of a polarization of society which is as acute as it ever has been, resulting in conflict, hate, and violence on an unprecedented scale. So far society has not found the means either to control the situation or to find a long-term remedy. The dichotomy of the city remains intransigent and still provides the bases for conflicting views about the value of the city as a whole.

Doubts have been further strengthened by the latest phase of urbanization, the explosion of cities in the developing world. It would be an error to see too much of a parallel between what is happening there and what happened in the European and American industrial metropolis, in spite of some demographic similarities. The differences lie mainly in the economic framework into which the massive movement of people is expected to fit, as well as in the expectations of the migrants. There are few studies of the perception of these cities by those who are attracted to them; most comments are by Western observers. And the difficulties of interpretation are further compounded by the fact that so much of the organizational and cultural superstructure has been imposed on these cities by Western culture. Nevertheless, the attraction of these cities cannot be overestimated; it is the most potent factor in their growth. The urban experience is highly valued, even for those who partake of it temporarily, as in many African cities. It is too soon to assess how far sophisticated Western urban ideas have really been fused to indigenous cultures, but on balance local populations would consider the metropolis to be an enormous plus in their society, even if it is only a half-realized dream full of hope and promises rather than realization.

It would be naïve to suggest that the metropolis is either wholly good or wholly bad. It is never more than an expression of the society which gave birth to it, though the close juxtaposition of all its qualities does deepen the contrast between the best things in society and the worst. It is the ambivalence which arouses passionate feelings for and against. Nevertheless, we should not allow the manifold disadvantages of metropolis to blind us to the positive aspects. As in the past, so today there is no lack of evidence of the expression of the highest peaks of cultural achievement. Civilization has found its apogee in metropolis. I must agree with the reaffirmation made by Robson and Regan of their belief in the great city as the culmination of progress:

There is much to love and admire in a great city. It is the home of the highest achievements of man in art, literature and science: the source from which the forces of freedom and emancipation have sprung. It is the place where the spirit of humanism and of democracy have grown and flourished, where man's quest for knowledge and justice has been pursued most constantly and truth revealed most faithfully and fearlessly. (p. 127)

What better note on which to end?

Bibliography and References

ABRAMS, C. (1966), *Housing in the Modern World* (Cambridge, Mass.).

ADAMS, R. McC. (1966), *The Evolution of Urban Society* (London).

ADDAMS, Jane (1910), *Twenty-Three Years at Hull House* (New York).

ANGEL, S., BERRYMAN, S., and DE GEOEDE, K.H. (1977), 'Housing systems in Bangkok', *Ekistics*, 44, pp. 79–84.

ARISTOTLE (1942), trans. B. Jowett (Oxford).

BACON, E.N. (1968), *The Design of Cities* (New York).

BANHAM, P.R. (1971), *Los Angeles: the Architecture of Four Ecologies* (London).

BARKER, F. and JACKSON, P. (1974), *London: 2000 Years of a City and its People* (London).

BAYLISS, D. (1970), 'Forecasting and Technology', in P. Cowan (ed.), *Developing Patterns of Urbanisation* (Edinburgh), pp. 169–85.

BELL, D. (1976), *The Coming of the Post-Industrial Society* (London).

BERRY, B.J.L. (1961), 'City Size Distribution and Economic Development', *Economic Development and Cultural Change*, 9, pp. 573–88.

——GOHEEN, P.G. and GOLDSTEIN, H. (1968), *Metropolitan Area Definition: a Revaluation of Concepts and Statistical Practice*. US Census Bureau Working Paper No. 28 (Washington).

BLUMENFELD, H. (1967), 'The Modern Metropolis', in *Cities: A* Scientific American *Book* (London), pp. 49–66.

BOOTH, C. (1888), 'The Conditions of the People of East London and Hackney, 1887', *Journal of the Royal Statistical Society*, 51, pp. 276–339.

BOSE, N.K. (1964), *A Social Survey of Bombay* (Bombay).

BRAUDEL, F. (1984), *Civilisation and Capitalism from the Fifteenth to the Eighteenth Century*, iii: *Perspective of the World* (London).

BRAY, W.M., SWANSON, E.H., and ISLINGTON, I.S. (1975), *The New World* (London).

BRIGGS, A. (1963), *Victorian Cities* (London).

BROWNING, C.E. (1962), 'Primate Cities', in F.R.P. Pitts (ed.), *Urban Systems and Economic Development* (Eugene, Oreg.), pp. 16–27.

BRUNN, S.D. and WILLIAMS, J.F. (1983), *Cities of the World* (New York).

BRUTZKUS, E. (1983), 'Ecumenopolis Reconsidered', *Ekistics*, 50, pp. 300–7.

Bureau of Census (1986), *States and Metropolitan Area Data Book*. US Department of Commerce (Washington, DC).

CARCOPINO, J. (1967), 'The Rome of the Antonines', in Toynbee (1967), pp. 118–37.

CASTELLS, E. (1988), 'High Technology and Urban Dynamics in the United States', in Dogan and Kasarda (1988), i, pp. 85–110.

CHANDLER, T. and FOX, G. (1974), *3000 Years of Urban Growth* (New York).

CHENG, X. (1988), 'Giant Cities and the Urban Hierarchy in China', in Dogan and Kasarda (1988), i, pp. 225–52.

CHILDE, V. G. (1950), 'The Urban Revolution', *Town Planning Review*, 21, pp. 3–17.

CHRISTALLER, W. (1966), *Central Places in Southern Germany*, trans. C. W. Baskin (Englewood Cliffs, New Jersey).

CLOUT, H. and WOOD, P. (1986), *London: Problems of Change* (London).

Council for Science and Society (1987), *Access for All: Technology and Urban Movement* (London).

COWAN, P. (1969), *The Office: a Facet of Urban Growth* (London).

DAMESICK, P. (1980), 'The Inner-City Economy and Post-Industrial London', *London Journal*, 6, pp. 23–35.

DAVIES, K. (1955), 'The Origin and Growth of Urbanisation in the World', *American Journal of Sociology*, 60, pp. 429–37.

——(1972), *World Urbanisation 1950–1970*, University of California Institute of International Studies Monographs 4 and 9 (Berkeley, Calif.).

DAVIS, M. (1987), 'Supranational Cities: Aspects of Urbanisation in the Last Quarter of the Twentieth Century' (University of London Ph.D. thesis).

DOGAN, M. (1988), 'Giant Cities as Maritime Gateways', in Dogan and Kasarda (1988), i, pp. 30–55.

——and KASARDA, J. D. (1988), *The Metropolitan Era*, i: *A World of Giant Cities*; ii: *Mega-Cities* (Newbury Park, Calif.).

DOUGLAS, D. (1967), 'The Paris of Abelard and St. Louis', in Toynbee (1967), pp. 178–93.

DOXIADIS, C. A. (1968), *Ekistics: an Introduction to the Study of Settlement* (London).

DWYER, D. J. (1975), *People and Housing in the Third World* (London).

ENGELS, F. (1962), *Conditions of the Working Classes in 1844* (London).

FARIA, E. (1988), 'São Paulo', in Dogan and Kasarda (1988), ii, pp. 294–309.

FOX, K. (1985), *Metropolitan America* (London).

FROBEL, F. (1980), *The New International Division of Labour* (London).

GAPPERT, G. (ed.) (1987), *The Future of Winter Cities, Urban Affairs*, No. 31 (Beverly Hills).

——and KNIGHT, R.V. (1982), *Cities in the Twenty-First Century, Urban Affairs*, No. 23 (Beverly Hills).

GARNET, S. (1988), 'The Height of Ambition', *Guardian*, 5 Feb.

GEORGE, M.D. (1954), *London Life in the Eighteenth Century* (London).

GERTLER, M.S. (1988), 'The Limits of Flexibility; Comments on the Post-Fordian Vision of Production and its Geography', *Transactions of the Institute of British Geographers*, 13, pp. 419–32.

GLAZER, N. (1973), 'Notes on Southern California', in E. Chinoy (ed.), *The Urban Future* (New York), pp. 119–33.

GLC (1981), *Report and Review of Office Policy in Central London* (London).

GOTTMANN, J. (1961), *Megalopolis: The Urbanized North Eastern Seaboard of the United States* (Cambridge, Mass.).

——(1977), 'The Role of the Capital City', *Ekistics*, 44, pp. 240–3.

——(1978), *Forces Shaping the City*, Newcastle University Department of Geography, 50th Jubilee Lecture (Newcastle).

——(1983), *The Coming of the Transactional Society* (University of Maryland, Baltimore).

GRAY, R. (1978), *A History of London* (London).

HALL, J.M. (1976), *London, Metropolis and Region* (London).

HALL, P. (1984), *World Cities*, 3rd edn. (London).

——(1988), *Cities of Tomorrow* (London).

——and BREHENY, M. (1988), 'Urban Decentralisation and Retail Development: Anglo-American Comparisons', *Built Environment*, 13, pp. 244–61.

——THOMAS, R., GRACEY, H., and DREWETT, R. (1973), *The Containment of Urban England* (London).

HERODOTUS (1910), *History*, trans. G. Rawlinson (London).

HICKS, U. (1974), *The Large City: a World Problem* (London).

ITO, T. and NAGASHIMA, C. (1979), 'Tokaido, Megalopolis of Japan', *Geojournal* 4, pp. 231–46.

JAMES, H. (1982), *English Hours* (Oxford).

JEFFERSON, M. (1939), 'The Law of the Primate City', *Geographical Review*, 26, pp. 226–32.

JONES, E. (1964), 'Aspects of Urbanisation in Venezuela', *Ekistics*, 18, pp. 420–5.

——(1988), 'London', in Dogan and Kasarda (1988), ii, pp. 97–122.

——and VAN ZANDT, E. (1974), *Cities; Yesterday, Today and Tomorrow* (New York).

JONES, G.S. (1971), *Outcast London* (Oxford).

JUVENAL (1967), *Satires*, trans. P. Green (Harmondsworth).

KHALIFA, A.M. and MOHIEDDIN, M.M. (1988), 'Cairo', in Dogan and Kasarda (1988), ii, pp. 235–67.

KING, A.D. (1984), *Capital City: Physical and Social Aspects of London's Role in the World Economy* (Brunel University Monographs in Social and Environmental Studies).

KINGSLEY, C. (1850), *Alton Locke, Tailor and Poet* (Oxford).

LAMBERT, A. (1971), *The Making of the Dutch Landscape* (London).

LATHUM, R. (1958), *The Travels of Marco Polo* (London).

LEE, T. (1977), *Race and Residence* (Oxford).

LEES, A. (1985), *Cities Perceived: Urban Society in European and American Thought, 1820–1940* (Manchester).

LEONTIDOU, L. (1989), *The Mediterranean City in Transition: Social Change and Urban Development* (Cambridge).

LINSKEY, A. S. (1965), 'Some Generalisations Concerning Primate Cities', *Annals of the Association of American Geographers*, 55, pp. 506–13.

LLOYD, P.C. (1976), *Slums of Hope? Shanty Towns of the Third World* (London).

LOPEZ, R.S. (1963), 'Crossroads within the Walls', in O. Handlin and J. Burchard (eds.) *The Historian and the City* (Cambridge, Mass.), pp. 27–73.

MA, L.T.C. and HARTEN, E.W. (eds.) (1981), *Urban Development in Modern China* (Boulder, Colo.).

MCGEE, T.G. (1967), *The South-East Asian City* (London).

MANNERS, G. (1974), 'The Office in Metropolis', *Economic Geography*, 50, pp. 93–110.

——(1986), 'Decentralising London, 1945–75', in Clout and Wood (1986).

MAYER, H.M. and WADE, R.C. (1969), *Chicago: Growth of a Metropolis* (Chicago).

MEADOWS, D.H., MEADOWS, D.L., and ANDERS, J. (1972), *The Limits of Growth: a Report of the Club of Rome Project on the Predicament of Mankind* (London).

MEIER, R. (1985), 'The Future of Urbanisation' in J. Brotchie, P. Newton, P. Hall and P. Nijkamp (eds.), *The Future of Urbanisation* (London).

MILES, S.R. (1970), *Metropolitan Problems* (London).

MISRA, R.P. (ed.) (1978), *The Million Cities of India* (London).

MUMFORD, L. (1940), *The Culture of Cities* (London).

MURPHY, R. (1988), 'Shanghai', in Dogan and Kasarda (1988), ii, pp. 157-83.

NAKAMURA, H. and WHITE, J. N. (1988), 'Tokyo', in Dogan and Kasarda (1988), ii, pp. 23-36.

O'CONNOR, A.M. (1983), *The African City* (London).

OLSEN, D. (1976), *The Growth of Victorian London* (London).

PAPAIOANOU, J.G. (1980), 'And Yet we Move towards Ecumenopolis', *Ekistics*, 50, pp. 306-15.

PETERSON, R. (trans.) (1956), *Reasons of State* (London).

PIREAUX, C. (1967), 'Alexandria under the Ptolemies', in Toynbee (1967).

PIRENNE, H. (1925), *Medieval Cities*, trans. F.D. Halsey (New York).

PLINY (1963), *Letters to Gallus*, trans. B. Radice (London).

POSTGATE, N. (1977), *The First Empires* (Oxford).

RASSMUSSEN, S.E. (1948), *London the Unique City* (London).

ROBSON, W. and REGAN, D. (eds.) (1972), *Great Cities* (London).

ROSENTHAL, F. (1958), *The Muqraddinah of Ibn Khaldun* (New York).

RUNCIMAN, S. (1967), 'Constantinople' in Toynbee (1967), pp. 150-65.

RUSSELL, B. (1958), 'In Praise of Idleness', in E. Larrabee and R. Meyerson (eds.), *Mass Leisure* (London), pp. 94-108.

SALT, J. (1988), 'High-Skilled International Migrants', *Geoforum*, 19, pp. 381-400.

SCHNEIDER, W. (1963), *Babylon is Everywhere* (London).

SHEPPARD, F. H. W. (1971), *London 1808-70: the Infernal Wen* (London).

SOMERVELL, D. C. (ed.) (1946), *A. Toynbee, A Study of History* (London).

STERNLIEB, G. and HUGHES, J.W. (1988), 'New York', in Dogan and Kasarda (1988), ii, pp. 27-55.

STOKES, C. J. (1962), 'Theory of Slums', *Land Economics*, 38, pp. 188-97.

STOW, J. (1908), *Survey of London* (Oxford).

SUMMERSON, J. (1978), *Georgian London* (London).

SUTCLIFFE, A. (ed.) (1984), *Metropolis 1890-1914* (London).

SWANSON, E. H., BRAY, W., and FARRINGDON, I. (1975), *The New World* (Oxford).

TALBOT-RICE, T. (1967), 'St. Petersburg', in Toynbee (1967).

THRIFT, N. (1986), 'The Geography of International Economic Disorder', in R. J. Johnston and P. J. Taylor (eds.), *A World in Crisis? Geographical Perspectives* (London).

TOYNBEE, A. (ed.) (1967), *Cities of Destiny* (London).

——(1970), *Cities on the Move* (London).

TROLLOPE, A. (1861), *North America* (London).

TUAN, Y.F. (1968), 'A Preface to Chinese Cities', in R.P. Beckinsale and J.M. Houston (eds.), *Urbanisation and its Problems* (Oxford), pp. 218–53.

TURNER, J.F.C. (1968), 'Architecture that Works', in G. Bell and J. Tyrwhitt (eds.), *Human Identity in the Urban Environment* (London), pp. 352–65.

TYRWHITT, J. (1968), 'The City of Ch'ang-an', *Town Planning Review*, 39, pp. 419–32.

ULLMAN, E. (1947), 'Theory of the Location of Cities', *American Journal of Sociology*, 46, pp. 853–64.

VICKERS, M. (1977), *The Roman World* (Oxford).

VRIES, J. DE (1979), 'Merchant Bankers', in A. Bullock (ed.), *The Faces of Europe* (Oxford), pp. 23–56.

WALLER, P.J. (1983), *Town, City and Nation: England 1850–1914* (Oxford).

WEBBER, M. M. (1963), 'Order in Diversity: Community without Propinquity', in L. Wingo, jun., *Cities and Space* (Baltimore).

——(1964), 'Urban Place and Non-Urban Realm', in M. Webber *et al.* (eds.), *Explorations in Urban Space* (Philadelphia), pp. 79–153.

WEBER, A.F. (1967), *The Growth of Cities in the Nineteenth Century* (Ithaca, NY).

WEISMAN, W. (1970), 'A New View of Skyscrapers in History', in E. Kaufman (ed.), *The Rise of American Architecture* (London), pp. 115–62.

WHEATLEY, P. (1963), 'What the Greatness of a City is Said to Be', *Pacific Viewpoint*, 4, pp. 164–88.

——(1967), 'Proleptic Observations on the Origins of Urbanisation', in R. Steel and R. Lawton (eds.), *Liverpool Essays in Geography* (Liverpool), pp. 315–45.

——(1976), 'Levels of Spatial Awareness in Islamic Cities', *Ekistics*, 42, pp. 354–66.

WILLIAMS, R. (1973), *The Country and the City* (London).

WILSHER, P. and RIGHTER, R. (1975), *The Exploding City* (London).

WILSON, A. (1971), *The Future City* (Leeds).

Wood, P. (1986), 'Economic Change', in Clout and Wood (1986), pp. 60–74.

Woolley, C. L. (1929), *Ur of the Chaldees* (London).

Wright, A. F. (1968), 'Ch'ang-an', in Toynbee (1967), pp. 138–49.

Zipf, G. W. (1941), *Human Behaviour and the Principle of Least Effort* (Reading, Mass.).

Zweig, S. (1941), *The World of Yesterday* (London).

Index